W9-APS-041

PARTS 1 & 2 · Second Editions

The

Digital
Photography

The step-by-step secrets for how to
make your photos look like the pros'! Book

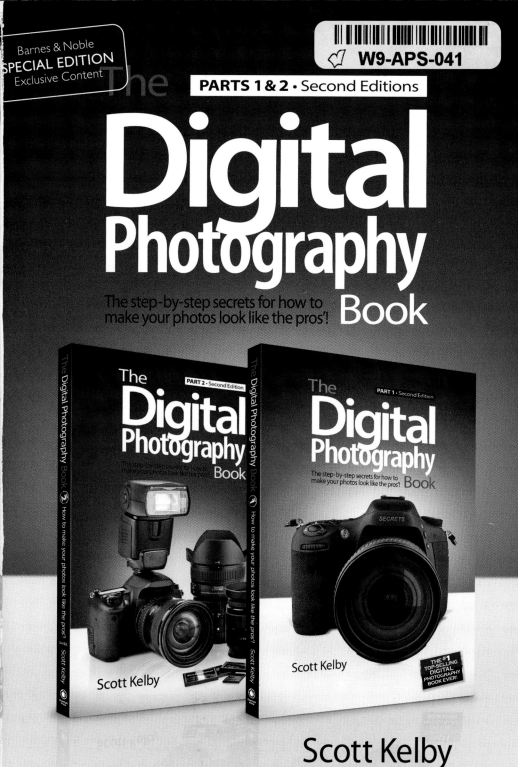

Scott Kelby

The Digital Photography Book, Parts 1 and 2
Barnes & Noble Exclusive Edition

The Digital Photography Book, parts 1 and 2 Team

CREATIVE DIRECTOR
Felix Nelson

ART DIRECTOR
Jessica Maldonado

TECHNICAL EDITORS
Kim Doty
Cindy Snyder

EDITORIAL CONSULTANTS
David Hobby
David Ziser
Steve Dantzig

PRODUCTION MANAGER
Dave Damstra

PHOTOGRAPHY
Scott Kelby

STUDIO AND
PRODUCTION SHOTS
Brad Moore

PUBLISHED BY

Peachpit Press

©2013, 2014 Scott Kelby

Composed in Myriad Pro (Adobe Systems Incorporated) and LCD (Esselte) by Kelby Media Group Inc.

Trademarks
All terms mentioned in this book that are known to be trademarks or service marks have been appropriately capitalized. Peachpit Press cannot attest to the accuracy of this information. Use of a term in the book should not be regarded as affecting the validity of any trademark or service mark.

Photoshop, Elements, and Lightroom are registered trademarks of Adobe Systems, Inc.
Nikon is a registered trademark of Nikon Corporation.
Canon is a registered trademark of Canon Inc.
Sony is a registered trademark of Sony Corporation.

Warning and Disclaimer
This book is designed to provide information about digital photography. Every effort has been made to make this book as complete and as accurate as possible, but no warranty of fitness is implied.

The information is provided on an as-is basis. The author and Peachpit Press shall have neither the liability nor responsibility to any person or entity with respect to any loss or damages arising from the information contained in this book or from the use of the discs or programs that may accompany it.

ISBN 13: 978-0-133-74207-7

ISBN 10:   0-133-74207-5

Published separately as *The Digital Photography Book, Part 1, Second Edition* (978-0-321-93494-9) and *The Digital Photography Book, Part 2, Second Edition* (978-0-321-94854-0)

15 14 13 12 11 10 9 8 7 6 5 4 3 2 1

Printed and bound in the United States of America

www.peachpit.com
www.kelbytraining.com

The Digital Photography Book

The step-by-step secrets for how to make your photos look like the pros'! **Book**

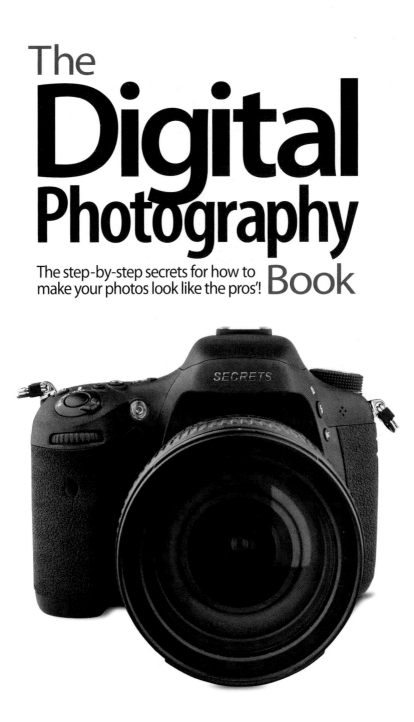

Scott Kelby

The Digital Photography Book, part 1

The Digital Photography Book, part 1 Team

CREATIVE DIRECTOR
Felix Nelson

ART DIRECTOR
Jessica Maldonado

TECHNICAL EDITORS
Kim Doty
Cindy Snyder

EDITORIAL CONSULTANT
Bill Fortney

PRODUCTION MANAGER
Dave Damstra

PHOTOGRAPHY
Scott Kelby

STUDIO AND
PRODUCTION SHOTS
Brad Moore

PUBLISHED BY

Peachpit Press

©2013 Scott Kelby

Composed in Myriad Pro (Adobe Systems Incorporated) and LCD (Esselte) by Kelby Media Group Inc.

Trademarks
All terms mentioned in this book that are known to be trademarks or service marks have been appropriately capitalized. Peachpit Press cannot attest to the accuracy of this information. Use of a term in the book should not be regarded as affecting the validity of any trademark or service mark.

Photoshop, Elements, and Lightroom are registered trademarks of Adobe Systems, Inc.
Nikon is a registered trademark of Nikon Corporation.
Canon is a registered trademark of Canon Inc.
Sony is a registered trademark of Sony Corporation.

Warning and Disclaimer
This book is designed to provide information about digital photography. Every effort has been made to make this book as complete and as accurate as possible, but no warranty of fitness is implied.

The information is provided on an as-is basis. The author and Peachpit Press shall have neither the liability nor responsibility to any person or entity with respect to any loss or damages arising from the information contained in this book or from the use of the discs or programs that may accompany it.

ISBN 13: 978-0-321-93494-9

ISBN 10: 0-321-93494-6

15 14 13 12 11 10 9 8 7 6 5 4 3 2 1

Printed and bound in the United States of America

www.peachpit.com
www.kelbytraining.com

Dedicated to the amazing
Dr. Stephanie Van Zandt
for her excellent advice, for taking
such good care of my wife, and
for delivering the sweetest
little baby girl in the whole world.

Acknowledgments

Although only one name appears on the spine of this book, it takes a team of dedicated and talented people to pull a project like this together. I'm not only delighted to be working with them, but I also get the honor and privilege of thanking them here.

I've written more than 50 books, and in each book I write, I always start by thanking my amazing, wonderful, beautiful, hilarious, and absolutely brilliant wife Kalebra. She probably stopped reading these acknowledgments 30 or more books ago because I keep gushing on and on about her, and despite how amazingly beautiful, charming, and captivating she is, she's a very humble person (which makes her even more beautiful). And even though I know she probably won't read this, I just have to thank her anyway because not only could I not do any of this without her, I simply wouldn't want to. She's just "it." It's her voice, her touch, her smile, her heart, her generosity, her compassion, her sense of humor, and the way she sneaks around behind the scenes trying to make sure my life is that much better, that much more fun, and that much more fulfilling—you just have to adore someone like that. She is the type of woman love songs are written for, and as any of my friends will gladly attest, I am, without a doubt, the luckiest man alive to have her as my wife. I love you madly, sweetheart!

I also want to thank my crazy, fun-filled, wonderful 16-year-old son Jordan. He won't read this either, because as he says, "It embarrasses him." And since I know he won't read it (or even let me read it to him), I can safely gush about him, too. Dude, you rock! You are just about the coolest son any dad could ask for—you dig Bon Jovi, you're always up for a game of *Black Ops*, you play drums (just like your dad), you love to go to the movies with me, and you get as excited about life as I do. You are nothing but a joy, and I'm so thrilled to be your dad (plus, you're such a great big brother to your little sister). I am very, very proud of you little pal (which is a relative term, since you're 6'1" now).

I also want to thank my beautiful, hilarious daughter Kira, who is the best-natured, happiest little girl in the whole wide world. You're only seven years old, and you've already been reflecting your mom's sweet nature, her beautiful smile, and her loving heart for many years now. You're too young to really know what an amazing mother you have, but before long, just like your brother, you'll realize that your mom is someone very special, and that thanks to her you're in for a really fun, exciting, hug- and adventure-filled life.

Also, thanks to my big brother, Jeff. Brothers don't get much better than you, and that's why Dad was always so proud of you. You are truly one of the "good guys" and I'm very, very lucky to have you in my life.

My personal thanks to my friend and fellow photographer Brad Moore, who shot most of the product shots for this edition of the book and worked as first assistant on many of the shots I took throughout the book. You're absolutely invaluable and an awful lot of fun.

Special thanks to my home team at Kelby Media Group. I love working with you guys and you make coming into work an awful lot of fun for me. I'm so proud of what you all do—how you come together to hit our sometimes impossible deadlines, and as always, you do it with class, poise, and a can-do attitude that is truly inspiring. I'm honored to be working with you all.

Thanks to my Editor Kim Doty, who is just the greatest editor ever, and I couldn't imagine doing these books without her. Also, thanks to Jessica Maldonado (my awesome book designer and our newest co-host on *Photoshop User TV*) for giving the book such a tight, clean layout, and for all the clever little things she adds that make the book that much better. Thanks to my in-house Tech Editor Cindy Snyder, who puts everything through rigorous testing and tries to stop me from slipping any of my famous typos past the goalie.

Thanks to my best buddy Dave Moser, whose tireless dedication to creating a quality product makes every project we do better than the last. Thanks to Jean A. Kendra for her steadfast support, and an extra special thanks to my Executive Assistant Susan Hageanon for keeping everything running smoothly while I'm out traveling and writing books (and for making sure I actually have the time I need to write books in the first place).

Thanks to my publisher Nancy Aldrich-Ruenzel, my way cool Editor and friend Ted Waitt (BT), marketing maverick Scott Cowlin, and marketing gunslinger Sara Jane Todd, along with the incredibly dedicated team at Peachpit Press. It's a real honor to get to work with people who really just want to make great books. Also, thanks to the folks at iStockphoto.com for enabling me to use some of their wonderful photography in this book when I didn't have the right image to illustrate my point.

I owe a special debt of gratitude to my good friend Bill Fortney for helping tech edit the first edition of this book, and it's infinitely better because of his comments, ideas, and input. Bill is just an amazing individual, a world-class photographer, a testament to how to live one's life, and I'm truly honored to have gotten the chance to work with someone of his caliber, integrity, and faith.

My sincere and heartfelt thanks to all the talented and gifted photographers who've taught me so much over the years, including Moose Peterson, Vincent Versace, Bill Fortney, David Ziser, Jim DiVitale, Helene Glassman, Joe McNally, Anne Cahill, George Lepp, Cliff Mautner, Kevin Ames, David Tejada, Frank Doorhof, Eddie Tapp, Jack Reznicki, and Jay Maisel. Thank you for sharing your passion, ideas, and techniques with me and my students.

Thanks to my mentors whose wisdom and whip-cracking have helped me immeasurably, including John Graden, Jack Lee, Dave Gales, Judy Farmer, and Douglas Poole.

Most importantly, I want to thank God, and His Son Jesus Christ, for leading me to the woman of my dreams, for blessing us with such amazing children, for allowing me to make a living doing something I truly love, for always being there when I need Him, for blessing me with a wonderful, fulfilling, and happy life, and such a warm, loving family to share it with.

Other Books by Scott Kelby

The Digital Photography Book, parts 2, 3 & 4

Professional Portrait Retouching Techniques for Photographers Using Photoshop

Light It, Shoot It, Retouch It: Learn Step by Step How to Go from Empty Studio to Finished Image

The Adobe Photoshop Lightroom Book for Digital Photographers

The Adobe Photoshop Book for Digital Photographers

The Photoshop Elements Book for Digital Photographers

It's a Jesus Thing: The Book for Wanna Be-lievers

The iPhone Book

About the Author

Scott is Editor, Publisher, and co-founder of *Photoshop User* magazine, is Publisher of *Light It!* digital magazine, and is co-host of the weekly videocasts *The Grid* (a photography talk show) and *Photoshop User TV*.

He is President of the National Association of Photoshop Professionals (NAPP), the trade association for Adobe® Photoshop® users, and he's President of the software training, education, and publishing firm Kelby Media Group.

Scott is a photographer, designer, and an award-winning author of more than 50 books, including T*he Digital Photography Book*, parts 1, 2, 3, & 4, *The Adobe Photoshop Book for Digital Photographers*, *Professional Portrait Retouching Techniques for Photographers Using Photoshop*, *The Adobe Photoshop Lightroom Book for Digital Photographers*, *Light It, Shoot It, Retouch It: Learn Step by Step How to Go from Empty Studio to Finished Image*, and *The iPhone Book*.

For the past three years, Scott has been honored with the distinction of being the world's #1 best-selling author of books on photography. His books have been translated into dozens of different languages, including Chinese, Russian, Spanish, Korean, Polish, Taiwanese, French, German, Italian, Japanese, Dutch, Swedish, Turkish, and Portuguese, among others.

Scott is Training Director for the Adobe Photoshop Seminar Tour, and Conference Technical Chair for the Photoshop World Conference & Expo. He's featured in a series of training DVDs and online courses, and has been training photographers and Adobe Photoshop users since 1993. He is also the founder of Scott Kelby's Annual Worldwide Photowalk, the largest global social event for photographers, which brings tens of thousands of photographers together on one day each year to shoot in over a thousand cities worldwide.

For more information on Scott, visit him at:

His daily blog: **www.scottkelby.com**
Twitter: **http://twitter.com/@scottkelby**
Facebook: **www.facebook.com/skelby**
Google+: **Scottgplus.com**

CHAPTER FIVE

91

Shooting Sports Like a Pro

Better Bring Your Checkbook

CHAPTER NINE   159

Taking Travel & City Life Shots Like a Pro
Tips for Travel Photography

CHAPTER TEN   179

How to Print Like a Pro and Other Cool Stuff
After All, It's All About the Print!

Chapter Eleven   197

Ten Things I Wish Someone Had Told Me
When I First Started Out in Photography

CHAPTER TWELVE   211

Photo Recipes to Help You Get "The Shot"
The Simple Ingredients That Make It All Come Together

Chapter One

Pro Tips for Getting Really Sharp Photos

If Your Photos Aren't Sharp, the Rest Doesn't Matter

Having photos that are sharp and in focus is so vitally important to pro photographers that they actually have coined a term for them. They call them "tack sharp." When I first heard that term tossed around years ago, I naturally assumed that it was derived from the old phrase "sharp as a tack," but once I began writing this book and doing some serious research into its history, I was shocked and surprised at what I found. First of all, it's not based on the "sharp as a tack" phrase at all. Tack sharp is actually an acronym. TACK stands for Technically Accurate Cibachrome Kelvin (which refers to the color temperature of light in photographs), and SHARP stands for Shutter Hyperfocal At Refracted Polarization. Now, these may seem like highly technical terms at first, but once you realize that I totally made them up, it doesn't seem so complicated, does it? Now, you have to admit, it sounded pretty legitimate at first. I mean, I almost had ya, didn't I? Come on, you know I had you, and I'll bet it was that "color temperature of light" thing I put in parenthesis that helped sell the idea that it was real, right? It's okay to admit you were fooled, just like it's okay to admit that you've taken photos in the past that weren't tack sharp (just in case you were wondering, the term "tack sharp" is actually formed from the Latin phrase *tantus saeta equina* which means "there's horsehair in my tantus"). Anyway, what's really important at this point is whatever you do, keep your spotted palomino away from anything with a sharp, pointy end used to attach paper to a bulletin board. That's all I'm saying.

The Real Secret to Getting Sharp Photos

Hey, before we get to "The Real Secret to Getting Sharp Photos," I need to let you in on a few quick things that will help you big time in getting the most from this book (sorry about duping you with "The Real Secret to Getting Sharp Photos" headline, but don't worry—that subject and more are coming right up, but first I have to make sure you totally understand how this book works. Then it will all make sense and we can worry about sharp photos). The idea is simple: You and I are out on a photo shoot. While we're out shooting, you have lots of questions, and I'm going to answer them here in the book just like I would in real life—straight and to the point, without teaching you all the technical aspects and behind-the-scenes technology of digital photography. For example, if we were out shooting and you turned to me and said, "Hey Scott, I want to take a shot where that flower over there is in focus, but the background is out of focus. How do I do that?" I wouldn't turn to you and give you a speech about smaller and larger apertures, about how exposure equals shutter speed plus aperture, or any of that stuff you can read in any book about digital photography (and I mean any book—it's in every one). In real life, I'd just turn to you and say, "Put on your zoom lens, set your aperture at f/2.8, focus on the flower, and fire away." That's how this book works. Basically, it's you and me out shooting, and I'm giving you the same tips, the same advice, and the same techniques I've learned over the years from some of the top working pros, but I'm giving it to you in plain English, just like I would in person, to a friend.

The Other Most Important Secret

JOEY WRIGHT

Again, ignore that headline. It's just a cheap come-on to get you to keep reading. Anyway, that's the scoop. Now, here's another important thing you need to know: To get the kind of quality photos I think you're looking for, sometimes it takes more than changing an adjustment in the camera or changing the way you shoot. Sometimes, you have to buy the stuff the pros use to shoot like a pro. I don't mean you need to buy a new digital camera, but instead, some accessories that the pros use in the field every day. I learned a long time ago that in many fields, like sports for example, the equipment doesn't really make that big a difference. For example, go to Wal-Mart, buy the cheapest set of golf clubs you can, hand them to Tiger Woods, and he's still Tiger Woods—shooting 12 under par on a bad day. However, I've never seen a field where the equipment makes as big a difference as it does in photography. Don't get me wrong, hand Jay Maisel a point-and-shoot camera and he'll take point-and-shoot shots that could hang in a gallery, but the problem is we're not as good as Jay Maisel. So, to level the playing field, sometimes we have to buy accessories (crutches) to make up for the fact that we're not Jay Maisel. Now, I don't get a kickback, bonus, or anything from any of the companies whose products I recommend. I'm giving you the same advice I'd give you if we were out shooting (which is the whole theme behind this book). This is *not* a book to sell you stuff, but before you move forward, understand that to get pro results sometimes you have to use (and that means buy) what the pros use.

Perhaps Even More Important Than That!

Still a fake headline. Don't let it throw you. Now, although we want pro-quality photos, we don't all have budgets like the pros, so when possible, I break my suggestions down into three categories:

 I'm on a budget. These are denoted with this symbol. It simply means you're not loose with money (meaning you're probably married and have kids).

 I can swing it. If you see this symbol, it means photography is your passion and you don't mind if your kids have to work a part-time job once they get to college to buy books. So you're willing to spend to have some better-than-average equipment.

 If you see this symbol, it means you don't really have a budget (you're a doctor, lawyer, venture capitalist, U.S. Senator, etc.), so I'll just tell you which one I would buy if I was one of those rich bas*%$#s. (Kidding. Kind of.)

To make things easy, I put up a webpage at **kelbytraining.com/books/vol1gear** with direct links to these goodies if you're so inclined. Again, I don't get a red cent if you use these links or buy this stuff, but I don't mind because I made such a killing on you buying this book. Again, I kid. Now, where do these links actually go? (See next page.)

If You Skip This, Throw Away Your Camera

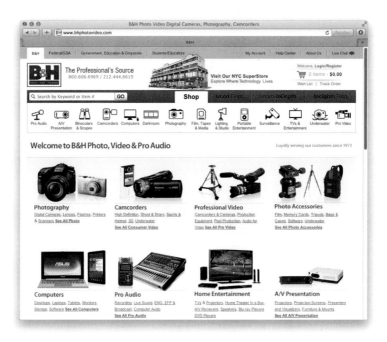

Hey, how do you like that grabber of a headline? Sweet! Totally a scam, but sweet nonetheless. Now, those links on the webpage lead to one of two places: (1) to the individual manufacturer who sells the product, if they only sell direct, or (2) to B&H Photo's website. So, why B&H? Because I trust them. I've been buying all my personal camera gear from them for years (so do all my friends, and most of the pros I know) and since you're now going to be one of my shooting buddies, this is where I would tell you to go without a doubt. There are three things I like about B&H, and why they have become something of a legend among pro photographers: (1) They carry just about every darn thing you can think of, no matter how small or insignificant it may seem. Lose your Nikon brand lens cap? They've got 'em in every size. Lose your neck strap with Canon stitched on it? They've got them, too. Lose that tiny little cap that covers the input for your remote shutter release? They've got it. (2) When you call them, you talk to a real photographer, and my experience is that they give you the real straight scoop on what to buy. I've called up with something in mind, and have had their reps tell me about something better that's cheaper. That's rare these days. And finally (3), their prices are very, very competitive (to say the least). If you're ever in New York City, make it a point to drop by their store. It is absolutely amazing. It's like Disneyland for photographers. I could spend a day there (and I have). Anyway, they're good people. Now, does the headline scam thing continue on the next page? You betcha.

If You Do This Wrong, It Will Lock Up

It's not as good as the last fake headline, but we're only one more page away from the real chapter content, so I'm backing it off a little. Now, once you turn the page you'll notice lots of photos of Nikon, Canon, and Sony cameras, and it might make you think that I'm partial to these three brands. It's not just me. Apparently most of the world is partial to these three brands, so you'll see lots of shots of them. Now, what if you don't shoot with a Nikon, Canon, or Sony camera? No sweat—most of the techniques in this book apply to any digital SLR camera, and many of the point-and-shoot digital cameras as well, so if you're shooting with an Olympus or a Sigma, don't let it throw you that a Nikon, Canon, or Sony is pictured. This book is about taking dramatically better photos, not about how to set up your Nikon, Canon, or Sony, even though since most people are shooting with one of these, I usually show one of these cameras or menus (but mainly only tell you how to set things up on a Nikon or Canon). So, if I'm talking about white balance, and I'm show-ing the Canon white balance menu, but you're not shooting with a Canon, simply breathe deeply and say to yourself, "It's okay, my [insert your camera name here] also has a white balance setting and it works pretty much like this one." Remember, it's about choosing the right white balance, not exactly which buttons to push on your camera, because if we were really out shooting together, we might not have the same brand of camera.

It's Time to Get Serious

I have good news: Not only are we at the end of this "fake headline" thing, you'll also be happy to know that from here on out, the rest of the book isn't laced with the wonderfully inspired (lame) humor you found on these first few pages. Well, the intro page to each chapter has more of this stuff, but it's only one page and it goes by pretty quickly. My books have always had "enlightened" chapter intros (meaning I wrote them when I was plastered) and the chapter names are usually based on movies, song names, or band names (the actual chapter name appears below the fake chapter name). The other reason I do it is because I need a chance to write something that doesn't use any of the terms shutter, aperture, or tripod. In a book like this, there's not much room to interject personality (if you want to call it that), and since the rest of the book is me telling you just what you need to know, there's little time for my brand of humor. In fact, in life there's little time for my brand of humor, so I sneak it in there. I have so little. Anyway, as you turn the page, keep this in mind: I'm telling you these tips just like I'd tell a shooting buddy, and that means oftentimes it's just which button to push, which setting to change, and not a whole lot of reasons why. I figure that once you start getting amazing results from your camera, you'll go out and buy one of those "tell me all about it" digital camera books. In all seriousness, I truly hope this book ignites your passion for photography by giving you some insight into how the pros get those amazing shots, and showing you how to get results you always hoped you'd get from your digital photography. Now pack up your gear, it's time to head out for our shoot.

Getting "Tack Sharp" Starts with a Tripod

There's not just one trick that will give you the sharp photos the pros get—it's a combination of things that all come together to give you "tack sharp" shots. (Tack sharp is the term pro photographers use to describe the ultimate level of sharpness. Sadly, we aren't the best at coming up with highly imaginative names for things.) So, while there are a number of things you'll need to do to get tack-sharp photos, the most important is shooting on a tripod. In fact, if there's one single thing that really separates the pros from the amateurs, it's that the pros always shoot on a tripod (even in daylight). Yes, it's more work, but it's the key ingredient that amateurs miss. Pros will do the little things that most amateurs aren't willing to do; that's part of the reason their photos look like they do. Keeping the camera still and steady is a tripod's only job, but when it comes to tripods, some do a lot better job than others. That's why you don't want to skimp on quality. You'll hear pros talking about this again and again, because cheap tripods simply don't do a great job of keeping your camera that steady. That's why they're cheap.

Scott's Gear Finder

Oben AC-2310LA 3-Section Tripod (around $115)

Manfrotto 458B NeoTec Pro Tripod (around $375)

Gitzo GT3541L Series 3 Mountaineer Tripod (around $745)

A Ballhead Will Make Your Life Easier

Here's the thing: when you buy a pro-quality tripod, you get just the tripod. It doesn't come with a tripod head affixed like the cheap-o tripods do, so you'll have to buy one separately (by the way, this ballhead thing isn't necessarily about getting sharp images, but it is about keeping your sanity, so I thought I'd better throw it in). Ballheads are wonderful because with just one knob they let you quickly and easily aim and position your camera accurately at any angle (which you'll find is a huge advantage). Best of all, good ballheads keep your camera locked down tight to keep your camera from "creeping" (slowly sliding one way or the other) after you've set up your shot. Like tripods, a good ballhead isn't cheap, but if you buy a good one, you'll fall in love with it.

Scott's Gear Finder

Manfrotto 498RC4 Midi Ballhead (around $110)

Oben BC-2 Ballhead (around $180)

Really Right Stuff BH-40 LR Ballhead ($375)

Don't Press the Shutter (Use a Cable Release)

Okay, so now you're lugging around a tripod, but your photos are looking much sharper. Not tack sharp yet, but much sharper. What will take you to the next level of sharpness? A cable release. This is simply a cable that attaches to your digital camera (well, to most semi-pro or high-end consumer DSLRs anyway) and it has a button on the end of it. That way, when you press this button on the end of the cable, it takes the photo, but without you actually touching the shutter button on the camera itself. So, why is this such a big deal? It's because, believe it or not, when you press the shutter button on the camera, it makes the camera move just enough to keep your photos from being tack sharp. I know, it sounds like a little thing, but this one is bigger than it sounds. Using it is easier than you might think, and these days most cameras support wireless remotes too, and they're fairly inexpensive, as well. Now your photos are just that much sharper.

Forgot Your Cable Release? Use a Self Timer

If you don't want to spring for a cable release (or wireless remote), or if you're out shooting and forgot yours (which has happened to me on numerous occasions), then the next best thing is to use your digital camera's built-in self timer. I know, you normally think of using this so you can run and get in the shot real quick, but think about it—what does the self timer do? It takes the shot without you touching the camera, right? Right! So, it pretty much does the same job of keeping your camera from moving—you just have to wait about 10 seconds. If you hate waiting (I sure do), then see if your camera allows you to change the amount of time it waits before it shoots. I've lowered mine to just five seconds (see the Nikon menu above). I press the shutter button and then five seconds later, the shot fires (I figure that five seconds is enough time for any movement caused by my pressing the shutter release to subside).

A BETTER CABLE RELEASE

If you're thinking of getting a cable release to reduce vibration, you're better off getting an electronic cable release rather than one that actually presses the shutter button with a plunger-style wire. Because, even though it's better than you pressing the button with your big ol' stubby vibration-causing finger, it doesn't compare with an electronic (or wireless) version that doesn't touch the camera at all.

Getting Super Sharp: Mirror Lock-Up

Nikon   Canon

All right, we're starting to get a bit obsessed with camera shake, but that's what this chapter is all about—removing any movement so we get nothing but the sharpest, cleanest photo possible. The next feature we're going to employ is called Exposure Delay Mode on a Nikon or Mirror Lockup on a Canon. What this essentially does is locks your camera's mirror in the up position, so when you take the shot, the mirror does not move until after the exposure is made—limiting the movement inside your camera during the exposure, and therefore giving you that much sharper a photo. How much does this matter? It's probably second only to using a solid tripod! So, you'll need to find out where the mirror lock-up control is for your camera (most of today's DSLR cameras have this feature because you also use this to clean your sensor). Once you set your camera to mirror lock-up, on a Nikon you now have to press the shutter release button (on your remote or cable release) once, on a Canon you have to press it twice—once to lift the mirror, and then a second time to actually take the shot. Now, this technique sounds a bit nitpicky. Does it make that big a difference? By itself, no. But add this to everything else, and it's another step toward that tack sharp nirvana.

Turn Off Vibration Reduction (or IS)

The big rage in digital lenses these days are the Vibration Reduction (VR) lenses from Nikon and the Image Stabilization (IS) lenses from Canon, which help you get sharper images while hand-holding your camera in low-light situations. Basically, they let you hand-hold in more low-light situations by stabilizing the movement of your lens when your shutter is open longer, and honestly, they work wonders for those instances where you can't work on a tripod (like weddings, some sporting events, when you're shooting in a city, or just places where they simply won't let you set up a tripod). If you're in one of those situations, I highly recommend these VR or IS lenses, but depending on which one you use, there are some rules about when you should turn them off. For example, we'll start with Nikon. If you are shooting on a tripod with a Nikon VR lens, to get sharper images, turn the VR feature off (you do this right on the lens itself by turning the VR switch to the Off position). The non-technical explanation why is that these VR lenses look for vibration. If they don't find any, they'll go looking for it, and that looking for vibration when there is absolutely none can cause (you guessed it) some small vibration. So just follow this simple rule: When you're hand-holding in anything but bright daylight (where your shutter speeds will already be really fast), turn VR or IS on. When you're shooting on a tripod, for the sharpest images possible, turn VR or IS off. Now, there are some Nikon VR lenses and some older Canon IS lenses that can be used on a tripod with VR or IS turned on. So, be sure to check the documentation that came with your VR or IS lens to see if yours needs to be turned off.

Shoot at Your Lens' Sharpest Aperture

Another trick the pros use is, when possible, shoot at your lens' sharpest aperture. For most lenses, that is about two full stops smaller than wide open (so the f-stop number you use will go higher by two stops). For example, if you had an f/2.8 lens, the sharpest apertures for that lens would be f/5.6 and f/8 (two full stops down from 2.8). Of course, you can't always choose these apertures, but if you're in a situation where you can (and we'll talk about this later in the book), then shooting two stops down from wide open will usually give you the sharpest image your lens can deliver. Now, that being said, this isn't true for all lenses, and if that's not the case with your lens, you'll find your lens' sweet spot (its sharpest aperture) in short order if you keep an eye out for which aperture your sharp-est images seem to come from. You can do that by looking at your photos' EXIF data (the background information on your shots embedded by your digital camera into the photos themselves) in Photoshop by going under Photoshop's File menu and choosing File Info. Then, click on Camera Data. It will show the aperture your shot was taken at. If you find most of your sharpest shots are taken with a particular aperture, then you've found your sweet spot. However, don't let this override the most important reason you choose a particular aperture, and that is to give you the depth of field you need for a particular shot. But it's just nice to know which f-stop to choose when your main concern is sharp-ness, not controlling depth of field.

Good Glass Makes a Big Difference

Does buying a really good lens make that big a difference in sharpness? Absolutely! I went shooting with a friend in Zion National Park in Utah. He had just bought a brand new Canon EF 24–70mm f/2.8L II, which is a tack-sharp lens. It's not cheap, but like anything else in photography (and in life), the really good stuff costs more. His other lens was a fairly inexpensive telephoto zoom he had been using for a few years. Once he saw the difference in sharpness between his new, good quality lens and his cheap lens, he refused to shoot with the telephoto again. He had been shooting with it for years, and in one day, after seeing what a difference a really sharp lens made, he wouldn't shoot with his old lens again. So, if you're thinking of buying a zoom lens for $295, sharpness clearly isn't your biggest priority. A quality lens is an investment, and as long as you take decent care of it, it will give you crystal clear photos that inexpensive lenses just can't deliver.

When talking about the quality of lenses, we don't use the word "lens." It's too obvious. Instead, we say stuff like, "Hey, Joe's got some really good glass," or, "He needs to invest in some good glass," etc. Try this the next time you're at the local camera store, and see if the guy behind the counter doesn't get that "you're in the club" twinkle in his eye.

Avoid Increasing Your ISO on a Tripod

When you're shooting on a tripod, even in very dim or low light, don't increase your ISO (your digital equivalent of film speed). Keep your ISO at the lowest ISO setting your camera allows (ISO 200, 100, as shown on the Nikon menu above, or 50, if your camera's ISO goes that low) for the sharpest, cleanest photos. Raising the ISO adds noise to your photos, and you don't want that (of course, if you're hand-holding and have no choice, like when shooting a wedding in the low lighting of a church, then increasing the ISO is a necessity, but when shooting on a tripod, avoid high ISOs like the plague—you'll have cleaner, sharper images every time).

BREAKING THE RULES

So what do you do if you can't use a tripod (e.g., the place where you're shooting won't allow tripods)? In this case, if there's plenty of light where you're shooting, you can try using very fast shutter speeds to minimize hand-held camera shake. Set your camera to shutter priority mode and choose a speed that matches or exceeds the focal length of your lens (a 180mm lens means you'll shoot at 1/200 of a second).

Zoom In to Check Sharpness

Nikon   Canon

Here's a sad fact of digital photography—everything looks sharp and in focus when you first look at the tiny LCD screen on the back of your digital camera. When your photo is displayed at that small size, it just about always looks sharp. However, you'll soon learn (once you open your photo on your computer) that you absolutely can't trust that tiny little screen—you've got to zoom in and check the sharpness. On the back of your camera there's a zoom button that lets you zoom in close to see if the photo is really in focus. Do this right on the spot, right after you take the shot, so you still have a chance to retake the photo if you zoom in and find out it's blurry. The pros always check for sharpness this way, because they've been burned one too many times.

CUSTOM QUICK ZOOM SETTINGS

Some of today's digital SLR cameras have a quick zoom option, where you can set a particular amount you want your zoom to zoom in to. Check your owner's manual to see if your digital camera has a custom quick zoom setting.

Sharpening After the Fact in Photoshop

If you've followed all the tips in this chapter thus far, and you've got some nice crisp photos, you can still make your photos look even that much sharper by adding sharpening in either Adobe Photoshop (the software darkroom tool the pros use) or Adobe Photoshop Elements (the semi-pro version). Now, which photos need to be sharpened using Photoshop? All of them. We sharpen every single photo we shoot using Photoshop's Unsharp Mask filter. Okay, it sounds like something named "unsharp" would make your photos blurry, but it doesn't—the name is a holdover from traditional darkroom techniques, so don't let that throw you. Using it is easy. Just open your photo in Photoshop, then go under Photoshop's Filter menu, under Sharpen, and choose Unsharp Mask. When the dialog appears, there are three sliders for applying different sharpening parameters, but rather than going through all that technical stuff, I'm going to give you five sets of settings that I've found work wonders.

(1) **For people:** Amount 150%, Radius 1, Threshold 10

(2) **For cityscapes, urban photography, or travel:** Amount 65%, Radius 3, Threshold 2

(3) **For general everyday use:** Amount 120%, Radius 1, Threshold 3

(4) **For super-sharpening** (for sports photos, landscapes, stuff with lots of details): Amount 95%, Radius 1.5, Threshold 1

(5) **For images I've already made smaller and lower resolution,** so I can post them on the web: Amount 85%, Radius 1, Threshold 4

Did You Resize That for the Web?
Then Resharpen!

If you take a shot, open it in Photoshop (or Photoshop Elements), and apply the Unsharp Mask filter to it (see the previous page), and then you lower the image size and resolution so you can post it on the web, you need to apply the Unsharp Mask filter again with just a little bit of sharpening. Here's why: when you lower the image size and resolution, it loses some of its sharpness during that resize, so I always go back and apply a tiny bit of sharpening to bring back what I just lost. I generally use this Unsharp Mask setting as a starting place: Amount: 70%, Radius: 1.0, Threshold: 10, but before I click the OK button, I simply look at the photo to make sure that it doesn't look oversharpened. If it looks a bit too sharp now, just lower the Amount to 50 and see how that looks. Still too sharp? Drop it down to 40, or even 30 (I've never gone below 30, but this is a call only you, as the "sharpener," can make).

Hand-Held Sharpness Trick

Anytime you're hand-holding your camera in anything but nice direct sunlight, you're taking your chances on getting a sharply focused photo because of camera shake, right? Well, the next time you're hand-holding in less than optimal light, and you're concerned that you might not get a tack-sharp image, try a trick the pros use in this sticky situation— switch to continuous shooting (burst) mode and hold down the shutter release to take a burst of photos instead of just one or two. Chances are at least one of those dozen or so photos is going to be tack sharp, and if it's an important shot, it can often save the day. I've used this on numerous occasions and it has saved my butt more than once. (Sony's continuous shooting mode button is pictured above. See Chapter 5 for more on shooting in continuous [burst] mode with both Nikon and Canon cameras.)

Getting Steadier Hand-Held Shots

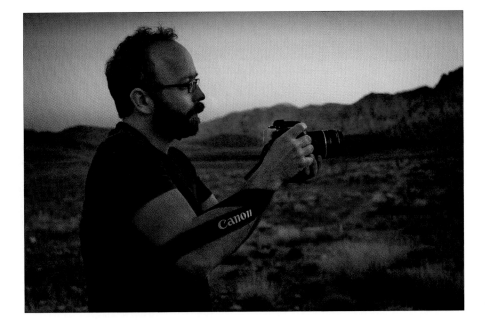

I picked up this trick from photographer Joel Lipovetsky when we were out on a shoot and I saw him hand-holding his camera with his camera strap twisted into what he called "The Death Grip." It's designed to give you extra stability and sharper shots while hand-holding your camera by wrapping your camera strap around your arm (just above the elbow), then wrapping it around the outside of your wrist (as shown above) and pulling the strap pretty tight, which makes your camera more stable in your hand. You can see how it wraps in the photo above, but the pose is just for illustrative purposes—you still would hold the camera up to your eye and look through the viewfinder as always. Thanks to Joel for sharing this surprisingly cool tip.

LEAN ON ME!

Another trick the pros use (when they're in situations where they can't use a tripod) is to either: (a) lean themselves against a wall to help keep themselves steady—if they're steady then the camera's more steady, or (b) lean or lay their lens on a railing, a fence, or any other already stationary object as kind of a make-shift tripod. Keep an eye out for these tripod substitutes whenever you're without yours—it can make a big difference.

SHUTTER SPEED: 1/60 SEC   F-STOP: F/5.6   ISO: 800   FOCAL LENGTH: 70mm | PHOTOGRAPHER: SCOTT KELBY

Chapter Two

Shooting Flowers Like a Pro

There's More to It Than You'd Think

You're probably surprised to see a chapter in here about shooting flowers because flowers seem like they'd be easy to shoot, right? I mean, they're just sitting there—not moving. They're colorful. They're already interesting, and people love looking at them. It should be a total no-brainer to get a good flower shot. But, ya know what? It's not. It's a brainer. It's a total brainer. Ya know why? It's because of pollination. That's right, it's the pollination that naturally occurs in nature that puts a thin reflective film over flowers that can't normally be seen with the naked eye, but today's sensitive CMOS and CCD digital camera sensors capture this reflectance and it appears as a gray tint over our images. Not only does it turn the photos somewhat gray (which causes flowers to lose much of their vibrant color), you also lose sharpness as well. Now, there is a special photographic filter (called the Flora 61B from PhotoDynamics) that can help reduce the effects of this pollination and both bring back the sharpness and reduce the graying effect, but because of U.S. trade sanctions imposed by the Federal Trade Commission, we can no longer buy this filter direct. Especially because I totally made this whole thing up. I can't believe you fell for this two chapters in a row. Seriously, how are you going to get good flower photos if you're falling for the old Flora 61B trick? Okay, I'm just teasing you, but seriously, getting good flower shots is an art, and if you follow the tips I'm laying out in this chapter, the very next flower shots you take will be that much better (especially if you don't mind the graying and loss of sharpness caused by pollination). See, there I go again. It's a sickness.

Don't Shoot Down on Flowers

On an average day, if you were to walk by some wildflowers in a field, or along a path in a garden, you'd be looking down at these flowers growing out of the ground, right? That's why, if you shoot flowers from a standing position, looking down at them like we always do, your flower shots will look very, well…average. If you want to create flower shots with some serious visual interest, you have to shoot them from an angle we don't see every day. That usually means not shooting down on them, and instead getting down low and shooting them from their level. This is another one of those things the pros routinely do and most amateurs miss. Hey, if you're going to shoot some great flower shots, you're going to have to get your hands dirty (well, at least your knees anyway). The shots above show the difference: on the left, the typical "shooting down on flowers" shot; on the right, the same flower in the same light using the same focal length lens shot 30 seconds later, but I shot it from the side (down on one knee) instead of shooting down on it. You can see the difference shooting a non-typical angle makes. So, to get great flower shots, start by not shooting down on them. By the way, while you're down there, try getting really low (down below the flowers) and shoot up at them for a fascinating angle you rarely see!

Shooting Flowers with a Zoom Lens

You don't have to have a macro (close-up) lens to take great flower shots—zoom lenses work just great for shooting flowers for two reasons: (1) you can often zoom in tight enough to have the flower nearly fill the frame, and (2) it's easy to put the background out of focus with a zoom lens, so the focus is just on the flower. Start by shooting in aperture priority mode (set your mode dial to A or Av), then use the smallest aperture number your lens will allow (in other words, if you have an f/5.6 lens, use f/5.6). Then try to isolate one flower, or a small group of flowers that are close together, and focus on just that flower. When you do this, it puts the background out of focus, which keeps the background from distracting the eye and makes a stronger visual composition.

SAVE YOUR KNEES WHEN SHOOTING FLOWERS

If you're going to be shooting a lot of flowers, there's an inexpensive accessory that doesn't come from the camera store, but you'll want it just the same—knee pads. They will become your best friend. Find them at Home Depot, Lowe's, or any good gardening store.

Use a Macro Lens to Get Really Close

If you've ever wondered how the pros get those incredibly close-up shots (usually only seen by bees during their pollination duties), it's with a macro lens. A macro lens (just called "macro" for short) lets you get a 1:1 view of your subject and reveal flowers in a way that only macros can. A macro lens has a very shallow depth of field—so much so that when photographing a rose, the petals in the front can be in focus and the petals at the back of the rose can be out of focus. I'm not talking about an arrangement of roses in a vase—I'm talking about one single rose. By the way, you *must* (see how that's set off in italics?), must, must shoot macro on a tripod. When you're really in tight on a flower, any tiny bit of movement will ruin your photo, so use every sharpening technique in Chapter 1 to capture this amazing new world of macro flower photography.

TURN YOUR ZOOM LENS INTO A MACRO ZOOM

It's easy—just add a close-up lens (like we talk about on the next page) onto your regular zoom lens. As I mention, these close-up lenses (also called two-element close-up diopters) are cheaper than buying a full-blown macro lens, plus adding it to your zoom gives you zoom capability, as well. You can buy single-element close-up filters, but they're generally not as sharp at the edges, but for flowers the edges usually aren't as important anyway.

Can't Afford a Macro? How 'bout a Close-Up?

I learned about this from my buddy (and famous wildlife and nature photographer) Moose Peterson, and what it lets you do is turn your telephoto zoom lens into a macro lens for 1/4 of the price, and 1/10 the weight and size. It looks just like a thick filter (it's about 1" thick), and it screws onto both Canon and Nikon lenses just like a traditional filter, but it turns your zoom lens into a macro zoom. What's great about this little close-up lens is that:

(1) it takes up so little room in your camera bag;

(2) it weighs just a few ounces;

(3) and best of all—it's pretty inexpensive (well, compared to buying a decent macro lens, which would run you at least $500).

It's called the Canon Close-Up Lens (even though it's from Canon, you can get a version that screws onto a Nikon lens. It's the only thing I know of from Canon that's designed for Nikon cameras. I use the Canon Close-Up Lens 500D to attach to my 70–200mm Nikon VR lens [it's 77mm], and it works wonders). So, how much is this little wizard? Depending on the size of the lens you're going to attach it to, they run anywhere from about $75 to $145. That ain't bad!

When to Shoot Flowers

©ISTOCKPHOTO/ANTONY SPENCER

There are three ideal times to shoot flowers:

(1) **On cloudy, overcast days.** The shadows are soft as the sun is hidden behind the clouds, and the rich colors of the flowers aren't washed out by the harsh direct rays of the sun. That's why overcast days are a flower photographer's best friend. In fact, there's probably only one other time that's better than shooting on an overcast day, and that is…

(2) **Just after a rain.** This is a magical time to shoot flowers. Shoot while the sky is still overcast and the raindrops are still on the petals (but of course, to protect your digital camera [and yourself], don't actually shoot in the rain). If you've got a macro lens, this is an amazing time to use it. While you're shooting macro, don't forget to shoot the raindrops on leaves and stems as well, while they're reflecting the colors of the flowers (of course, don't forget to shoot on a tripod if you're shooting macro).

(3) **If you shoot on sunny days**, try to shoot in the morning and late afternoon. To make the most of this light, shoot with a long zoom lens and position yourself so the flowers are backlit, and you'll get some spectacular (but controlled) back lighting.

Don't Wait for Rain—Fake it!

This one may sound cheesy at first, but you'll be shocked at how well this works. Instead of waiting for a rainy day to shoot, take a little spray bottle with you, fill it with water, and spray the flowers with water yourself. I found a nice little spray bottle in Walgreens' beauty section (I know what you're thinking, "Walgreens has a beauty section?" Believe it or not, they do) for a couple of bucks, and it works wonders. Just a couple of quick spritzes with the spray bottle and you've got some lovely drops of water on your petals, and no one will ever know you didn't wait patiently for Mother Nature to intervene. Get a small enough bottle and you can carry it in your camera bag (empty, of course). By the way, I've used this spray bottle technique to shoot some yellow roses I bought for my wife, and by using a macro lens you'd swear I was shooting on the White House lawn after a spring shower. Try this once—you'll become a believer.

TIP THAT DOESN'T BELONG IN THIS BOOK

There's another hidden benefit of carrying a small spray bottle in your camera bag: getting wrinkles out of clothes. Just give your shirt, blazer, photographer's vest, etc., a couple of spritzes before bed and when you wake up in the morning, the wrinkles are gone. I know, this has little to do with photography, but I had this empty space at the bottom here, so I figured I'd pass this on.

Flowers on a Black Background

One of the most dramatic compositions for shooting flowers is to position a single flower on a black background. You can add a black background in Photoshop, but in most cases that is just way too much work. Instead, do what the pros do—put a black background behind your flower when you shoot it. My buddy Vincent Versace, one of the leading nature photographers (and instructors) in the business, told me his trick—he wears a black jacket while out shooting flowers, and if he sees a flower he wants on a black background, he has his assistant (or a friend, or his wife, or a passerby, etc.) hold the back of his jacket behind the flower. I know, it sounds crazy—until you try it yourself. If you're shooting flowers indoors (I shoot nearly every arrangement I buy for my wife, or that we receive from friends), buy a yard of either black velvet or black velour (velvet runs around $10–15 per yard; velour runs around $5–10 per yard) and literally put it behind your flowers. You can prop it up on just about anything (I hate to admit it, but I've even propped up my velour background by draping it over a box of my son's Cookie Crisp cereal). Leave a few feet between your flowers and the black background (so the light falls off and the black looks really black) and then shoot away. Now, what kind of light works best? Keep reading to find out.

Flowers on a White Background

Another popular look for a flower photographer is to shoot on a white background. You could buy a seamless roll of paper from your local camera store (it's pretty cheap), but it's usually much wider than you need. Plus, unless you're shooting flowers for a florist, you're usually not going to want to see the vase. That's why I go to Office Depot and buy two or three 20x30" sheets of white mounting board (it looks like poster board, but it's much thicker and stiffer). I usually position one behind the flowers (in a vase), and then use the other to reflect natural light (from a window with indirect sunlight) back onto the white background so it doesn't look gray. Again, put about 3 feet between your flowers and the background, and use that natural light to capture your flowers on what appears to be a solid white background you added in Photoshop, but it was even easier because you did it in the camera.

PUT THAT SHOWER CURTAIN TO WORK

If you buy the white shower curtain mentioned in the tip on the next page, here's another way to stretch your shopping dollar—use it as your white background. As long as you're using a shallow depth of field, you'll never know that white background is a shower curtain. Just don't shoot at f/11 or f/16 or people will say things like, "Hey, nice shower curtain," or, "Did you shoot that in the bathroom?"

The Perfect Light for Indoor Flower Shots

If you're shooting flowers indoors, you don't have to buy an expensive lighting rig (finally, something you don't have to spend a bunch of money on), because flowers love diffused natural light. By diffused, I mean that it's not getting direct sunlight, so any soft light coming in from a window works just great. If your window is really, really dirty, that's even better because it makes the light even more diffuse. So look for a window in your house, studio, office, etc., that has non-direct sunlight coming in. Then set your flowers near that window, and position them so you're getting side lighting (if the natural light hits the flowers head on, they'll look kind of flat—you need that extra dimension that side lighting brings). Set up your tripod so you're shooting the flowers at eye level (remember, don't shoot down on flowers). Now you're ready to shoot in some beautiful, soft light, and you didn't spend a dime (at least on lighting, anyway).

HOW TO CREATE THE PERFECT NATURAL LIGHT BY CHEATING

If you're faced with nothing but harsh direct sunlight through your open window, you can cheat—just go to Wal-Mart, Kmart, or Target and buy two things: (1) a frosted white shower curtain (or shower curtain liner), and (2) some tacks or push pins. Go back to your harsh light window, tack up your frosted shower curtain, and enjoy the best diffused natural light you've seen. Don't worry—I won't tell anybody.

Where to Get Great Flowers to Shoot

©ISTOCKPHOTO/BRIGIDA SORIANO

This may sound like the "Duh" tip of the book, but I can't tell you how many times I've told a photographer about this and they say, "Gee, I never thought of that." To get some really great flowers to shoot, just go to a local florist and buy them (see, there's that "duh" part). You can pick exactly which individual flowers you want (I like shooting roses, calla lilies, and daisies myself), and chances are the flowers you're getting are in great shape (they're fresh). You can reject any flower they pull out that has brown spots or is misshapen (I love that word, "misshapen"), and you don't have to pay to have them arranged. You can often walk out for less than 10 bucks with some amazing-looking subjects to shoot at the height of their freshness (though sometimes you have to wait a day or so until your roses are in full bloom).

WANT BETTER-LOOKING FLOWER SHOTS? CHOOSE BETTER-LOOKING FLOWERS

When you're walking through a field of flowers, you're going to see some with broken petals, half-eaten petals, missing petals, and some that are a little bit wilted. Keep walking. Don't stop at the first "okay-looking" flower you run across. Great flower shots start with flowers that are healthy looking, with beautiful petals and crisp green stems. Be picky about which ones you choose to shoot.

Stopping the Wind

If you're shooting flowers outdoors, you're bound to run into the natural enemy of flower photography—wind. There's nothing more frustrating than standing there, tripod set, camera aimed and focused, and you're waiting for the wind to die down enough to get the shot. This is especially bad if you're shooting macro, where the slightest movement spells disaster (well, not disaster, but a really blurry photo). You can try the old use-your-body-to-block-the-wind trick (which rarely works, by the way), but you're actually better off letting the camera fix the problem. Switch to shutter priority mode (where you control the shutter speed and your camera takes care of adjusting the rest to give you a proper exposure), then increase the shutter speed to at least 1/250 of a second or higher. This will generally freeze the motion caused by wind (unless it's hurricane season). If the higher shutter speed doesn't do the trick, then you have to go to Plan B, which is making the wind the subject. That's right, if you can't beat 'em, join 'em—use a very slow shutter speed so you see the movement of the flowers (you'll actually see trails as the flower moves while your shutter is open), and in effect you'll "see" the wind, creating an entirely different look. Give this seeing-the-wind trick a try, and you might be surprised how many times you'll be hoping the wind picks up after you've got your regular close-ups already done.

Consider Just Showing One Part

Although most of the time we'll be capturing one or more flowers in our frame, you can create flower images with a lot of impact by zooming in really tight and just showing part of a flower. One single petal (if it's a larger flower) or 1/3 or 1/2 of the flower can really create a dynamic-looking image. One of the reasons why these images are so interesting is because this close-up view of flowers is one we normally don't see. This doesn't take any special technique—you just have to zoom in really close (and if you have a macro lens, it's even easier getting in really tight on just part of the flower).

SHUTTER SPEED: 1/25 SEC   F-STOP: F/2.8   ISO: 1000   FOCAL LENGTH: 82mm | PHOTOGRAPHER: SCOTT KELBY

Chapter Three

Shooting Weddings Like a Pro

There Is No Retaking Wedding Photos. It Has Got to Be Right the First Time!

If you're living your life and you think to yourself, "Ya know, I've got it pretty easy," then it's time to shoot a wedding. Don't worry, this isn't something you're going to have to go looking for—if you've got even one long lens (200mm or longer), it will find you. That's because in a lot of people's minds, if you have a long lens, you're a serious photographer. It's true. Seriously, try this: show up at an event with a 200mm to 400mm lens on your camera and people will literally get out of your way. They assume you've been hired by the event and that you're on official photography business, and they will stand aside to let you shoot. It's the equivalent of walking into a factory with a clipboard—people assume you're legit and they let you go about your business. Add a photographer's vest and it's like having an official press pass to anything (try this one—you'll be amazed). Anyway, if you have a long lens, before long someone you know will get married but they won't have a budget for a professional photographer (like your cousin Earl). He'll ask, "Can you shoot our wedding photos?" Of course, you're a nice person and you say, "Why sure." Big mistake. You're going to work your butt off, miss all the food, drinks, and fun, and you'll experience stress at a level only NORAD radar operators monitoring North Korea ever achieve. A wedding ceremony happens once in real time. There are no second takes, no room for mess-ups, no excuses. Don't make Earl's bride really mad—read this chapter first.

Tricks for Low-Light Shooting in a Church, Part 1

Although you usually should use a tripod when shooting the formals (the group shots after the ceremony with the bride, groom, family members, etc.), when shooting the wedding ceremony in a low-light situation like a church, you'll probably need to hand-hold your shots. This is a problem because hand-holding in low-light situations is almost a guarantee of having blurry photos. Here's why: When there's low lighting, your camera compensates for it by slowing down the shutter speed to take in more light so it can make a proper exposure. So, your exposure will still be right, but chances are your photos will wind up being blurry because the shutter speed isn't fast enough. Any tiny little movement on your part equals blurry photos. So, how do the pros get those crisp low-light shots in a setting like a church? Well, one thing they do is increase their digital camera's ISO setting, which raises the camera's shutter speed (you generally need a shutter speed of at least 1/60 of a second for non-blurry photos). Luckily, today's DSLR cameras let you shoot at high ISOs with little visible noise. So, how high can you go? At least ISO 800, but you can usually get away with as high as ISO 1600 in most situations (or more, depending on your camera model—generally, the more expensive the camera, the less noise you'll see shooting at high ISOs). So, now that you know what to do, here's how to do it: Aim at the low-light scene you want shoot, press your shutter button halfway down, and look in your viewfinder to see what your shutter speed will be. If it's slower than 1/60 of a second, you're going to need to crank up the ISO until you see your shutter speed hit at least 1/60 of a second or faster (then hold your camera very steady).

Tricks for Low-Light Shooting in a Church, Part 2

The second trick wedding pros use to shoot in low-light situations is to shoot with a fast lens to let in more light (by that, I mean a lens where the largest available f-stop is something like f/1.4 or f/1.8, or maybe f/2.8—lower numbers are better). Once you have one of these lenses, shooting at these fast f-stops (let's use f/1.8, for example) lets a lot more light in, which gives you faster shutter speeds so you don't have to raise your ISO nearly as much (or at all). Since we know that raising our ISO adds at least some noise to our photos, if we have a choice, we'd rather use a fast lens than crank up our ISO. Now, depending on how dark it is where you're shooting, you might still have to increase the ISO amount, even when using one of these fast lenses at it's wide-open (lowest number) setting, but you'll have to raise it less, which means less noise.

Do You Really Need the f/1.4 Lens?

So, now you know that wedding pros use fast lenses to shoot in lower light with less noise, so having one of these in your wedding shoot camera bag makes a lot of sense. However, how fast of a lens do you really need? The two most popular fast lens sizes for wedding photographers these days are probably the 50mm prime and the 85mm prime (prime means it's not a zoom lens, it's stuck at that one focal length). Okay, so now do you need the f/1.4 or the f/1.8? This I can help with: At the time this book was published, a Nikon 50mm f/1.8 lens sold for around $125 (over at B&H). However, to get just 2/3 of a stop more light, the Nikon 50mm f/1.4 sold for around $330 (nearly triple the price). Besides the obvious price difference, you need to be more accurate with your focus shooting at f/1.4 than you do shooting at f/1.8 (shooting a close object with either is going to create a very shallow depth of field. For example, if you shoot a close-up portrait at f/1.4, the tip of your subject's nose could be in focus, but then their eyes would be a bit out of focus, and their hair would be way out of focus). For that reason, I'm personally more likely to shoot at f/1.8 (it gives me a little more latitude, and a little more area in focus). As for quality, there's a lot of debate as to whether anyone can really see the quality difference between the f/1.4 or the f/1.8, so for most folks, I recommend going with the less expensive f/1.8 lens (so, who would I recommend buy the f/1.4 model? That's easy—rich doctors).

Getting Soft, Diffused Light with Flash, Part 1

If you're shooting your weddings with a flash indoors, you're likely to get harsh shadows and unflattering, flat light, but it doesn't have to be that way. The trick for getting soft, diffused light is to get a flash diffuser of some sort. One of the most popular ones these days is the Westcott Micro Apollo Softbox (shown above), which runs around $30. Another popular flash diffuser is Gary Fong's Lightsphere Collapsible, which sells for around $45. Both attach over your flash unit, and do a great job of softening the light and dispersing it evenly. This will make a big difference in the quality of the light that falls on your bride, groom, and bridal party, and you'll get much more professional results for a very small investment.

WAY COOL TIP

If you're shooting in very high ISOs, you'll want to know about a popular Photoshop plug-in for wedding photographers called Dfine 2.0 (from Nik Software). Besides reducing noise, a happy side effect is that it also smooths skin.

Getting Soft, Diffused Light with Flash, Part 2

The other method of getting soft, diffused, and better yet, directional light using a flash (the key word here is directional, because it keeps your flash shots from looking flat) works if you're using an external flash unit (and not the built-in flash on your camera, which is pretty limited, as you'll soon see). The advantage of an external flash unit is that you can change the angle and direction of the flash. The reason this is cool is that instead of aiming your flash right into your subject's face (which gives the most harsh, flat light you can imagine), you can bounce the light off one of two places: (1) The ceiling. If the room you're shooting in has a white ceiling (and chances are the ceiling is white), then you can aim your flash head up at the ceiling at a 45° angle (as shown above, and provided that the ceiling isn't more than 10 feet tall) and the ceiling will absorb the harsh light, and what will fall on your subject is much softer, smoother light and, best of all, it won't cast hard shadows behind your subject. Instead, your soft shadows will cast on the ground (and out of your frame). Now, want to take this up another notch? Then instead of aiming at the ceiling, (2) have an assistant (a friend, relative, etc.) hold a reflector on your left or right side, slightly above shoulder height, and angle your flash head into that. So now, the reflector eats up the harsh light, but better yet, since the reflector is at an angle, it casts soft directional light on an angle, too. This puts soft shadows on one side of the bride's (groom's, bridesmaid's, etc.) face, giving a more pleasing and less flat lighting effect (think of it as side lighting).

Use Your Flash at Outdoor Weddings

One trick that wedding photographers have been using for years is to use fill flash outdoors on sunny days. I know, it sounds crazy to use a flash when the sun is bright in the sky, but wedding photographers add flash to these daylight shots to help eliminate those hard, harsh shadows in their subjects' faces, and make the bride and groom look more natural under these undesirable lighting conditions (plus it usually adds nice catchlights in the eyes of your subjects, as well). Always check the results in your LCD monitor to make sure your light is properly balanced. Here's a shot of me taken while shooting a recent wedding. Notice the flash doesn't fire straight into the wedding party's faces. Instead, the head is rotated to the right (or left) and tilted 45°, so the flash fills in the shadows yet doesn't have that harsh look you'd get by aiming the flash straight at your subjects. As long as you're not more than 8 or 10 feet away from your subject, don't worry—the flash will still be effective, even though it's not aiming straight on.

ANOTHER COOL FLASH TIP

Here's another tip that will make your flash seem less "flashy" when shooting outdoors: use your camera's flash exposure compensation button and change the flash exposure compensation to –1 (it works the same way regular exposure compensation works, but for flash exposures). Your flash will still help lift out the shadows, but now without being so obvious.

Finding That Perfect Bridal Light

At most weddings there is a spot with really spectacular light just waiting for you to walk over and find it, but once you find it, you have to know how to use it. That light, of course, is natural light coming in through a window (it's hard to make a photo look bad in that light). Look for a window that doesn't have direct sunlight (a window facing north usually works well to provide some soft, diffused light). So, once you find this wonderful natural side light coming in from a window, where do you place the bride? Ideally, about 6 to 8 feet from the window, so the light falls evenly and softly upon her (almost sounds like a song, doesn't it?). This is a great spot for shooting some pre-wedding shots of the bride alone, the bride with her mother, and the bride with her father.

Don't Spend Too Much Time On the Formals

SCOTT KELBY AND ©ISTOCKPHOTO/ALEKSANDR LOBANOV

A very famous wedding photographer gave me some great advice one day about shooting the formals (the posed group portraits, usually taken after the ceremony, of the bride and groom posed with the wedding party, with just the bridesmaids, just the groomsmen, just the bride's parents, just the groom's parents, and so on). He said, "Get the formals over fast. You have to do them, but nobody cares about them." They don't usually include a special or touching moment and they're rarely photos anybody talks about after the wedding (unless, of course, you forget to do them). So, get everybody together, knock those shots out, and move on to the important job of capturing the moments that do matter.

Formals: Who to Shoot First

After the ceremony, in most cases you'll shoot the formal portraits of the bride and groom posed with everyone from bridesmaids to grandparents. The hard part is rounding up all the people you'll need to shoot with the bride and groom at the exact time you need them. This can take 30 minutes or three hours—it's up to you and how organized you are. Here's a tip to make things move as quickly as possible: gather everyone that will appear in any shot together right from the start. While they're all sitting there, shoot the formal bride and groom portraits first (you'll see why in just a moment). Once you've got those out of the way, shoot the largest groups of people (the huge family portraits), and then once you're done with a group (like the grandparents for example), send them off to the reception. So, in short—start with everyone, and then as you shoot them, release them to go to the reception until you're left with just the bride and groom again. If you don't do it this way, you'll wind up standing around for long periods of time waiting for Uncle Arnie, who's somewhere in the reception hall. The reason you shoot the bride and groom first is that the pressure to get the bride and groom to the reception hall increases exponentially as time goes by, because generally they hold the meal until the bride and groom have arrived. So, everyone is sitting in the reception hall waiting on you—the photographer. You then wind up rushing the most important portraits of them all (the ones the couple will actually buy—their formal portraits). Make your life easy—start big, then get small.

Formals: Build Off the Bride and Groom

There's a popular format for creating all your formals—have the bride and groom in the center, and have them stay put. They don't move—instead you have groups of other people (bridesmaids, groomsmen, the best man, maid of honor, parents, grandparents, etc.) move in and out around them. Use the bride and groom as building blocks and everything will be much easier (well, as far as posing your large groups goes anyway).

How to Pose the Bride with Other People

When you're posing other people with the bride, including the groom, to create the level of closeness you'll want in your photos, be sure to position the heads of the bride and the other person very close to each other. This doesn't sound like it would be a problem, until you actually start posing people. When they fall into what feels like a natural pose, they leave way too much room between their head and the bride's head. While this may look perfectly natural in person, the photos will lack a closeness that will be really obvious. I've seen this again and again, and I constantly have to remind people, even the groom, to move their head in very close to the bride's. To them, it just feels unnatural being that close while posing, but if they don't do it, your shots will look stiff and unnatural. Keep an eye out for this on your next wedding shoot and you'll be amazed at how the level of closeness between your subjects goes up, giving you much more powerful images.

The Trick to Keeping Them from Blinking

If you shoot a group of five people or more, it's almost guaranteed that one or more people will have their eyes shut. It's another natural law of wedding photography, but you're not going to have to worry about that very much, because you're about to learn a great trick that will eliminate most, if not all, instances of people blinking or having their eyes closed. When you're ready to shoot the shot, have everybody close their eyes, and then on the count of three have them all open their eyes and smile. Then, wait one more count before you take your shot. When I'm shooting these groups, here's what I say, "Okay, everybody close your eyes. Now open them on 3-2-1…open!" Then I wait one count after they open their eyes before I take the shot. It works wonders.

Formals: Where to Aim

©ISTOCKPHOTO/KEVIN RUSS

When shooting large groups for the formal portraits, you'll want to make sure that you use an aperture setting that keeps everyone in focus. Try f/11 for a reasonable depth of field for groups. Now, where do you focus? If you have more than one row of people deep, the old rule (which still stands true today) is to focus on the eyes of the people in the front row. You have more depth behind than in front, so make sure you focus on them, and the rest should be okay, but if that front row is out of focus, the whole shot is a bust.

Formals: How High to Position Your Camera

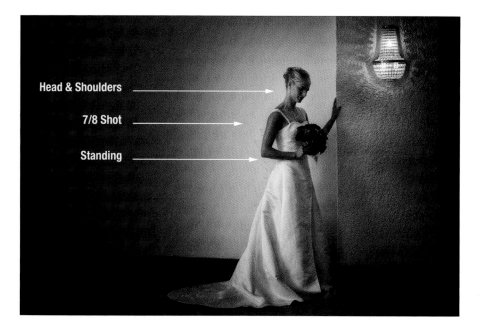

When you're shooting your formal shots, the height that you position the camera is actually very important, because if it's not positioned correctly, your subject's body can look distorted or some parts can look larger than normal (in general, this is just not good stuff). So, finding the right height for professional portraits is critical. Here are a few guidelines to help you get the pro look:

Standing, Full-Length Portrait: Position your camera (on your tripod) at the bride's waist height (yes, you'll have to squat down/bend over, etc., but the final result will be worth it). Keep your lens straight (don't aim up toward the bride's face).

⅞ Shots (from the Calf Up): Position your camera (on your tripod) at the bride's chest level and shoot with your lens straight from there.

Head and Shoulders Shots: Position your camera (on your tripod) either at the bride's eye level or slightly above.

Formals: Don't Cut Off Joints

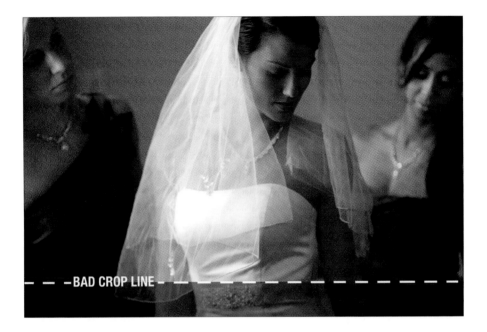

When you're framing your formals in your viewfinder, for a more professional look, be careful not to cut off anyone at the joints (in other words, don't let the bottom of the frame cut anyone off at the elbow or knee. On the side of the frame, don't cut anyone off at the wrist or elbow either). Basically, stay away from the joints. If you have to crop an arm or leg off, try to do it as close to the middle of the arm or leg as possible, staying clear of the joints. 'Nuf said.

Formals: The Trick to Great Backgrounds

In formal portraits, the backgrounds are just that—backgrounds. And the key to a great background is using a very simple one. The simpler, the better. So don't look for an outdoor shot with a waterfall, 36 different kinds of plant life, and flowers blossoming from hanging vines, etc. Look for simplicity or it will greatly distract from your portraits, and give your formals an uncomfortable look (yet nobody will know why). Plus, if for any reason you have to retouch the background later in Photoshop, the less busy the background, the easier your retouch will be.

BACKGROUND TIP

Here's another good tip: vary your background for your formals. It may not seem like a big deal at the time, but when you see the same background over and over and over again in the final wedding album, it can become really tedious. Once you've shot a few sets on one background, if there's another simple background nearby, try it in order to keep the album from looking like a cookie cutter.

Reception Photos: Making Them Dance

There's a problem with taking photos of people dancing. If you shoot them with a flash (and most likely you will), it will freeze their movement, so they'll look like they're just standing still, but in somewhat awkward poses. It still amazes me how people doing a line dance can be pictured as people in a police lineup—the camera just doesn't capture motion, unless you tell it to. There are really two techniques: The first is in the camera. Use a slow shutter speed so the people have a motion blur, which makes them look like (you guessed it) they're dancing. (If you want the main person in your shot, like the bride, to be in focus, you can use panning, where you take the camera and follow their move-ment.) If you didn't remember to employ this technique during your reception shoot, then you can add this motion blur in Photoshop. The first step is to duplicate the Background layer. Then go under the Filter menu, under Blur, and choose Motion Blur. Set the Angle to 0°, then increase the Distance until things look like they're really moving. If you want to keep one person in focus, get the Eraser tool, choose a really big, soft-edged brush (like the soft round 200-pixel brush) and erase over the person you're focusing on (like the bride, etc.) so that person appears in focus, while everyone else is dancing and moving around having a good time.

Your Main Job: Follow the Bride

The main focus at any wedding is the bride, so make darn sure your main focus at the pre-wedding, the ceremony, the formals, and the reception is the bride. Follow the bride just like you would follow the quarterback if you were shooting a football game. Especially if you're going to be selling these photos, as it will be the bride (either directly or indirectly) who will be buying the prints. So, make darn sure that she's the clear star of the show (photos of Uncle Arnie at the reception don't sell well, if you get my drift).

Shooting the Details (& Which Ones to Shoot)

The photojournalism style of wedding photography is very big right now (where you tell the story of the wedding in photos as if you were covering it for a newspaper or magazine). One of the cornerstone elements of this technique is to make sure to photo-graphically capture the tiny details of the wedding, especially behind the scenes before the wedding. Here's a list of things you might want to capture (shoot), which can either stand alone in the wedding album or be used as backgrounds for other photos:

- The bride's shoes

- The bride's dress hanging on a hanger

- The bride's tiara, necklace, etc.

- The wedding invitation

- The sheet music played at the wedding

- The guestbook (once a few people have signed it)

- Their champagne glasses

- Name cards at the reception

- Their wedding rings (perhaps posed on the invitation with some rose petals casually placed nearby)

- The airline tickets for their honeymoon

- The sheet music, or CD jewel case, to the music for their first dance

- The groom's boutonniere

- The bride's bouquet

- Any fine detail in her dress

Change Your Vantage Point to Add Interest

Want to create a shot everyone will remember? Shoot it from a high vantage point (look for a second story window you can shoot down from, or a balcony on the second floor, a bridge, etc.). If you can't find an existing high vantage point, then you can always create your own by bringing (or borrowing) a ladder to shoot from. Of course, be careful, because being on a ladder with expensive camera equipment is the stuff Hollywood comedies are made of. This high vantage point trick is ideal for shooting bridesmaids, groomsmen, the bride and groom, and even the bride alone (as shown here, where I shot the bride while standing on a ladder).

What to Shoot with a Wide-Angle Lens

At weddings, there are three things you're definitely going to want to shoot with a wide-angle lens. One is the rice throwing (of course, they don't actually throw rice anymore). You'll want to shoot this with a wide-angle lens so you get the bride, groom, and—just as important—the crowd throwing the rice (or birdseed, or blowing bubbles, etc.) behind and around them. Another thing you'll want a wide-angle lens for is shooting the interior of the church. The bride is going to expect a photo that takes it all in and your wide-angle lens will be your Get Out of Jail Free card when it comes to covering this all-important shot. Lastly, you'll want your wide-angle lens for shooting the bouquet toss and garter toss, so you can get both the tosser and the anxious crowd waiting to capture the prize (so to speak). Go wide, shoot from in front of the bride, and you'll get it all in one shot (but don't just take one shot—this is where a burst of shots will pay off).

Keep Backup Memory Cards on You

It's not unusual for a pro wedding photographer to shoot 750 shots in one wedding, covering the four major parts of a wedding (the pre-wedding shots, the ceremony, the formals, and the reception), so it's likely you'll be shooting a similar amount (maybe less, maybe more, but it will be literally hundreds of shots). The last thing you want to happen is to run out of film (in other words—you don't want to fill up your digital camera's memory card unless you have an empty backup card ready to step right in so you can keep shooting). The trick here is to keep a spare backup memory card physically on you at all times. Keep one right there in your pocket (or purse) so the moment your card reads full, you're just seconds away from continuing your shoot. It's a natural law of wedding photography that your memory card will become full at the most crucial moment of the ceremony, and if you have to stop to go find your backup card (in your camera bag across the room, in the car, or in the reception hall), you're going to miss the most important shot of the day (I learned this the hard way). So always keep a backup physically on you, so you're only 10 seconds away from shooting again.

Back Up Your Photos Onsite

COURTESY OF SANHO

A wedding happens once. You don't get a redo, so make sure that backing up your photos on location is a part of your workflow. If you fill a memory card, and pop in a new one, the next thing you should be doing is backing up that full card to a hard drive, like the Sanho 250-GB HyperDrive ColorSpace UDMA2 Multimedia Player/Storage Device (shown above), which lets you pop a CompactFlash card directly into the unit and back up your photos onto it without having a computer nearby. As soon as you fill a card, pop it into the Sanho HyperDrive and hit the copy button. In just a few minutes, your memory card (with those irreplaceable photos) is backed up. Also, as soon as you return to your studio, immediately copy all the photos on the backup drive onto a removable hard drive, so now you have two backups of the wedding photos. This backing up is so important—without a backup, you're placing a lot of faith in those memory cards. Imagine how you'd feel having to tell a bride and groom that your memory card somehow became corrupted and you lost the shots of their ceremony. You can sidestep that crisis (and a potential lawsuit) by making one or two simple backups.

Scott's Gear Finder

The 250-GB Sanho HyperDrive (around $370)

The 750-GB NEXTO DI Photo Storage Portable Backup Drive (around $450)

If Shooting JPEGs, Use a Preset White Balance

If you're shooting with your digital camera set to RAW format, you don't need to worry about the white balance (leave it set at Auto White Balance, you can always change it later, in Photoshop), but if you're like many pro wedding photographers, you're shooting in JPEG Fine format (so you can take more shots and write to the memory card faster). If that's the case, then you're better off choosing a preset white balance in the camera that matches the lighting situation you're shooting in (that way, the overall color of your photo looks balanced for the light). If you don't set the right white balance, your photos can look too yellow or too blue. Luckily, choosing a white balance is easier than you'd think, and it will save you loads of time later when you're processing your photos in Photoshop. Just go to the menu on your digital camera, scroll to the white balance control, and choose Incandescent if you're shooting in a standard reception hall, or Daylight if you're shooting an outdoor wedding. If you're using a flash, set your white balance to Flash. It's that easy to get your color in line.

SHUTTER SPEED: 1/125 SEC   F-STOP: F/8   ISO: 100   FOCAL LENGTH: 70mm   PHOTOGRAPHER: SCOTT KELBY

Chapter Four

Shooting Landscapes Like a Pro

Pro Tips for Capturing the Wonder of Nature

If you ever get to shoot in some truly amazing outdoor locations, like the Grand Canyon or Yosemite National Park, it's really a very humbling photographic experience. The reason why is you're looking at this amazing vista, at the sheer grandeur of it all, and it looks so awe inspiring you'd figure a chimp could even take a great photo of it. I mean, it's just so spectacular, how could you mess it up? Then you set up your tripod, look in your viewfinder, and it happens—you begin to silently sob. You're sobbing because you bought all this expensive camera gear, with multiple camera bodies and lenses that cost more than a Toyota Prius hybrid, you've got more filters than a Ritz Camera store, and your camera bag weighs approximately 54 lbs. You saved all year, took your two-week vacation from work, bought round-trip airfare, and rented a huge SUV big enough to haul you, your family, and all your expensive gear out into the sweltering summer heat of the canyon. Now you're looking through your viewfinder and what you see doesn't look half as good as the stinkin' postcards in the park's gift shop that sell for $1.25 each. Tears begin to stream down your face as you realize that you're not going to get the shot you came for. And whose fault is all this? Ansel Adams—that's who. He screwed up the Grand Canyon, Yosemite, and a dozen other locations for us all. But even though we're not Ansel Adams, we can surely get better photos than the ones in the gift shop, right? Well, it starts with reading this chapter. Hey, it's a start.

The Golden Rule of Landscape Photography

LOCATION: MONTEREY, CA

There's a golden rule of landscape photography, and you can follow every tip in this chapter, but without *strictly* following this rule, you'll never get the results the top pros do. As a landscape photographer, you can only shoot two times a day: (1) Dawn. You can shoot about 15 to 30 minutes before sunrise, and then from 30 minutes to an hour (depending on how harsh the light becomes) afterward. The only other time you can shoot is (2) dusk. You can shoot from 15 to 30 minutes before sunset, and up to 30 minutes afterward. Why only these two times? Because that's the rule. Okay, there's more to it than that. These are the only times of day when you get the soft, warm light and soft shadows that give professional quality lighting for landscapes. How stringent is this rule? I'll never forget the time I was doing a Q&A session for professional photographers. The other instructor was legendary *National Geographic* photographer Joe McNally. A man in the crowd asked Joe, "Can you really only shoot at dawn and dusk?" Joe quietly took his tripod and beat that man to death. Okay, that's an exaggeration, but what Joe said has always stuck with me. He said that today's photo editors (at the big magazines) feel so strongly about this that they won't even consider looking at any of his, or any other photographer's, landscape work if it's not shot at dawn or dusk. He also said that if he takes them a shot and says, "Look, it wasn't taken during those magic hours, but the shot is amazing," they'll still refuse to even look at it. The point is, professional landscape photographers shoot at those two times of day, and only those two times. If you want pro results, those are the only times you'll be shooting, too.

Become Married to Your Tripod

Okay, so now you know that as a pro landscape shooter your life is going to be like this: you get up before dawn, and you miss dinner about every evening (remember, there's no shame in coming to dinner late). If you're okay with all that, then it's time to tell you the other harsh reality—since you'll be shooting in low light all the time, you'll be shooting on a tripod all the time. Every time. Always. There is no hand-holding in the professional landscape photography world. Now, I must warn you, you will sometimes find landscape photographers out there at dawn some mornings shooting the same thing you are, and they're hand-holding their cameras. They don't know it yet, but once they open their photos in Photoshop, they are going to have the blurriest, best-lit, out-of-focus shots you've ever seen. Now, what can you do to help these poor hapless souls? Quietly, take your tripod and beat them to death. Hey, it's what Joe McNally would do. (Kidding. Kind of.)

TRIPODS: THE CARBON FIBER ADVANTAGE

The hottest thing right now in tripods is carbon fiber. Tripods made with carbon fiber have two distinct advantages: (1) they're much lighter in weight than conventional metal tripods without giving up any strength or stability, and (2) carbon fiber doesn't resonate like metal, so you have less chance of vibration. However, there's a downside: as you might expect, they're not cheap.

Shoot in Aperture Priority Mode

Nikon

Canon

The shooting mode of pro outdoor photographers is aperture priority mode (that's the little A or Av on your digital camera's mode dial). The reason why this mode is so popular is that it lets you decide how to creatively present the photo. Here's what I mean: Let's say you're shooting a tiger with a telephoto zoom lens and you decide you want the tiger (who's in the foreground of the shot) to be in focus, but you want the background out of focus. With aperture priority mode, it's easy—set your aperture to the smallest number your lens will allow (for example, f/2.8, f/4, f/5.6, etc.) and then focus on the tiger. That's it. The camera (and the telephoto lens) does the rest—you get a sharp photo of the tiger and the background is totally out of focus. So, you just learned one of the three aperture tricks: low numbers (and a zoom lens) leave your subject in the foreground in focus, while the background goes out of focus. Now, what do you do if you want the tiger and the background to both be in focus (you want to see the tiger and his surroundings clearly)? You can move your aperture to either f/8 or f/11. These two settings work great when you just want to capture the scene as your eye sees it (without the creative touch of putting the background majorly out of focus). Far away backgrounds (way behind the tiger) will be a little bit out of focus, but not much. That's the second trick of aperture priority mode. The third trick is which aperture to use when you want as much as possible in focus (the foreground, the middle, the background—everything): just choose the highest number your lens will allow (f/22, f/36, etc.).

Composing Great Landscapes

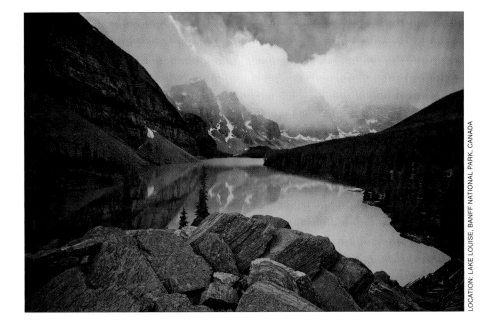

LOCATION: LAKE LOUISE, BANFF NATIONAL PARK, CANADA

The next time you pick up a great travel magazine that features landscape photography or look at some of the work from the masters in digital landscape photography, like David Muench, Moose Peterson, Stephen Johnson, Bill Fortney, and John Shaw, take a moment to study some of their wonderful, sweeping images. One thing you'll find that most have in common is that these landscape shots have three distinct things: (1) A foreground. If shooting a sunset, the shot doesn't start in the water—it starts on the beach. The beach is the foreground. (2) They have a middle ground. In the case of a sunset shot, this would be either the ocean reflecting the sun, or in some cases it can be the sun itself. And lastly, (3) they have a background. In the sunset case, the clouds and the sky. All three elements are there, and you need all three to make a really compelling landscape shot. The next time you're out shooting, ask yourself, "Where's my foreground?" (because that's the one most amateurs seem to forget—their shots are all middle and background). Keeping all three in mind when shooting will help you tell your story, lead the eye, and give your landscape shots more depth.

ANOTHER ADVANTAGE OF SHOOTING AT DAWN

Another advantage of shooting at dawn (rather than at sunset) is that water (in ponds, lakes, bays, etc.) is more still at dawn because there's usually less wind in the morning than in the late afternoon. So, if you're looking for that glassy mirror-like reflection in the lake, you've got a much better shot at getting that effect at dawn than you do at dusk.

The Trick to Shooting Waterfalls

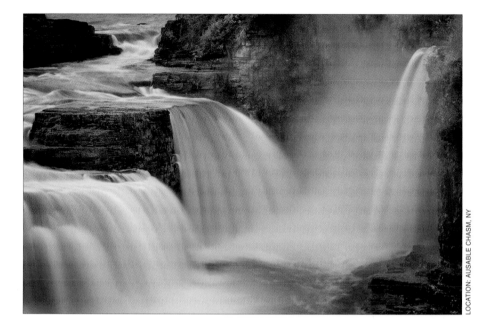

LOCATION: AUSABLE CHASM, NY

Want to get that silky waterfall or that stream effect you see in those pro photos? The secret is leaving your shutter open (for at least a second or two), so the water moves while everything else (the rocks and trees around the waterfall or stream) remains still. Here's what you do: switch your digital camera to shutter priority mode (the S or Tv on your camera's mode dial), and set the shutter speed to 1 or 2 full seconds. Now, even if you're shooting this waterfall on a bit of an overcast day, leaving your shutter open for a few seconds will let way too much light in, and all you'll get is a solid white, completely blown-out photo. That's why the pros do one of two things: (1) They shoot these water-falls at or before sunrise, or just after sunset, when there is much less light. Or they (2) use a stop-down filter. This is a special darkening filter that screws onto your lens that is so dark it shuts out most of the light coming into your camera. That way, you can leave the shutter open for a few seconds. Such little light comes in that it doesn't totally blow out your photo, and you wind up with a properly exposed photo with lots of glorious silky water. Now, if you don't have a stop-down filter and you run across a waterfall or stream that's deep in the woods (and deep in the shade), you can still get the effect by trying this: put your camera on a tripod, go to aperture priority mode, and set your aperture to the biggest number your lens will allow (probably either f/22 or f/36). This leaves your shutter open longer than usual (but that's okay, you're in deep shade, right?), and you'll get that same silky-looking water.

A Tip for Shooting Forests

LOCATION: MAUI, HI

Want a great tip for shooting forest scenes? Don't include the ground in your shots. That's right, the ground in the forest is often surprisingly messy (with dead branches, and leaves, and a really cluttered look) and that's why so many pro forest shots don't include the ground—it distracts from the beauty of the trees. So, easy enough—frame your shots so they don't include the ground, and you're shooting better forest shots right off the bat. Now, if the ground looks good, then by all means include it, but if it's a mess, you've got a way to save the shot. Here's another forest shooting tip: overcast days are great for shooting forests because it's difficult to get a decent forest shot in bright, harsh sunlight. However, there is one exception to this rule: if there's "atmosphere" (fog or mist) in the forest on bright days, the sun's rays cutting through the fog or mist can be spectacular.

THIS ISN'T A FOREST TIP. IT'S FOR WATERFALLS

So why is this tip here instead of on the waterfalls page? I ran out of room on that page. The tip is this: when shooting waterfalls, if you don't have a stop-down filter, then you can try putting your polarizing filter on instead. This serves two purposes: (1) it cuts the reflections in the waterfall and on the rocks, and (2) since it darkens, it can eat up about two stops of light for you, so you can shoot longer exposures with it than you could without it. Also, choosing slower shutter speeds exaggerates the silky water effect, so try a few different shutter speeds (4 seconds, 6 seconds, 10 seconds, etc.) and see which one gives you the best effect for what you're currently shooting.

Where to Put the Horizon Line

LOCATION: MONUMENT VALLEY NAVAJO TRIBAL PARK, MONUMENT VALLEY, UT

When it comes to the question of "Where do I place the horizon?" the answer is pretty easy. Don't take the amateur route and always place the horizon in the dead center of the photo, or your landscape shots will always look like snapshots. Instead, decide which thing you want to emphasize—the sky or the ground. If you have a great-looking sky, then put your horizon at the bottom third of your photo (which will give you much more emphasis on the sky). If the ground looks interesting, then make that the star of your photo and place the horizon at the top third of your photo. This puts the emphasis on the ground, and most importantly, either one of these methods will keep your horizon out of the center, which will give your shots more depth and interest.

REALLY BORING SKY? BREAK THE RULE

If you're shooting a landscape shot with a sky where nothing's really happening, you can break the 1/3 from the top horizon line rule and eliminate as much of the sky from view as possible. Make it 7/8 ground and 1/8 sky, so the attention is totally off the sky, and onto the more interesting foreground.

Getting More Interesting Mountain Shots

LOCATION: CANYONLANDS NATIONAL PARK, MOAB, UT

One theme you'll see again and again throughout this book is to shoot from angles we don't see every day. For example, if your subject is mountains, don't shoot them from the road at the bottom of the mountain. This is exactly how we see mountains every day when we drive by them on the interstate, so if you shoot them like that (from the ground looking up), you'll create shots that look very normal and average. If you want to create mountain shots that have real interest, give people a view they don't normally see—shoot from up high. Either drive up as high as you can on the mountain, or hike up as high as is safe, then set up your camera and shoot down on or across the mountains. (This is the same theory as not shooting down on flowers. We don't shoot down on flowers because that's the view we normally have of them. In turn, we don't shoot up at mountains, because we always see them from that same view. It's boring, regular, and doesn't show your viewer something they haven't seen a hundred times before.)

The Trick for Warmer Sunrises and Sunsets

Nikon   *Canon*

Here's a trick I picked up from Bill Fortney for getting even warmer sunrises and sunsets: For Nikon shooters, go to your camera's Shooting menu and choose Cloudy as your white balance. Press the right arrow button to get the White Balance Cloudy submenu, and move the dot in the middle of the grid to the right three spots (to A3), and then click OK. This does an amazing job of warming these types of photos. If you're a Canon shooter, go to your camera's menu and choose Cloudy as your white balance. Go back to the menu, select WB SHIFT/BKT, move the dot in the middle of the grid to the right three spots (to A3), and then press the Set button. *Note*: Don't forget to turn this setting off when you're not shooting sunrises or sunsets. Okay, it wouldn't be the worst thing in the world (it won't ruin all your subsequent shots), but your world will be a little warmer.

Turn on "The Blinkies" to Keep More Detail

Okay, they're technically not called "the blinkies" (that's our nickname for them), they're actually called highlight warnings (or highlight alerts) and having this turned on, and adjusting for it, is a critical part of getting properly exposed landscape shots. This warning shows exactly which parts of your photo have been overexposed to the point that there's no detail in those areas at all. You'll be amazed at how often this happens. For example, even on an overcast day, clouds can blow out (turn solid white with no detail) easily, so we keep our camera's highlight warning turned on. Here's how it works: When the high-light warning is turned on and you look at the shot in your LCD monitor, those blown out areas will start to blink like a slow strobe light. Now, these blinkies aren't always bad—if you shoot a shot where the sun is clearly visible, it's going to have the blinkies (I don't mean sunlight, I mean the red ball of the sun). There's not much detail on the suface of the sun, so I'd let that go. However, if your clouds have the blinkies, that's a different story. Probably the quickest way to adjust for this is to use your camera's exposure compensation control (covered on the next page). For now, let's focus on making sure your highlight warning (blinkies) is turned on. If you have a Nikon camera, press the playback button so you can see the photos on your memory card. Now, push the down arrow button to see file information, then the right arrow button until the word Highlights appears below your photo on the LCD monitor. If you have a Canon camera, press the playback button to view your images and then press the Info button to see the blinkies.

How to Deal with the Dreaded Blinkies

If you look on your camera's LCD monitor and you see the blinkies appearing in an area that's important to you (like in the clouds, or in someone's white shirt, or in the snow, etc.), then you can use your digital camera's exposure compensation control. Basically, you're going to lower the exposure until the blinkies go away. It usually takes a few test shots (trial and error) to find out how much you have to back down, but normally this only takes a few seconds. Here's how it works:

Nikon: Press the exposure compensation button that appears just behind your shutter button (as shown above). Then move the command dial until your exposure compensation reads –1/3 (that's minus 1/3 of a stop). Now take the same shot again and see if the blinkies are gone. If they're not, do the same thing, but lower the amount another 1/3, so it reads –2/3 of a stop, and so on, until the blinkies are gone.

Canon: Turn the mode dial to any creative zone mode except manual, turn the power switch to the quick control dial setting, then set the exposure compensation by turning the quick control dial on the back of the camera and using the settings mentioned above.

How to Show Size

©ISTOCKPHOTO/JIM VEILLEUX

If you've ever had a chance to photograph something like the California redwood trees or a huge rock formation out in Utah's Monument Valley, you've probably been disappointed that when you looked at those photos later, you lost all sense of their size. In person, those redwoods were wider around than a truck. In your photos, they could've been the regular pines in your backyard, because they lost their sense of size. That's why, when trying to show the size of an object, you need something in that shot to give the object a sense of scale. That's why many photographers prefer to shoot mountains with people in the scene (hikers, climbers, etc.) because it instantly gives you a frame of reference—a sense of scale that lets the viewer immediately have a visual gauge as to how large a mountain, or a redwood, or the world's largest pine cone really is. So, the next time you want to show the sheer size of something, simply add a person or a familiar object to your shot and you've got an instant frame of reference everyone can identify with. It'll make your shots that much stronger. (*Note:* By the way, this also works for things that are very small. Put the object in someone's hands, and it instantly tells the story.)

Don't Set Up Your Tripod. Not Yet

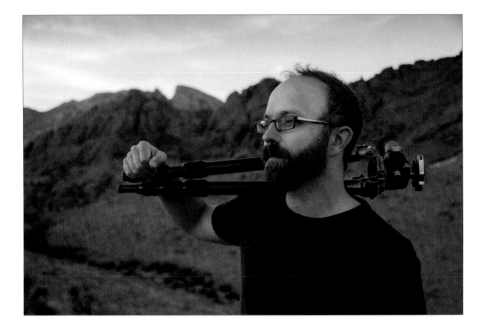

Okay, so you walk up on a scene (a landscape, a mountain range, a waterfall, etc.) and you set up your tripod and start shooting. What are the chances that you just happened to walk up on the perfect angle to shoot your subject? Pretty slim. But that's what most people do—they walk up on a scene, set up their tripod right where they're standing, and they start shooting. It's no big surprise that they wind up with the same shot every-body else got—the "walk-up" shot. Don't fall into this trap: before you set up your tripod, take a moment and simply walk around. View your subject from different angles, and chances are (in fact, it's almost guaranteed) that you'll find a more interesting perspective in just a minute or two. Also, hand-hold your camera and look through the viewfinder to test your angle out. Once you've found the perfect angle (and not just the most conve-nient one), you can then set up your tripod and start shooting. Now the odds are in your favor for getting a better than average take on your subject. This is one of the big secrets the pros use every day (legendary landscape photographer John Shaw has been teaching this concept for years)—they don't take the walk-up shot. They first survey the scene, look for the best angle, the best view, the interesting vantage point, and then (and only then) they set up their tripod. It sounds like a little thing (surveying the scene before you set up), but it's the little things that set the pros apart.

The Trick to Getting Richer Colors

One tool the pros use to get richer, more vivid colors is the polarizing filter. Of all the add-ons used by landscape pros, the polarizing filter is probably the most essential. This filter screws onto the end of your lens and it basically does two things: (1) it cuts the reflections in your photo big time (especially in water, on rocks, or on any reflective surface), and (2) it can often add more rich blues into your skies by darkening them and generally giving you more saturated colors throughout (and who doesn't want that?). Two tips: (1) polarizers have the most effect when you're shooting at a 90° angle from the sun, so if the sun is in front of you or behind you, they don't work all that well, and (2) you'll use the rotating ring on the filter to vary the amount (and angle) of polarization (it's also helpful so you can choose to remove reflections from either your sky or the ground). Once you see for yourself the difference a polarizing filter makes, you'll say something along the lines of, "Ahhhh, so that's how they do it."

POLARIZING TIP

If there's a lens the polarizing filter doesn't love, it's the super-wide-angle lens (like a 12mm or 10.5mm, etc.). Because the field of view is so wide, the sky winds up having uneven shades of blue, and because of that, many pros avoid using polarizers with super-wide-angle lenses. Also, when it comes to polarizers, it pays to buy a good one—that way it will be truly color balanced. It doesn't pay to scrimp here.

What to Shoot in Bad Weather

Okay, so you're thinking that it's an overcast or drizzly day, and you're going to spend the day inside working on your photos in Photoshop. That's not the worst idea in the world, but you'll miss some great shooting opportunities, like:

(1) **Right after a rain,** while it's still cloudy and dark, is the perfect time to shoot foliage, forests (the green leaves look more saturated and alive, even leaves on the ground look good, plus the water droplets on the leaves and flowers add interest), mossy rivers, and waterfalls (you can use slower shutter speeds while the sun is buried behind the overcast rain clouds).

(2) **If it's storming,** there's a good chance that right after the rain stops, and the clouds break, and the sun peeks through, there's a very dramatic shot coming. It may only last a couple of minutes, and it will either start storming again or clear up and just get really sunny (an outdoor photographer's enemy), so be ready for those few magical moments between storms. They're worth waiting for.

(3) **Before the storm "lets loose,"** you can get some really amazing skies, with angry clouds and sometimes colorful light or strong light beams. Most people miss these shots, so be ready (just don't shoot in the rain, to protect you and your gear).

Atmosphere Is Your Friend

LOCATION: GREAT SMOKY MOUNTAINS NATIONAL PARK, TN

Besides just keeping us here on earth, the atmosphere (low-hanging clouds or fog) can make for some really interesting landscape photos (we're talking soft, diffused light heaven). In fact, some of my personal favorite shots are taken when the fog rolls in between mountains (but, of course, you need to shoot this from above the fog on a higher mountaintop). I've shot horses on the beach with the fog rolling in and it creates almost a Hollywood fantasy effect that looks great on film (digital film, anyway). Also, beams of light in the forest, beaming through moisture in the air, or through thick fog, can be just amazing. Get up early (or miss dinner) to make the most of these atmospheric effects.

PROTECT YOUR GEAR TIP

Fog and moisture are fancy names for water, and digital cameras flat out do not like water, so make sure your gear is not getting silently soaked. You can buy rain gear for your camera from B&H, but in a pinch, use the shower cap from your hotel room and put it around your camera—it's not pretty, but it works.

Getting Rid of Lens Flare—The Manual Way

Another great reason to wear a baseball cap when you shoot (besides the two obvious reasons: [1] it protects you from the harmful rays of the sun, and [2] it looks cool) is to help eliminate (or at the very least, reduce) lens flare. If you're using a lens hood on your camera, that can certainly help, but I've found that often it alone is not enough. That's where your ballcap comes in—just take it off and position it above the right or left top side of your lens (depending on where the sun is positioned). Then look through your camera's view-finder to see (1) right where to position your ballcap so it blocks the lens flare from the sun (it's easier than you think), and (2) to make sure your ballcap doesn't show up in your photo (I've had more than one photo with the edge of a ballcap in the frame. I guess that's why they make Photoshop—to remove silly stuff like that). I'm still surprised how well this totally manual technique for removing lens flare works.

The Landscape Photographer's Secret Weapon

So, earlier you learned about the polarizer and how essential that filter is. This filter, the neutral density gradient filter, isn't necessarily essential but it is the secret weapon of professional landscape photographers. It lets them balance the exposure between the ground and the sky to capture a range of exposure which, without it, their camera could never pull off (it's either going to expose for the ground or for the sky, but not both at the same time). For example, let's say you're shooting a landscape at sunset. If you expose for the sky, the sky will look great but the ground will be way too dark. If you expose for the ground, then the sky will be way too light. So, how do you get both the sky and the ground to look right? With a neutral density gradient filter (a filter that's dark at the top and smoothly graduates down to transparent at the bottom). What this essentially does is darkens the sky (which would have been overexposed), while leaving the ground untouched, but the brilliance of it is the gradient—it moves from darkening (at the top of the filter) and then graduates smoothly down to transparent. That way it only darkens the sky, but it does so in a way that makes the top of the sky darker, and then your sky gradually becomes lighter until the filter has no effect at all by the time it reaches the ground. The result is a photo where both the sky and ground look properly exposed.

Keeping Your Horizons Straight

There is nothing that looks worse than a crooked horizon line. It's like when you don't get the fleshtone color right in a photo—it just jumps out at people (and people can't resist pointing this out. It doesn't matter if you've taken a photo with composition that would make Ansel Adams proud, they'll immediately say, "Your photo's crooked"). A great way to avoid this is by using the Virtual Horizon feature on your camera (if your camera has this feature, like the Nikon D600 shown above on the left) or with a double level—a simple little gizmo that slides into your flash hot shoe (that little bracket on the top of your camera where you'd attach an external flash). This double level gizmo has a mini-version of the bubble level you'd find at Home Depot and it lets you clearly see, in an instant, if your camera is level (and thus, your horizon line). The double level version works whether your camera is shooting in portrait or landscape orientation and is worth its weight in gold (of course, that's not saying very much, because I doubt the thing weighs even one ounce, but you get my drift). As luck would have it, they're more expensive than they should be— between $25 and $80—but still very worth it.

Shooting on Cloudy Days

LOCATION: TORC WATERFALL, KILLARNEY NATIONAL PARK, IRELAND

This is another one of those things that may initially elicit a "Duh" response, but I've been out shooting with more photographers than I can think of who didn't think of this simple concept when shooting on gray, overcast days—shoot to avoid the sky. I know, it sounds silly when you're reading it here, but I've heard it time and time again, "Ah, the sky is so gray today, I'm not going to shoot." Baloney. Just take shots that limit the amount of visible sky. That way, if you make a tonal adjustment later in Photoshop (that's a fancy way of saying, "I'm going to make the sky look bluer than it really was on that gray, over-cast day"), you won't have to work very hard. This just happened on my last shoot, where we'd have 20 minutes of blue sky and then an hour and a half of gray, overcast sky. I just really limited the amount of sky in my photos (I was shooting urban city photos), and then it took just seconds to fix in Photoshop. Here's what I did:

Step One: I opened one of the photos where the sky looked nice and blue, then took the Eyedropper tool (I), and clicked on the blue sky to make that my Foreground color.

Step Two: I then opened a photo with small amounts of gray, overcast sky and with the Magic Wand tool (W) clicked in the sky to select it (which took all of two seconds).

Step Three: I added a new blank layer above my Background layer and filled the selection with my Foreground color. That's it—my gray sky was blue.

Tips for Shooting Panoramas, Part 1

MIKE KUBEISY

There is something so fascinating about what happens when you stitch together five or six (or more) landscape photos into one long, single image. It's as close as you can get (with a photograph anyway) to recreating the experience of being there. Now, although this will take more than one page to describe, shooting panos right is easy, so if you're serious about panos, follow these rules. However, if you have Photoshop CS4 or higher (or Elements 6 or higher), Photomerge is so vastly improved, you can simply just overlap each shot by 20% when you shoot your pano.

(1) **Shoot your pano on a tripod.** (*Note:* Panos work best shot on a tripod, and if you're shooting at sunrise or sunset, they're a must. That being said, you can shoot hand-held if the light is bright enough, like if you're shooting in daylight or really bright cloudy light.)

(2) **Shoot vertically** (in portrait orientation) rather than horizontally (in landscape orientation). It'll take more shots to cover the same area, but you'll have less edge distortion and a better looking pano for your extra effort.

(3) **Switch your camera's white balance to Cloudy.** If you leave it set to Auto, your white balance may (will) change between segments, which is bad, bad, bad.

(4) **There's more**—go to the next page...

Tips for Shooting Panoramas, Part 2

MIKE KUBEISY

(5) **Press your shutter button halfway down** to set your exposure, then look in your viewfinder and make note of the f-stop and shutter speed. Now switch your camera to manual mode and dial in that f-stop and shutter speed. If you don't, and you shoot in an auto exposure mode of any kind, your exposure may (will) change for one or more of the segments.

(6) **Once you focus on the first segment,** turn off auto focus for your lens. That way, your camera doesn't refocus as you shoot the different segments.

(7) **Overlap each segment by 20–25%.** That's right, make sure that about 1/4 of your first shot appears in the second shot. Each segment needs to overlap by at least 20% so Photoshop's stitching software can match things up. This is very important.

(8) **Shoot fairly quickly**—especially if clouds are moving behind your landscape. Don't be lollygagging for two minutes between each shot. Git 'er done, or something could change (lighting, clouds, etc.) in your pano, which will really mess things up.

(9) **Use a shutter release,** or at the very least a self timer, so you don't have any camera movement as you're shooting each segment. Nothing's worse than one segment that is blurry.

Tips for Shooting Panoramas, Part 3

LOCATION: SEINE RIVER AND ÎLE DE LA CITÉ, PARIS, FRANCE

Now, if you followed the rules set out on the previous two pages, the rest is easy:

Step One: Open Photoshop and then go under Photoshop's File menu, under Automate, and choose Photomerge.

Step Two: In the resulting dialog, click the Browse button in the center, navigate to your pano photo segments, choose them all, and click Open.

Step Three: At the bottom of the Source Files section, make sure the Blend Images Together checkbox is turned on and turn on Vignette Removal. Leave the Layout set to Auto and click OK.

Step Four: Photoshop will then stitch the photos together into one seamless panorama (you may need to crop off any transparent areas). If you see a small seam at the top, between two segments, use the Clone Stamp tool (S) to cover it by pressing-and-holding the Option (PC: Alt) key and clicking in a nearby area of sky that looks similar to sample that area. Then, choose a soft-edged brush from the Brush Picker and clone (paint) over the little seam to hide it. If you still have some gaps in the corners, select them, then go under the Edit menu and choose Fill. In the Fill dialog, change the Use pop-up menu to Content-Aware and click OK. Use the Clone Stamp tool to clean up any problems.

Faking Panoramas

LOCATION: OUTSIDE BAR HARBOR, ME

If you have Photoshop or Photoshop Elements, there's a great way to create a fake panorama: crop the photo so it becomes a panorama. Just get the Crop tool (C) and click-and-drag so it selects only the center of your photo, cropping off the top and bottom (as shown above). Then press Return (PC: Enter) and the top and bottom are cropped away, leaving you with a wide panoramic crop of your original photo. Hey, don't knock it until you've tried it.

Why You Need a Wide-Angle Lens

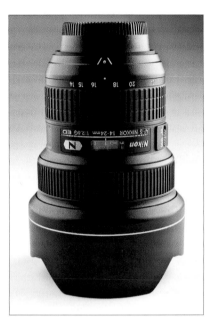

If you're shooting landscapes, you've probably come back from a shoot more than once and been disappointed that the incredible vista you saw in person didn't transfer to your photos. It's really tough to create a 2D photo (which is what still photos are—two-dimensional) that has the depth and feeling of being there. That's why I recommend one of two things:

(1) **Don't try to capture it all.** That's right, use a zoom lens and deliberately capture just a portion of the scene that suggests the whole. These can often be much more powerful than trying to fit everything into one photo, which can lead to a photo without a clear subject, and with distracting images and backgrounds. This is why I often shoot with a 70–200mm lens—to get in tight on a portion of the scene.

(2) **Buy a super-wide-angle lens.** Not a fish-eye lens—a super-wide-angle lens (like a 12mm). If you're trying to capture it all, a super-wide-angle (sometimes called ultra-wide-angle) lens is often just the trick you need to take in the big picture. My favorite outdoor lens is my 14–24mm zoom lens (which is also a good sports shooting lens, by the way). I must admit, I rarely use the 24mm end, because I use this lens when I'm trying to get "the big picture," so I use the 14mm end most of the time. You'll love what it does to clouds, almost giving them a sense of movement along the edges.

Want to Take Things Up a Notch? Shoot Low

When you're setting up your tripod at some famous landscape location, look at all the other people setting up their tripods. What do they all have in common (take a look at the image on page 65 again)? They're all standing behind their tripods, right? So, what's about to happen? They're all about to take a shot with pretty much the same vantage point and perspective. So, how do you make yours have more impact and stand out? Shoot down low. That's right—rather than extending the legs of your tripod all the way out, set up your tripod fairly low to the ground, to where you'll be shooting either sitting down or kneeling down (in some situations you might even want to lay down). This will give you a different perspective and it will accentuate the foreground. These two will often give your images more impact. Remember, if you just do what everybody else is doing, your shots will pretty much look like those of everybody else shooting right beside you. This is one way to tip the scales in your favor.

WHAT TO DO IF THE COLOR IN YOUR SHOT DOESN'T LOOK GOOD

Okay, this one's an "if all else fails" tip, but if you have a landscape shot that is well composed, and otherwise looks good, but the color is kind of lame, consider converting the image to black and white (using Photoshop, Elements, Lightroom, etc.). This can sometimes save a shot that has a lot going for it photographically, but the color just isn't compelling. Hey, it's worth a try.

SHUTTER SPEED: 1/1600 SEC   F-STOP: F/2.8   ISO: 200   FOCAL LENGTH: 400mm   PHOTOGRAPHER: SCOTT KELBY

Chapter Five

Shooting Sports Like a Pro

Better Bring Your Checkbook

This is the one chapter in the book where you have a choice. Do you want to get much better at shooting sports using the tips the pros use, but pretty much use your own existing gear? Or, do you want to seriously shoot sports for a living? Here's why I mention this: we're going to conduct a brief, totally scientific test which will quickly determine which path you should take. Ready? Let's begin. Question 1: This book retails for $24.99. When you turned the book over to look at the price, how did you react? You thought: (a) $24.99, that's cheap enough—I think I'll buy it; (b) I dunno, it's $24.99—I hope this is worth it; (c) $24.99, that's pretty steep, but I really need to learn this stuff; or (d) $24.99! $24.99! I can't believe they're charging $24.99! Well, I'm not happy about it, but I have to have this book. Answer: If you answered a, b, c, or d, you're not ready to enter the world of professional sports photography, because professional sports photographers spend so much on their equipment that they would never even think of looking at the price of anything. Ever. They see something they want and they just take it to the checkout counter and buy it, never questioning its price, because they figure they've spent so much on their photography equipment, there's no way any book, or flat screen TV, or luxury car could ever cost anything close. So what are we mere mortals to do? We use the tricks in this chapter to get better shots with what we've got. Of course, a few accessories wouldn't hurt, right?

Pro Sports Shooting Is Dang Expensive

©ISTOCKPHOTO/SPXCHROME

Of all the photographic professions, professional sports photography is probably the most expensive, so if you think you want to go this route, better bring your checkbook. The main reason it's so expensive is because many sporting events are held indoors (or in domed stadiums) or at night, so you'll need the most expensive (fastest) lenses money can buy (well, only if you want to shoot at a professional level). For example, you're going to need some long telephoto lenses (ideally, a 400mm) and since you'll generally be shooting in lower-light situations, they'll need to be f/2.8 to f/4 lenses. If you haven't priced a 400mm f/2.8 lens lately, they're around $11,500 (Canon) and $9,000 (Nikon). Plus, you'll need a monopod (those lenses are too heavy to hand-hold), so figure another $300 for that. Also, you'll need at least two camera bodies, which both have to be able to shoot at high ISOs indoors with very low noise and, ideally, shoot at least 10 or more frames per second (which means, as a Canon shooter, you're going to spend around $6,800 for an EOS-1D X or, as a Nikon shooter, you're going to spend around $6,000 for a D4. Did I mention you need two?). By the time you add up two camera bodies, a fast long lens, a fast shorter lens (like a 70–200mm f/2.8), a monopod, a 1.4x tele-extender (to get your zoom in even closer), lots of very fast memory cards (plan on shooting well over 1,000 photos for a typical base-ball or football game), and rolling cases to move all this gear, you're in the $25,000 and up range, just for starters.

Which Lenses to Use

TROY BREIDENBACH

When you're shooting sports, carrying a load of lenses and a big camera bag (even a camera backpack) will strain your back and just add to your frustration. Instead, go light with just two lenses:

(1) A wide-angle zoom lens (something that goes at least 24mm wide, like a 24–70mm). You'll need these wide angles to capture full stadium shots, full court shots, close-up group shots, etc.

(2) A 300mm or 400mm telephoto lens (or a 200–400mm zoom). At the very least, you'll need a 200mm lens, but plan on doing a *lot* of running because if the players aren't right in front of you, they'll be too far away to make pro-quality shots.

You're not going to want to change lenses, so ideally you'd put one lens on one camera body, and one lens on the other (more on this coming up). The only other thing you'll need to carry (besides extra memory cards and a backup battery) is a 1.4x teleconverter to get you even closer to the action (these magnify the amount of zoom, turning a 300mm telephoto into a 450mm). *Note:* Some pros advise against 2x teleconverters because they feel 2x photos are not as sharp and you lose up to two f-stops of light (it turns your f/2.8 into an f/5.6), making it harder to get the fast shutter speeds you need indoors. To move all this stuff around with the greatest of ease, try a Manfrotto Pro Photo Vest or a Think Tank Photo belt system, which is very popular with pro sports shooters.

This Lens Rocks for the Money

COURTESY OF NIKON, INC.

If you're just starting out shooting sports, I've got a great lens you might want to consider and both Canon and Nikon now make their own versions of this lens: it's the 70–200mm f/4. What's so great about this lens is (a) it has a great range for your first lens, and if you get a longer lens one day (like a 300mm or a 400mm), you can still use this lens on your second camera body, or when the play action gets close to you. Since it's an f/4 lens, rather than f/2.8, (b) the price is much better (the Canon 70–200mm f/4 IS is around $1,350 and the Nikon is around $1,400 [Sony doesn't make a 70–200mm f/4 at this time]. If that sounds kind of expensive, consider how much the same lens costs for the f/2.8 model—the Canon is $2,500 and the Nikon is around $2,400). Believe it or not, in the world of shooting sports, spending $1,400 for a good lens is actually considered a bargain. Don't shoot the messenger. Finally, (c) these weigh much less than their f/2.8 counterparts, which are fairly heavy (at least, that's what people always tell me when I hand them an f/2.8 lens to try). *Tip:* If you're primarily shooting in daylight, then you might want to also buy a 1.4x tele-extender to turn your 200mm reach into a 280mm (nearly a 300mm), but besides the price of it, there's another price you pay: you lose one stop of light (so your f/4 lens only lets you open it up to f/5.6 now). This is why I really only recommend getting a tele-extender for daylight sports shooters using an f/4 lens—at f/5.6 at night or indoors with that tele-extender, you'll have to crank your ISO a bunch (see page 99). Not that big a deal if you have an f/2.8 lens (because it becomes an f/4), but it kinda crosses the line for a lens that's already f/4.

Stability for Shooting Sports

DONN JONES

Sports photographers don't generally use tripods for a number of reasons: (1) they're not mobile enough for the fast-action shooting that typifies sports photography, (2) many professional sports won't allow the use of tripods, and (3) having a tripod set up near the playing field (in football, basketball, etc.) has the potential to injure a player. That's why sports shooters, especially those shooting with long lenses, use monopods instead. These one-legged versions of tripods generally wind up supporting those long lenses (the lens attaches directly to the monopod itself for support and to keep the lens and camera still during the low-light situations many sporting events are played under). Monopods are easy to move (or to quickly move out of the way if need be), and many professional sports that ban tripods allow monopods. Carbon fiber monopods are the most popular because, while they can hold a lot of weight, they are surprisingly lightweight. Now, not surprisingly, they're not cheap (nothing in sports photography is).

Scott's Gear Finder

Oben ACM-1400 4-Section Aluminum Monopod (around $40)

Manfrotto 680B Compact Monopod (around $70)

Manfrotto 695CX Carbon Fiber 5-Section Monopod (around $180)

Don't Plan on Changing Lenses

JEFF KELBY

Now, don't read this headline to mean you only need one lens for sports photography. It means just what it says, don't plan on changing lenses—plan on changing cameras. That's right, if you're really into sports photography, you'll miss "the shot" if you have to change lenses. That's why the pros have multiple camera bodies hanging around their necks—so they can change from a 400mm telephoto to a wide-angle lens in an instant. If they didn't do this, while they were changing lenses, the guy next to them would be getting "the shot" (which winds up on the cover of the magazine). If you want to compete with the big boys, you'll be hanging more than one camera body around your neck so you're ready to catch the shot with a moment's notice. I told you this digital sports photography thing was expensive.

Set Your White Balance for Indoor Sports

If you're going to be shooting sports indoors, you can count on your photos having a yellow or green tint, caused by the indoor lighting used at most indoor events. You can save yourself a lot of Photoshop editing down the road if you change your white balance to either Fluorescent or Tungsten/Incandescent now, in the camera. (Set it at Fluorescent and do a test shot, then take a look at your test shot in your LCD monitor. If the overall color looks too yellow or green, then try Tungsten/Indcandescent. See the Canon menu above.) By doing this, you're offsetting the yellow or green tint you would have had, which will keep you from pulling your hair out later. If you're shooting in RAW format, you can always reset the white balance later in your RAW processing software. But by setting the correct white balance in the camera, at least you'll see your photos in the proper color temperature when you view them in the LCD monitor on the back of your camera.

DON'T USE COLOR FILTERS

Your first thought might be to add a screw-on color balance filter to your lens to offset the indoor color cast, but don't do it. When you're shooting sports, you're already going to be challenged by lower than ideal lighting situations, and adding a filter takes away even more light. You're better off using a custom white balance setting because it only affects the color of light, not the amount.

Shoot at a ¹/₁₀₀₀ Sec. Shutter Speed or Faster

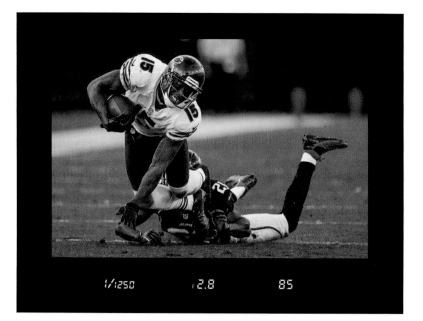

With sports photography, most of the time you're going to want to freeze the action of the athletes (or cars, or motorcycles), and to do that, ideally, you'll need a shutter speed of around 1/1000 of a second or faster (any slower than that and you'll probably have at least some blur. Although I've shot sports as low as 1/640 of a second and wound up with some sharp shots, they're not all sharp, so 1/1000 of a second is our goal). If you're shooting outside on a sunny day, this is no problem—just set your camera to aperture priority mode, use the lowest f-stop your camera will allow (ideally, f/2.8, if your lens will let you go that low, but if not, try for f/4 or f/5.6—lower is better), and you'll probably have shutter speeds of more than 1/4000 of a second or higher. If it's a partly cloudy day, you may drop down to 1/2000, and that's okay, too, as long as you stay above 1/1000. This all sounds too easy, right? Switch to aperture priority mode on your camera, use the lowest f-stop you can, and if you're shooting outside on a sunny day, hitting 1/1000 of a second is no problem. There's gotta be a catch, right? Nope. Well, there's just one thing: the key phrase is "outside on a sunny day." As long as that describes where you're shooting, there is no catch. However, when you shoot at night, or indoors in an arena, a domed stadium, or gym, that's when things get really sticky (see the next page).

Shooting at Night or Indoors?
Raise Your ISO!

The biggest challenge of shooting sports happens when you shoot at night, or if you shoot indoors in an arena, gym, or a domed stadium. That's because, without that bright sunlight, your shutter speed will drop like a rock. There's really only one way around this—you'll have to raise your ISO like crazy to get your shutter speed back up to 1/1000 of a second to freeze sports action. So, why do we worry so much about raising the ISO? Well, it's because the higher you raise your ISO, the more noise (grain) you'll see in your photos. Today's high-end sports cameras (like the Canon EOS-1D X and the Nikon D4) have very low noise, even at very high ISOs, but it's still sometimes visible. But, really, there's nothing we can do about it—the only way to get our shutter speed up at night or indoors is to raise our ISO until it raises our shutter speed enough. This is why "fast lenses" (like an f/2.8 or f/4) are so helpful—the faster the lens you have, the less you'll have to raise your ISO (and the less noise you'll have). So, how much of a difference does a fast lens really make? Well, if I'm shooting in an NFL football stadium at night with really bright stadium lighting, and I set my f-stop to f/4, I have to set my ISO around 4,000 to get my shutter speed up to 1/1000 of a second to freeze the action. If I have an f/2.8 lens instead, I can usually set it at just 1,600 ISO (much less noise). That one stop makes that big a difference (but man do they charge you a bundle for that one extra stop of light). So, our plan when shooting at night or indoors is to shoot at our widest aperture (lowest number f-stop possible for our lens) and then increase our ISO until we hit a 1/1000 of a second shutter speed. You will see some noise, but seeing some noise beats having a blurry photo every single time.

Getting Burned by Indoor Lighting

If you're shooting indoors at an arena or outdoors under the lights, you already know you're going to have to raise your ISO quite a bit to be able to freeze the action (see the previous page), but there's another area where you're likely to get burned under these lights: most stadiums and arenas don't have consistent light throughout the field of play. For example, it's not uncommon for the center of the field to be much brighter than either end of the field, or for one end of the court to be darker than the other. The reason why you want to keep an eye out for this is because when parts of the playing field are darker than others, your shutter speed will drop in those parts of the field, and that might mean blurry shots in the most important parts of the playing field (think about it—the scoring doesn't happen in the middle of the field for most sports, it usually happens at the ends). So, what you'll have to do is keep an eye on your shutter speed when shooting in those areas, and if you see your shutter speed drop below 1/1000 of a second, you'll need to raise your ISO while the action is happening in that area, and then lower it back down when they move to better-lit areas of the field. If it sounds like kind of a pain in the butt to have to keep an eye on this all night, you're absolutely right.

Shoot Wide Open

By shooting wide open, I mean shoot as close to your wide open aperture as possible (so if you have an f/2.8 lens, shoot at f/2.8 or one stop up). This will pay off in two ways:

(1) This will blur the background, creating a more dramatic, dynamic, and uncluttered photo of your subject. Busy backgrounds are a problem when shooting sports, and shooting with a telephoto lens at such a wide open aperture gives you a very shallow depth of field (meaning your subject in the foreground is in focus, while the background is out of focus).

(2) You'll be able to shoot at faster shutter speeds, which will greatly help when shooting indoors under artificial low-light situations.

Shooting in Burst Mode

Nikon   *Canon*

Much of the shooting you'll be doing in sports photography will require you to take bursts of shots (four or more shots per second) in order to make sure you get the shot while a play is in motion. So, you'll need to set your camera to shoot multiple shots while you hold down the shutter button (this is called burst mode on some digital cameras). By default, most cameras shoot one frame at a time, so you'll have to switch this burst mode on.

Nikon: Switch the camera's mode to continuous (where holding down the shutter release takes multiple photos) by first pressing the Menu button, choosing the Custom Settings menu, and then choosing Continuous High-Speed (to choose either 10 fps or 11 fps). Then, press the release mode dial lock release button on the top left of the camera and turn the release mode dial to CH.

Canon: Press the Drive or AF•Drive button, then rotate the quick control dial until you see an icon that looks like a stack of photos on the top LCD panel.

Now, you can simply hold down the shutter button to fire multiple shots.

RAW or JPEG for Sports Shooters?

Because of the fact that much of sports photography is taken in burst mode (see the previous page) and the fact that you only have so much memory space in your camera's multiple-shot buffer, the larger the photos you take, the quicker that buffer will become full. When it's full, you're done shootin' (well, at least until it has time to write the shots to your memory card, which empties the buffer again). That's why many pro sports pho-tographers choose to shoot in JPEG format rather than RAW. It's because JPEG files are considerably smaller in file size so more of them fit in the buffer (plus, since they're smaller, they write to your memory card faster, so you can effectively shoot more uninterrupted shots in JPEG format vs. RAW format). Now, there are some purists who feel so strongly about shooting in RAW for every occasion (including shots of their kid's birthday party at Chuck E. Cheese) that reading about anyone advocating any file format other than RAW sends them scrambling into a tower with a high-powered rifle to pick off pedestrians. To them, I just say, "Remember, RAW is a file format, not a religion." (By the way, I know a pop-ular *Sports Illustrated* magazine shooter who now sets his cameras to shoot RAW+JPEG, which captures both file formats at the same time. Just thought you'd like to know.)

Pan to Show Motion

For this entire chapter we've been talking about using super-fast shutter speeds to freeze the motion of sporting events, but there are times when it's more dramatic to emphasize the motion and let parts of the photo become intentionally blurry from movement. There are three keys to this technique:

(1) **Use a slow shutter speed**—ideally, either 1/30 of a second or 1/60 of a second. So, switch to shutter priority mode (using the mode dial on the top of your digital camera) and set the shutter speed accordingly.

(2) **Pan right along with your subject**—following them with your camera. Believe it or not, it's the camera's motion that creates the blurring background, because you're trying to move (pan) right along with the athlete so they remain sharp while everything around them appears blurred.

(3) **Use continuous shooting (burst) mode** for your best chance to capture a sharp shot—capturing multiple shots per second really pays off here.

One important thing to remember: Don't stop panning when the athlete leaves your frame—continue panning for a couple of seconds afterwards to get a smooth release.

Pre-Focus to Get the Shot

If you're covering an event where you have a pretty good idea where the action is going to happen (for example, you're covering baseball and you know the runner on second base is headed to third, or you're covering snowboarding and you know approximately where the snowboarder is going to land), pre-focus on that spot, so when it happens, all you have to do is press the shutter button. You can start by leaving auto focus on, and then focus on the spot where you expect the action to occur, then switch your lens to manual focus and leave the focus alone (it's set). Now you can pretty much relax and watch the event unfold. When the runner (jumper, skier, etc.) gets near your pre-focused point, just aim back to that area and fire—knowing the focus is locked onto that point. No waiting for auto focus to either get, or miss, the focus. You're good to go—just fire away.

Shoot Vertically for More Impact

Much of pro sports photography is shot vertically because it's easier to fill the frame with your subject (plus, it's ideal for magazine covers, ads, etc.). Just turn the camera sideways, get in tight (with your long lens) and make the magic happen (so to speak). This particularly holds true if you're shooting a single athlete, rather than two or more, where a horizontal shot might work best, but when it comes to shooting a single subject, your best bet is to go vertical. That being said, if you want to really cover your bases (like the way I worked that sports metaphor in there), shoot both as much as possible. As my tech editor Bill Fortney says, "The editor will always ask for the orientation you didn't shoot."

WELL, THERE IS AN EXCEPTION TO THIS "SHOOT VERTICALLY" THING

Today, much of the sports photography you see appears on the Internet, right (on sports websites, team homepages, Facebook, Twitter, etc.)? Wide images look better on the web because they wind up much larger (with more impact) in a web browser than tall shots. Plus, if you shoot wide, you can usually crop pretty easily to make it a tall shot, but it's really hard to crop a tall, vertical shot and make it a wide shot for the web. Which one's right for you? Ask yourself, "Where will these images be seen?" If it's just on the Internet, I'd shoot wide. If there's a chance it's going in print, vertical might get you the cover!

Don't Be Afraid to Crop Your Photos

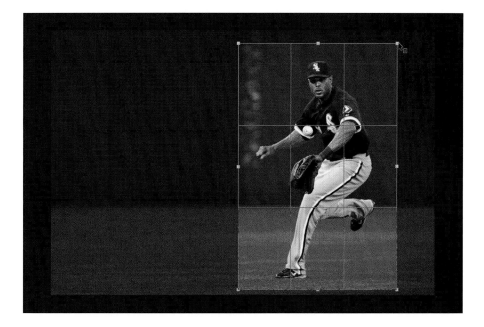

In general, I hate cropping, and if I have to crop a photo after I've taken it, it kind of makes me feel like I've failed at my most basic job as a photographer—deciding what to include in the photo (how the photo is composed). So, it makes me really mad if I have to crop and I do it very rarely, except for sports, where I crop all the time and feel no remorse whatsoever. I have to. All sports photographers (especially the pros) do. It's because, for most sports, the play often moves away from you in a split-second—a basketball player steals a pass, turns, and runs down the court; a quarterback throws a pass to a receiver 70 yards down the field from you; a baseball player hits a ball deep into the outfield. Even with a 400mm lens, outfielders look tiny in your frame, so we have to crop in tight after the fact (in Photoshop, Elements, Lightroom, etc.) to create dynamic-looking images. It's a part of sports photography—the tight crop, and the tighter the better! If you're reading this and thinking, "Oh, so that's how those sports shooters get those super-up-close shots that look so great!" The answer is "Yes!" and now you can do it, too! Also, the shorter the lens you have, the more you'll be doing it (you'll crop a lot less if you have a 400mm lens than you will if you only have a 200mm lens). This is another reason why having a high-megapixel camera is a big benefit to a sports photographer—you can crop the image in tight and still have plenty of resolution for print or for the web. One more thing: when you're cropping your image and you think to yourself, "Man, that's really a tight crop!" that's your cue to crop it even tighter!

You Need Two Eyes and a Ball

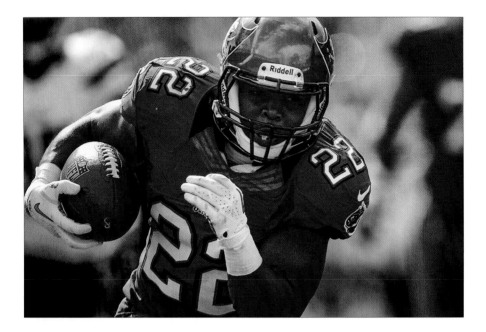

When you're shooting athletes, what's the most important thing to capture? Generally, it's their face. It's their facial expressions that tell the story, and it's their faces that people want to see, but if you really want to take it to the next level, try to include the ball in the shot, as well (if it's a sport that uses a ball, anyway. No sense in including a ball in a Formula One racing shot). There's an old adage used by sports photo editors (the folks who decide which images wind up in a sports magazine) that goes, "Give me two eyes and a ball." If you've got those two, you've got a shot that tells a story and that's going to capture the imagination of your viewer. So, keep that floating around in the back of your mind while you're shooting the game—"I need to see two eyes and a ball."

Don't Always Focus on the Winner

In sports photography (and in sports in general), it's only natural to follow the winner. If someone scores a critical point, you'll be capturing shots of the athlete that made the big score, right? If a team wins, you'll be shooting shots of the winning team celebrating. But if you follow that tradition of covering only the winner, you might miss some of the most dramatic shots with the most powerful story-telling angle, which are the expressions and reactions of the loser or the losing team. This is especially important if you just missed the action play—quickly switch to the reaction of the guy who missed the ball, or didn't block the shot, or missed the goal, etc. Sometimes their reactions are more fascinating than those of the person who makes the shot. Next time, try catching the expression of the golfer who missed the putt (or the golfer who lost because her opponent just sank a 40-footer), and see if it doesn't elicit as much or more emotion as a shot of the winner.

Composing for Sports

When composing your sports images, give your athlete somewhere to go. Don't compose the shot so your athlete is running out of the frame, compose it so there's room in front of the athlete to move to continue his visual story, so the athlete doesn't look boxed in. It's an uncomfortable look for sports, so when you're composing, be sure to leave some running room (i.e., for a shot of an athlete running left, compose the shot with him on the far-right side of the frame. That way, he visually has room to run). This simple compositional trick will make a big difference on the impact of the final image.

The Pros Know the Game

If you know the game you're shooting (for example, if you're a baseball fanatic and you're shooting a baseball game), you're going to get better shots than the next guy because you're going to know where the next play is likely to unfold. This is a huge advantage in sports shooting, and being able to anticipate when and where the big moment will unfold can make all the difference in getting "the shot." The key is you have to watch the game while you're shooting, so you can see the play unfolding and be ready to aim where you feel the action will take place. You won't always be right, but you'll be right enough that you'll get the shot more often than not. So, what if you're assigned to shoot a game you don't know well? Go online and watch some videos, go to the newsstand and buy some magazines on the topic, and study how the pros that cover that sport are shooting it—find out who the stars are in that sport and make sure you follow them (after all, the stars are most likely to be involved in the big plays, right?). It basically comes down to this: if you know the game, you're putting yourself in the best position to get "the shot." If you don't know the game, the only way you'll get "the shot" is by sheer luck. That's not a good career strategy.

SHUTTER SPEED: 1/125 SEC   F-STOP: F/13   ISO: 100   FOCAL LENGTH: 185mm   PHOTOGRAPHER: SCOTT KELBY

Chapter Six

Shooting People Like a Pro

Tips for Making People Look Their Very Best

Now, the subhead above says this chapter is how to make people look their very best, and that is kind of misleading because it's really about making your photos of people look better. If you've got some really ugly looking people in your photos, there's not much you or I can do to help these poor souls. They've been hit with the ugly stick, and they don't make a digital camera that will make these people, who didn't have a date for the prom, suddenly look like Mila Kunis or Channing Tatum (who, not coincidentally, were chosen as the Sexiest Woman Alive by *Esquire* magazine and Sexiest Man Alive by *People* magazine, just in case you cared). By the way, although I did not make last year's cut, if you read my bio at the beginning of this book, you learned that I was among *People* magazine's top 50 sexiest picks back in 2004. This surprises many people, including my wife, as she has no recollection of this whatsoever, but I'm actually thankful for that because she has also completely erased any memory of my brief but highly publicized affair with Angelina Jolie while we were filming the movie *Taking Lives* in Toronto. But I digress. Now this chapter isn't so much about studio portrait techniques, because if you're shooting in a studio, then you're a professional photographer and, honestly, this chapter (and this book for that matter) really isn't for you. This is really for getting better outdoor, or candid, or posed shots that are supposed to look candid, but really aren't, but you can tell they are because they're posed. Are you taking all this down?

The Best Lens for Portrait Photography

There are not many aspects of photography that have a specific focal length you should try to shoot with, but luckily portrait photography is one of them because there's kind of a "sweet spot" that pros generally choose, and that's anywhere between an 85mm focal length and a 105mm range (these are pretty much thought of as "classic" portrait focal lengths). The main reason these focal lengths are popular is that they are literally flattering to your subjects. At lengths 85mm and over, these lenses provide a really flattering perspective and compression that makes people look great (by the way, you can go farther than 105mm. In fact, my go-to portrait lens is my 70–200mm, and I normally shoot somewhere between 150mm and 200mm). Although this is the kind of topic people love to argue endlessly about in online photography forums, I can tell you that most pros I know shoot portraits with an 85mm telephoto lens or longer. By the way, another benefit of shooting with a longer focal length like this is that you don't wind up being right in your subject's face with your lens—the telephoto lens puts some breathing room between you and their face—and if your subject is more comfortable, that usually translates into better-looking images. (*Note:* Nikon, Canon, and Sony all make zoom lenses that fall somewhere in this portrait focal range, as do Sigma and Tamron, so you'll have plenty to choose from in that sweet spot of around 85mm to 105mm, up to 200mm. Also, don't forget, you can buy a 24–105mm, a 24–120mm, or a 70–200mm. Just don't shoot portraits in those lower ranges—use the long end of the zoom, starting at around 85mm and going up from there.)

Which Aperture to Use

One thing I love about portrait photography is that a lot of the decisions are made for you (like which lens/focal length to use), so you can focus on the harder parts of portrait photography—ensuring that you have great light and capturing the personality of your subject. So, now that you know which lens to use, believe it or not (and this is very rare), there is a special aperture (f-stop) that seems to work best for most portrait photography. When it comes to portraits, f/11 is the ticket because it provides great sharpness and depth on the face (and isn't that what portraits are all about?), which gives you a great overall look for most portrait photography (now, I say "most" because there are some artistic reasons why you might want to try a different aperture if you're trying to get a special effect, but for the most part you can choose aperture priority mode, set your aperture at f/11, and then worry about the really important stuff—the lighting, capturing your subject's personality, how much to bill your client, etc.). Okay, as always, there's an exception to every rule, so see page 118 for when f/11 wouldn't be your first choice.

Using Seamless Backgrounds

Backgrounds provide quite a challenge for portrait photographers because they generally get in the way of the portrait photographer's goal—capturing the personality, the drama, the soul (if you will) of the person they're shooting. That's why so many portrait photographers shoot their subjects on as plain a background as possible. In the studio, perhaps the least expensive option is to use a seamless background—these are very inexpensive because they're made of paper. That's right, it's just a big giant roll of paper, and a standard size (53"x36') will only run you about $22. That ain't bad for a professional studio background (you can find these backgrounds at your local camera store). Some photographers tape it to the wall, others nail it to the wall, but the best option is probably to buy an inexpensive stand that holds the roll up for you (you can get a decent one for around $70). Now, which colors should you use? For starters, stick with black (for dramatic portraits) or white (for everything else). The nice thing about a white seamless background is that it usually appears as a shade of gray. To make it really appear white like the one above, you'll have to aim one or more lights at the background or the light from your flashes will fall off, giving you a gray backround. Gray is not a bad background color (in fact, it's very popular), but if you're really going for white, make sure to position one or two lights behind your subject, aiming at the background itself. If you go with a black seamless background, you may need an extra light to backlight your subject (especially if they have dark hair), so they stand out against the black.

Using Canvas or Muslin Backgrounds

SCOTT KELBY AND ©ISTOCKPHOTO/SHUTTERWORX

Canvas or muslin backgrounds aren't quite as cheap—I mean as inexpensive—as seamless rolls, but they're inexpensive enough that you should consider using one as a formal background, as well (a decent canvas background only runs around $140). These backgrounds are seamless too, and I'd recommend buying one (at least to start) that's kind of neutral, like one that's mostly gray or mostly brown. These backgrounds add texture to your photo without distracting from the subject, and they're very popular for use in everything from formal business portraits to engagement photos. Again, an inexpensive stand will pay for itself in no time (they start at around $70), and you'll be amazed at how quickly you can change the look of your background by repositioning your lighting.

The Right Background Outdoors

When shooting portraits outdoors, you're not going to be able to use a muslin background or seamless paper (did I even have to say that?), and because of that you have to think about your background even more. The background rule for shooting portraits outdoors is to keep the background as simple as possible. The simpler the background, the stronger your portrait will be, so position your subject where the least possible amount of activity is going on behind them. Here's where you might want to break the f/11 rule, so you can throw the background out of focus by using an aperture like f/2.8 or f/4 with the portrait focal length you like best. Remember, when it comes to portrait backgrounds outdoors, less is more.

THE BACKGROUND LIGHTING RULE

When it comes to backgrounds, there's another simple rule you can follow that will keep you out of trouble. When you're choosing a simple background to shoot on, make sure your background is no brighter than your subject (in fact, darker is better because a dark subject on a bright background rarely works).

Where to Focus

Over the years, there have been conflicting thoughts as to where the optimal place is to focus your camera when shooting portraits (the cheek, the tip of the nose, the hairline, etc.). Luckily, today the consensus is fairly clear (you'll still find some cheek holdouts here and there, but don't let them throw you): focus directly on the subject's eyes. By shooting at f/11 and focusing on the eyes, this will give you a nice level of sharpness throughout the face (and most importantly, the eyes will be tack sharp, and in portraits that is absolutely critical).

Where to Position Your Camera

Portraits generally look best when you position your camera at the subject's eye level, so set your tripod up so you're shooting level with their eyes. This is particularly important when shooting children—don't shoot down on children (just like you don't shoot down on flowers), or you'll wind up with some very disappointing shots. So, with kids, you're either going to raise them up to your eye level (on a tall seat) or you're going to lower your tripod down to their eye level and shoot on your knees (I know—the indignities we have to suffer for our craft and all that…). Also, now that you're at the right height, about how far back should you position your tripod from your subject? Your focal length will pretty much dictate that for you, but if you're about 6 to10 feet from your subject, depending on your lens, you'll be in good shape.

Positioning Your Subject in the Frame

If you're shooting portraits, especially candid portraits or editorial style shots, there's a rule that many pros use about where to position the subject's eyes in the frame—position them 1/3 of the way down from the top of the frame. This is another one of those tricks that gives your portraits more visual interest, and it's easy enough to do since you just compose the shot so your subject's eyes are 1/3 of the way down from the top.

Tip for Framing Portraits

If you're looking for another tip for great portrait shots, try zooming in close so your subject's face nearly fills the entire frame. Also try zooming in close enough so that either the top of their hair, or even the top of their head, gets cut off and extends outside of the frame. This is a very popular look in professional headshots, and you see it all the time in magazines, in ads, and on the web, so don't be afraid to cut off their hair or the top of their head—it can make for a more dynamic portrait.

Getting Great Light Outdoors

Although there's plenty of light for shooting portraits outdoors in the middle of the day, most of that light is very direct and will wind up casting hard, unflattering shadows on your subject's face (not to mention that your subject will usually be squinting, sweating, or both). So, how do you get great outdoor portraits at two o'clock in the afternoon? It's easy—move your subject into the shade, where the light is softer, and the shadows are less prominent and much softer. Now, don't move into a cave—just move to a shady area near the direct sunlight (typical places include under a large tree, under the overhang of a building or house, on the porch of a house, under an umbrella, etc.). Just find a place you'd normally go to get out of the sun on a hot day, and you're ready to get portraits where your subject isn't squinting, and the light is soft and flattering. The photos above perfectly demonstrate the advantage of doing this. The shot on the left was taken in direct sunlight and the shot on the right, of the same model in a similar pose, was taken one minute later less than 30 feet away but in open shade. Notice how much softer and warmer the light is, how vibrant the color is, and how much better the same model looks. All I did was move her into the shade. It makes that big a difference.

Getting Great Light Indoors

What's the pros' trick for getting great portrait light indoors without setting up some extensive studio lighting? Use the best light ever created—natural light. This is such wonderful light that many pros insist on using nothing but natural light for their portraits. To take advantage of this wonderful light source, just position your subject beside a window in your house, office, studio, etc., that doesn't get direct light. The most ideal window light is a north-facing window, but any window getting nice, soft, non-direct sunlight will work. If the window is dirty, that's even better because it helps diffuse the light and makes it even softer. If the only window you have gets direct light, try using sheers (thin curtains that are almost see-through—you find these in hotel rooms quite often, and they make great light diffusers). You can position your subject standing or sitting, but make sure your subject is getting side light from the window—not harsh direct light. The soft shadows on the other side of the face will enhance the portrait and give it depth and interest.

DON'T FORGET THE SHOWER CURTAIN TRICK

That's it—don't forget the frosted shower curtain trick you learned in Chapter 2. It can work wonderfully well here too, and although your subject may think you're a little lame for pinning up a frosted shower curtain, the people who look at their portrait will only think, "What soft, magical lighting—your photographer must be a genius" (or something along those lines).

Taking Great Photos of Newborn Babies

By now you've probably heard how hard it is to photograph babies. That may be true, but newborn babies usually have a distinct advantage—they're asleep. That's right, newborns spend most of their days sleeping, so getting great shots of them is easier than you'd think, but you have to put them in the right setting or everyone who looks at the photos will say something along the lines of, "Aw, too bad she was asleep." Generally, people like babies to be wide awake and smiling in photos, but there's a very popular brand of newborn photography where the baby and mom (or dad) are sharing a quiet moment, and it really sets the stage for a touching portrait. I saw this first-hand when David Ziser (the world-class wedding and portrait photographer) spent one evening photographing my newborn daughter, Kira. Now, David had a huge advantage because my daughter just happened to be the cutest little baby in the whole wide world, but he did stack the deck in his favor with a simple, but extremely effective, technique—he had my wife and I both wear long-sleeved black turtleneck shirts (you can find these at Target). Then, he photographed Kira as my wife held her in her arms (I took a turn as well). David shot very tight (zoomed in), so what you basically got was a sweet little baby resting peacefully in her mother's (and father's) arms. You can use a diffused flash (more on this in Chapter 3), or you can use soft natural light from a side window.

Great Sunset Portraits

Everyone wants to shoot portraits at sunset because the sky is so gorgeous, but the problem generally is that (a) your subject either comes out as a silhouette because the sunset is behind them, or (b) you use a bright flash so your subject looks washed out. Here's how to get great portraits at sunset without washing out your subject: Start by turning off your flash and aim at the sky. Then hold your shutter button halfway down to take an exposure reading from the sky, and while still holding the shutter button halfway down (or you can turn on the exposure lock button on your digital camera), recompose the shot by aiming at your subject, but now turn the flash on (with the power of the flash way down low—maybe 1/4 power or less) and just that small amount of light from your flash is what you use to reveal your subject. This way, your subject gets fill flash, but the sky behind them still looks great. It's an old trick, but it's still around because it works so well.

Better Natural-Light Portraits with a Reflector

If you want better-looking outdoor portraits, get a reflector. It does just what it sounds like—it lets you reflect light back onto your subject—and one reason why this is so handy is that sunlight isn't always where you'd like it when you're shooting a portrait, so you use a reflector to bounce some of that sunlight over onto your subject, right where you need it. Reflectors are great because: (1) They're cheap. I use a Westcott 30" 5-in-1 circular collaps- ible reflector (it lets you have gold, silver, white, black, and a translucent light diffuser [for shooting in harsh direct light—you put it between the sun and your subject to soften and diffuse the light]) and they sell for around $30 (told you they were cheap). (2) That collaps- ible part is important as they fold into a small, flat circle. (3) They're very lightweight, so they're easy to take with you just about anywhere. (4) You'll be amazed at how this one $30 accessory can improve your portraits, either to provide fill light (like when your subjects are backlit [their backs are to the sun], so they're virtually a silhouette—you can bounce some of that sunlight back onto them almost like you're using a light), or when you just want to fill in some dark shadows on one side of your subject's face. The white side of the reflector is probably what you'll wind up using most, as it's the most subtle (and doesn't wind up blinding your subject or, at the very least, making them squint). The silver side is usually used inside a studio or when you need really "punchy" reflected light outdoors (it reflects a lot more light than the white side). The gold side is only for outdoor portraits and works best later in the day because it changes the color of the light it reflects to a very warm sunset-like gold.

Aiming Your Reflector

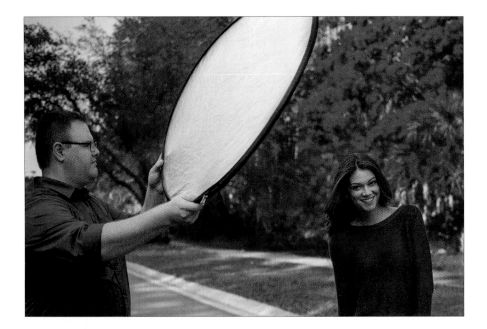

If you've ever watched somebody aim a reflector at their subject, they usually hold it down low and bounce the sunlight from above back onto their subject. That works fine if you're just trying to fill in some shadows, but if your reflector is providing most of the light (your subject is in the shade), then you're "uplighting" your subject (kind of like they do in monster movies to make the monster look more menacing, which probably isn't the look you're going for, unless of course you're lighting your mother-in-law. Not my mother-in-law, mind you, as she is a saint, but ya know, other mothers-in-law). Anyway, people generally look best when lit from above, so the person holding your reflector will need to hold it up high and bounce the light back onto your subject from up there, which is definitely more flattering. (Did I mention that it helps to have a friend hold your reflector? It does. Otherwise, it'll just be sitting there on the ground. Luckily, they do sell reflector stands if you don't have any friends, but if that's the case, reflecting light might not be your biggest concern right now. But I digress.) Have your friend hold the reflector up high and then have them slowly tip it down until you see it starting to light your subject's face. You'll have to direct your friend how far to tip it (ideally, you'd like it aiming down at your subject at a 45° angle), but luckily, while they're moving it, you can see the light move so this won't be too hard to figure out. When it looks good, have them hold it there while you make the shot. Simple enough.

Use a Reflector When the Lighting Is Flat

Another time you'll want to reach for your reflector is on a cloudy day because the light tends to be kind of flat (meaning, there are no shadows on one side of your subject's face. It's not horrible light—like harsh, direct sunlight—but it's not great light either, because great light generally has some direction to it). So, on a cloudy day, or if someone is in the shade, we use the reflector to redirect some sunlight onto one side of their face, so it creates a soft shadow on the other side. In this case, your friend holding the reflector will hold the reflector up high to catch the sun, then they'll stand, not in front of your subject, but to either the left or right of them, bouncing the light onto the side of their face and spilling a little bit over onto their cheek on the other side.

THE CLOSER THE REFLECTOR, THE SOFTER THE LIGHT

If your subject is standing in the shade and you want to bounce sunlight onto them, you'll want to know that if the reflector is close to them, the light will be nice and soft. But if the person holding your reflector has to stand 25 or 30 feet away to find some sunlight to bounce back onto your subject, when that light reaches your subject, it's going to be pretty harsh and unflattering. So, ideally, you'd position your subject so they're still standing in the shade, but fairly close to a sunny area. That way, your friend holding the reflector will be fairly close nearby so you'll get softer, better-quality reflected light.

SHUTTER SPEED: 1/1600 SEC   F-STOP: F/2.8   ISO: 200   FOCAL LENGTH: 300mm | PHOTOGRAPHER: SCOTT KELBY

Chapter Seven
Avoiding Problems Like a Pro
How to Avoid Digital Headaches

Pros are out shooting every day. And when I say out, if they're studio photographers they're actually usually shooting indoors, so in that case, of course I mean they're out shooting in the studio. Stick with me here, will ya? Anyway, these pros are out shooting every day, while most of the rest of us only get to shoot when our wives let us. I mean, we only get to shoot on certain occasions (like when our wives are out of town), so although we run across digital problems when we're shooting, since we won't have to deal with them again until our wives fly to Minnesota to visit their parents, we just let them slide. The pros don't because they have to deal with these things every day (meaning their in-laws live in the same town they do), so the way they keep from having migraine headaches the size of the Shuttle's booster rockets is by figuring out clever ways to deal with them on the spot. So, this chapter is kind of a shortcut because you're going to get the benefits of years of other people's headaches, but you're going to get to fix them right now, sidestepping one of the real downsides of shooting digital, and that primarily is having to shoot your cousin Earl's wedding (see, you should have listened to your wife when she told you not to get that long lens). Now, you may have noticed that I've been referring to wives as if all photographers were men, and clearly that's not the case. It's just that I am a man (a masculine, mannish, manly man) and therefore it would be silly for me to say, "My husband didn't want me to go shooting that day," when you know darn well he wouldn't mind. Wait—that's not what I meant.

Pro Tips to Avoid White Balance Problems

White balance problems often happen when you shoot indoors under fluorescent, incandescent, or just "them regular ol' light bulbs." Of course, you don't generally find out about them until you open the photos later on your computer and all the shots have either a yellowish, or greenish, or blueish color cast. By default, your camera is set to Auto White Balance, which works pretty well outdoors, but generally doesn't work worth a darn indoors. The pros use three methods to avoid white balance problems when they shoot: (1) They go into the camera and choose a preset white balance setting that matches the lighting they're shooting in (it's easier than you think—just go to your camera's white balance section, and choose either Incandescent [for regular indoor lighting] or Fluorescent [for typical office lighting]). You can choose preset white balance settings for outdoor shots as well, and you'll get more realistic colors there, too. (2) They create a custom white balance. Luckily, your camera will do most of the work for you if you just put a neutral gray card (you can find these at any camera store or B&H Photo) about 8 to 10 inches in front of your lens, and zoom in/out so the card fills your frame. Then, go to your camera's custom white balance menu and set it up to measure what it sees to create a custom white balance (it's easier than it sounds—just take a peek in your camera's manual). And, (3) they shoot in RAW format, so they don't worry about white balance, because they can choose the white balance after the fact, either in Adobe Photoshop's Camera Raw or in their RAW processing software (if they don't use Photoshop's RAW processor). This is just one advantage of shooting in RAW (see Chapter 10 for more on why RAW rocks).

Cold Weather Shooting Means Extra Batteries

Another thing the pros have learned is that digital camera batteries don't last nearly as long in cold weather. So if you're going out shooting in the snow, you'd better bring at least one or two backup batteries for your camera or it could turn into a very short shoot.

EXTRA BATTERIES ARE A SHOOT SAVER

I go out of my way to avoid using flash (I'm one of those natural light freaks), so my batteries last a good long time, and I seldom have to change batteries during a shoot. However, I have at least one backup battery for both of my cameras, and although I don't use them that often, when I have needed them, they've been a shoot saver big time. If there's a must-have accessory, it's an extra battery.

Don't Change Lenses in Dusty Weather

If you're shooting outdoors, take a tip from the pros and don't change lenses if you're in a dusty environment. That's the last thing you want getting down inside your digital camera, and although sometimes you can't see the dust swirling around you, your camera's sensors will see it, and then so will you (when you open the photos on your computer). If you must change lenses, try to go back to your car, or some indoor location, and switch lenses there. Remember, it doesn't take a whole lotta dust to make your camera really miserable—it's worth the extra effort to either plan carefully for shoots in desert or sandy conditions and go with just one lens, or to keep your car nearby so you can go inside, shut the door, and change the lens without fear of fouling your gear.

PROTECT YOUR GEAR TIP

You can buy protective gear for your camera for shooting in harsh or rainy weather conditions. But, if you find yourself in that kind of situation without that protection, you can do what my buddy Bill Fortney does and take a clear plastic shower cap from the hotel you're staying at, and use it to cover your camera and lens. It balls up right in your pocket, and it does a better job than you'd think.

Apply for Permits to Shoot with Your Tripod

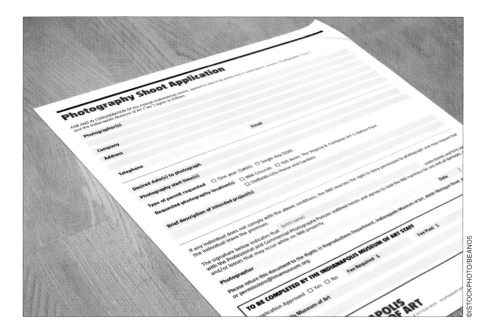

Many indoor locations (including museums, aquariums, public buildings, etc.) don't allow you to shoot on a tripod, even though these locations generally have very low "museum-like" lighting. However, in some cases, you can apply for a free permit to shoot on a tripod—such as the one shown above from the Indianapolis Museum of Art—you just have to ask in advance. I've had a number of instances where, by asking in advance, they would let me come in before or after hours to shoot when nobody's there (alleviating their fear that someone might trip on my tripod and sue them). Sometimes government buildings or museums will let you apply for a permit so you can shoot during their regular open hours, but often they'll have you come before or after hours, which I actually prefer. So, usually it's just me and a security guard shooting at five o'clock in the morning or nine o'clock at night, but at least I've got a stable shooting platform, I'm getting sharp shots because I'm on a tripod, and I don't have to worry about anyone tripping over my tripod, shooting their flash while I'm trying to shoot, or rushing me to get out of the way.

Be Careful What You Shoot

©ISTOCKPHOTO/JONATHAN HARPER

Especially since September 11th in the U.S., people can sometimes get freaky when they see someone shooting photos outside their building (which is common in downtown areas), and they're particularly touchy outside state and federal buildings. Recently, a photographer I know was shooting in a downtown area, and when he pulled his eye away from his viewfinder he was surrounded by three security guards. He didn't realize the building he was shooting was a federal building (it just looked like a fascinating old building to him), and the guards wanted to confiscate his camera's memory card. Luckily, he was able to convince the guards to let him just delete the photos from his card right in front of them, but if he hadn't, the police would have been involved within minutes (it was a federal building, after all). However, building security for corporations can be very aggressive as well (I've heard stories there, too), so just take a little care when shooting in downtown areas and be prepared to delete shots off your card if necessary. Also, as a general rule, in the U.S. and in other countries, you're taking your chances any time you shoot government buildings, airports, military bases, terrorist training camps, nuclear missile silos, Russian sub bases, etc.

A Tip for Shooting on an Incline

If you find yourself shooting on an incline with your tripod, here's a tip that can save your camera from instant death. Let's say you're shooting on a rock or on the side of a hill. Your tripod has three legs—place only one facing you. That way, if the camera starts to tip back, the single leg acts like an anchor and keeps it from falling. If the two-legged side is facing you, with the single leg on the rock or hillside, your camera will topple right over.

TIP FOR MORE STABLE SHOOTING ON A TRIPOD

When you're shooting on a tripod, depending on the terrain, you don't always wind up extending your tripod's legs all the way—sometimes you just extend one set of legs and not both. If that's the case, the pros extend the top ones (the legs nearest the camera) first, because they're thicker and provide more stability and balance than the thinner lower legs.

The Other Reason Pros Use a Lens Hood

The lens hood that comes with most good-quality lenses these days is designed to reduce or eliminate the lens flare that can creep into your lens when shooting outdoors in daylight, but pros keep a lens hood on even indoors (basically they keep it on all the time) for another reason—it protects the lens. Think about it—the glass end of your lens is pretty much flush to the end of the lens barrel, and if it comes in contact with anything that's not really, really soft, it can get scratched, cracked, or just fingerprinted or dirty. However, when you put a lens hood on the end, it puts a buffer between the glass and the scary world around it. It can save your lens if you drop it or knock it into someone or something.

Keeping Your Lens Out of Trouble

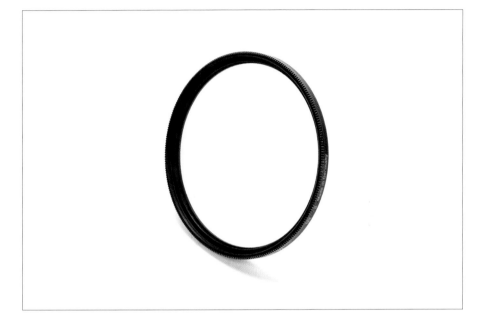

If you're going to be using good-quality lenses with your digital camera, then I highly recommend buying a UV filter for each lens. Although the UV part doesn't do all that much (it filters out UV rays to some extent, which makes your photos look better to some small extent), the real reason to use one is to protect your lens (specifically, the glass on your lens, which can get scratched easily or break if you drop it). Although this "buy a UV filter/don't buy one" controversy is heavily debated on the web, I can tell you from personal experience it saved one of my lenses from certain death. I was out on location and, while changing lenses, I somehow lost my grip and my lens crashed to the ground, glass first. My filter was severely damaged, but once I unscrewed it and took a look at my lens, it was totally unscathed. The filter took all the damage, and it's much cheaper to buy a new filter than it is to replace an expensive lens. So, while a UV filter might not do all that much for your photos, it does a lot for your peace of mind.

Limit Your LCD Time to Save Battery Life

One of the biggest drains on battery life is the color LCD monitor on the back of your digital camera. Although it's a very important part of digital photography, using it too often can really drain your battery, but here's something that can help—lower the number of seconds that your LCD displays right after you take the shot. After all, if you need to see a shot you just took again, you can just press the playback button on the back of your camera and it will reappear. Also, limit your chimping (admiring your photos on the LCD monitor or showing them off to others while making "Oooh! Oooh!" sounds).

Bracket If You're Not Sure About Exposure

In a tricky lighting situation, or a situation where you've just got to get the correct exposure for the shot, the pros make use of the camera's built-in exposure bracketing feature. This basically sets up your camera to shoot multiple versions (as many as five, if you like) of your current scene using different exposures (some lighter, some darker) with the idea that one of them will be just right. It starts by using the suggested exposure reading taken by your camera (which your camera believes is the correct exposure, by the way, but it can sometimes be fooled in tricky lighting situations), then it creates another image that is slightly underexposed, and another slightly overexposed (so you've bracketed both ends of the original exposure). This greatly increases your odds of getting the perfect exposure, and since digital film is free—hey, why not, right? You turn on bracketing right on the camera itself. For Nikon digital cameras, depending on the model, the bracketing button may be to the left of the viewfinder below the pop-up flash or on the release mode dial (it says "BKT" on the button). On Canons (like the 60D or the Rebel T4i), you have to turn on bracketing from the menu itself.

BRACKETING TIP

If you're shooting in RAW, bracketing becomes much less important because you have so much control after the fact (in your RAW conversion software), and because you can make as many copies, with different exposures, as you'd like.

Avoid Red Eye

Without going into all the technical (and physiological) reasons why people in our photos often get "red eye" when we use a flash, let's just look at how to avoid it. The main culprit is your camera's pop-up flash, which sits right above your lens and is an almost automatic recipe for red eye. The easy fix (the one the pros use anyway) is to either get that flash (ideally) off the camera and hold it a couple of feet away from the lens, or at the very least up much higher away from the lens, to reduce the chance for red eye. Another method is to bounce your flash off the ceiling, which is a great cure for red eye. Of course, all of these require you to have a separate external flash unit (and not just your camera's built-in pop-up flash). If you can't spring for an external flash, there are a few other popular strategies when you have no choice but to use your built-in pop-up flash: (1) Turn on some room lights, if possible. It lets your subject's pupils contract, and that causes less red eye than shooting in complete darkness. (2) If your camera has a red-eye reduction mode (where it sends a preemptive flash, which causes your subject's pupils to quickly contract, before it fires the main flash), that sometimes reduces red eye. (3) Ask your subject to look slightly away from the lens and that will certainly help, plus (4) moving your camera closer to your subject can also help reduce the dreaded red eye.

Remove Red Eye

Okay, let's say you forgot to try one of the strategies on the previous page and you wind up with an important photo that has red eye. Luckily, it's easier than ever to get rid of red eye. Whether you're using Photoshop, Lightroom, or Elements (the consumer version of Photoshop), you can use the Red Eye or Red Eye Correction tool to quickly get rid of red eye. Here's how they work: open the photo in Photoshop (or Lightroom, or Elements), then get the Red Eye tool, and simply click directly on the red area in one of the eyes. That's it—it does the rest. Then do the other eye. Not too shabby, eh? If clicking directly on the red part of the eye is too hard (the person is standing kind of far away so their eyes are kind of a small target), then just take the tool and click-and-drag to create a rectangle or oval around the whole eye area, and when you release the mouse button, it will do its thing. Either way you do it, that red eye is going to be gone in seconds. Just another reason why I love Photoshop.

Chapter Eight
Taking Advantage of Digital Like a Pro
It's More Than Just a Replacement for Film

I added this chapter to the book for a very important reason—I constantly run into people who treat their digital camera like a film camera that comes with free film. These people (freaks) don't realize that digital is much more than just a new type of "free-film camera" and digital cameras offer advantages that we (they, them, us, etc.) never had in film cameras. So, that's what I tried to do in this chapter—show how the pros take advantage of digital cameras to get the most out of their investment. Now, these pros have to squeeze every advantage out of their cameras for two reasons: (1) They have to monetize the results. They paid a lot of money for these tools for their business, and they have to have a verifiable means of tracking their ROI (return on investment). And (2) they have to be able to make enough money to pay both alimony and child support, because their spouses left them shortly after they went digital, because now they spend all their free time playing around with their photos in Adobe Photoshop. Hey, it's an easy trap to fall into, and I've been known to spend an hour or two in Photoshop myself. But that doesn't mean I've turned my back on my wife and child. I mean, wife and two children. My two boys. I mean, my son and daughter, right? Little what's-her-name? And of course, my son Gerald. Er, Jordan. That's it—Jordan. Great little boy, too. What's he now, six? Sixteen! No kidding, he's 16 already? Boy, they sure do grow up fast.

Level the Playing Field: Press That Button

Will digital photography really get you better photos? Absolutely. There are two huge advantages digital brings (if you take advantage of them), so I'm covering both of them on these first two pages. The first is that film is free. In the days of traditional film cameras, every time I pressed the shutter button, I heard in my head, "22¢." Each time I clicked off a shot, it cost me around 22¢. So whenever I considered taking a shot, I would consciously (or subconsciously) think, "Is this shot worth 22¢?" Of course, I wouldn't know for days (when the film came back from the processing lab), but it always made me pause. Now I can push the shutter button again and again and again, and in my head I just see a smiley face instead. Why? Because I'm insane. But besides that, it's because once you've bought your memory card, film is free. This really levels the playing field with professional photographers, because this has always been a huge advantage they had over the amateurs. The pros had a budget for film, so if they were shooting a portrait, they'd shoot literally hundreds of photos to get "the shot." Amateurs would shoot, maybe, a roll of 24. Maybe 36. So, here's a pro photographer shooting hundreds of shots vs. an amateur shooting 36. Who had the best chance of getting the shot? Exactly. Now, jump ahead to digital. It's portrait time—the pro will shoot hundreds of shots, right? Now, so can you, and it doesn't cost you a dime. When you shoot "with wild abandon" (as my friend Vincent Versace always says), you level the playing field. Your chances of getting "the shot" go way, way up, so fire away.

The LCD Monitor "Gotcha!"

Normal   Zoomed in to 100%

The second thing that levels the playing field is that, with the LCD monitor on the back of your camera, you can see if you "got the shot." And by "got the shot," I mean you can tell if your subject blinked when the photo was taken, if your flash actually fired, that sort of thing (I'm not trying to trivialize them—these are huge advantages), but there's a big potential "gotcha" that gets a lot of photographers. It happens because the LCD monitor is so small, it can also fool you. Everything looks in focus on a tiny 3" monitor (think of it this way: even the screen on your cell phone is bigger than this!). When you open that photo later on your computer, you might find out that the key shot from your shoot is out of focus (or your camera focused on the wrong object, so the background is in sharp focus, but your subject is blurry). This actually happens quite often because (all together now) everything looks in focus on an LCD monitor. So, you absolutely *must* zoom in and check your focus regularly during your shoot. If not, you're setting yourself up for a nasty surprise when you download the photos later (see page 17 for how to zoom in).

THE LCD MONITOR CHALLENGE

Another way the LCD monitor will make you a better photographer is through instant creative feedback. If you take your shot, look at the LCD, and what you see disappoints you, then it challenges you to come up with something better. It makes you work the shot, try new angles, get more creative, and experiment until you finally see on the monitor what you set out to capture in the first place.

Edit as You Shoot to Get More Keepers

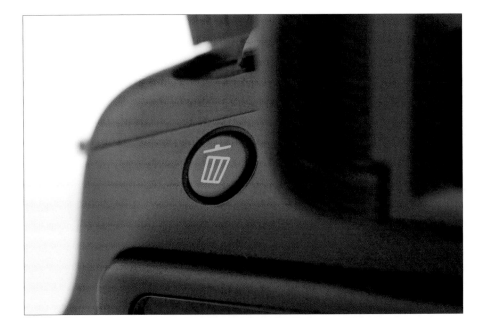

One of the tricks the pros use to keep an efficient workflow, and to keep from unnecessarily filling up their memory cards, is to edit out the bad shots as they go. If they take a shot and look on the LCD monitor and see that it's grossly underexposed, overexposed, has tons of blinkies, is clearly out of focus, or is just plain badly composed, they delete it right there on the spot. If you do this as well, later, when you download your photos onto your computer, you're only looking at shots that actually have a chance of being a keeper. Plus, you can take more shots per card, because the bad ones have been erased to make room for more potential good shots.

THE HIDDEN "EDIT AS YOU GO" ADVANTAGE

You may think this is silly (at first), but if you edit out all the really bad shots, when you finally do download and start looking at them, you'll feel better as a photographer. That's because you'll be looking at a better group of photos from the very start. The really bad shots have already been deleted, so when you start looking at the day's take, you'll think to yourself, "Hey, these aren't too bad."

Take Advantage of the Blinkies

I know I mentioned this earlier, but it bears repeating. Turning on your highlight warning (or highlight alert, the strobe-like flashing you see on your LCD monitor which shows the parts of your photo that are totally blown out and have no detail) and looking for the "blinkies" will yield you more keepers—no doubt. So, what do you do when you see the blinkies? Use your camera's exposure compensation control to back down the exposure 1/3 stop and shoot the same photo again. If you still see the blinkies, take it down another 1/3 stop and shoot it again. Keep shooting until the blinkies go away. *Note:* Some things will always have blinkies—like the sun—and that's okay. What you want to be concerned about is specifically "blinkies that matter" (blinkies in parts of the photo that you care about). A reflection of the sun on the chrome bumper of a car is an okay situation to let blinkies live. However, blinkies blinking on the forehead of your subject is not acceptable. Also, when looking at the LCD monitor, keep an eye on the overall exposure of the photo—don't let it get way underexposed just to stop a tiny blinky somewhere. Here's how to adjust using exposure compensation:

Nikon: Press the exposure compensation button just behind the shutter button, then move the command dial to the left until it reads –1/3 in the viewfinder readout.

Canon: Turn the mode dial to any creative zone mode except manual, press the shutter button down halfway, then set the exposure compensation by turning the quick control dial on the back of the camera.

The Viewfinder "Border Patrol" Trap

95% View

Extra 5%

Twigs
Sneaking
Into Your
Frame

One of the most common mistakes new photographers make is that they don't pay much attention to what's happening around the edges of their image (they're focused on the subject right smack dab in the middle of the frame) and all kinds of stuff creeps in from the sides that can ruin the entire image (things like tree branches, leaves, an old shoe [*an old shoe?*], or some other distracting thingy). We call the act of policing those oh-so-important edge areas "Border Patrol" (you're patrolling the borders for things that shouldn't be there). Anyway, this stuff that's sneaking in on the edges to ruin their shot may not be all their fault. Well, it's not all their fault (notice how I'm spinning this so it's not about you? See? I care). That's because the viewfinder on most digital cameras doesn't actually give you the full 100% of what the camera is capturing. That's right—very often you're only seeing 95% or less of what the camera's sensor is actually seeing (in fact, it's so rare that you see the full 100% image through the viewfinder that when you find a camera that does give you the full-image view, they list that as a feature). So, how do you deal with this? Two ways: (1) Always check the LCD screen on the back of your camera because it actually does show you the full view in most cases. That way, you can see right then, while you can still retake the shot, if something snuck into the edges of your frame. And, (2) now that you're aware that you are in charge of "Border Patrol" for your images, you'll be scanning the edges of your view before you press the shutter button, and that alone makes a big difference.

No Penalty Fee for Experimenting

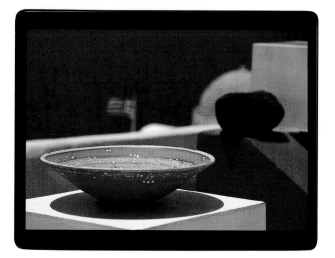

In the days of traditional film, the only people who could really afford to experiment were pros (or wealthy amateurs), because both the film and processing cost money, and experimenting was just that—taking a chance with money. Now, with digital, not only can you see the results of your experiment instantly (on your LCD monitor), but you can see the full-size results on your computer, and best of all—it doesn't cost a dime. Got a crazy idea? Try it. Want to shoot a subject from a really wild angle? Do it. Want to try something that's never been done before? Go for it. Now there's nothing holding you back from trying something new (except, of course, the intense humiliation that comes with experiencing utter and complete failure, but there's nothing digital can do to help you deal with that. Well, not yet anyway).

Don't Cram Too Much on One Card

One thing a lot of pros do to help avoid disaster is to not try to cram all their photos on one huge memory card, especially when shooting for a paying client. Here's why: Let's say you're shooting a wedding and you want to capture everything on one 64-GB card, so you don't have to switch cards. That's cool, as long as the card doesn't go bad (but sadly my friend, cards do go bad—not often, but it happens. It's a sobering fact of digital photography, but remember that traditional film can go bad as well—there is no "never fails" film). So, if you get back to your studio and find that your 64-gig card took a fatal dive, every photo from that wedding may be gone forever. You might as well just sit by the phone and wait for their lawyer to call. That's why many pros avoid the huge-capacity cards, and instead of using one huge 64-GB card, they use four 16-GB cards. That way, if the unthinkable happens, they only lose one card, and just one set of photos. With any luck, you can save the job with the 48 GB of photos you have on the other three cards, and avoid a really harrowing conversation with "the attorney representing the bride and groom."

SHOOTING RAW? LEAVE A LITTLE ROOM ON THAT MEMORY CARD

A word of warning: If you're shooting in RAW format, don't use up every shot on your memory card (leave one or two unshot) because you could potentially corrupt the entire card and lose all your shots. It happens because some RAW shots take more room on the card than others, but your camera calculates how many shots are left based on an average size, not actual size. So, don't chance it—leave one or two unshot.

Take Advantage of Poster-Sized Printing

You don't have to have a large-format printer to get large-format prints, because today there are loads of professional, reputable online color labs that will print stunning, full-color, poster-sized prints (16x20", 20x30", etc.) and even color correct them for you, for much less than you'd think. You just upload an image, pick your size, and they print it and ship it right to you (I use Mpix [www.mpix.com], and if I get my image uploaded to them by 11:00 a.m., I have the large print in my hands the next morning). For a 20x30" poster-sized print, it runs around $25. Send one of these to your client after an important shoot and it will blow their mind! By the way, the process is so much easier than most people think—you literally just drag-and-drop the file—and once you print one, you'll be totally hooked (and so will your clients).

WHERE TO "GO BIG!"

Here are a couple of services that I use for large-format prints:

- **Mpix** (www.mpix.com)—Been using them for years. I swear by them.
- **Artistic Photo Canvas** (artisticphotocanvas.com)—I use them for large prints on canvas.

You're Probably Going to Lose Your Lens Hood

It's the one thing that falls off your camera more than all the other parts combined. I have no idea why camera manufacturers have been able to pull off mini-miracles where you can make great photos literally in just candlelight and shoot 14 frames per second, with HD video built right in, but the engineering feat of designing a lens hood that doesn't fall off two or three times during a shoot (or walking around a city while on vacation) is simply out of their reach. So, to keep you from pondering this maddening thought at the worst possible time (or losing your lens hood altogether, as I have. Twice. By the way, the replacement was $47), do this instead: buy a cheap roll of gaffer's tape (it's black tape that's good and sticky, but you can peel it off cleanly and it doesn't mess up your camera's finish). Tear off a few small strips and apply them directly to the lens hood itself. Then, when you're out shooting, tear off two short, thin pieces and use them to secure your lens hood to the lens itself. Since I've been doing this, it hasn't fallen off once. You don't know how nice this is until it doesn't happen any more. You can order gaffer's tape online from dozens of places—from B&H Photo to Amazon to www.tapejungle.com.

Is It Better to Underexpose or Overexpose?

There have been some theories bouncing around a few of the photography forums on the web that claim that you should underexpose by a stop for digital photography. First off, let me say this: your goal (my goal, our common goal) is to get the proper exposure. That's our goal. Always. But if that's not possible, if given a choice between overexposing (a photo that's a bit too light) and underexposing (a photo that's a bit too dark), go with overexposing—you'll have less noise. That's because noise is most prevalent in the shadows, and if you have to lighten an underexposed photo, in Photoshop (see tip below) you're lightening (increasing) the noise in the photo. That's why it's better to shoot lighter (overexposed), because darkening a photo doesn't increase noise the way lightening it does. So, if you'd rather have one than the other—overexpose (but again, our goal is to do neither. That's why we bought these fancy cameras with their highly advanced metering systems).

WHAT TO USE PHOTOHOP FOR

If you're shooting in RAW, then you're going to use Photoshop to process your RAW photos, but once you leave Camera Raw and you're in the regular part of Photoshop, the idea is to use Photoshop to finish your photos—not fix them. You want to spend your Photoshop time being creative and having fun, not fixing things you should have done correctly in the camera.

Keep from Accidentally Erasing Memory Cards

This is a small tip, but one that can save your hide when you're out shooting in the field. If you keep your spare memory cards in a card holder (and for the sake of your cards, I hope you do), there's a simple routine the pros use to keep track of which cards are full and which cards are empty and available for quick use. They turn the full cards backward in the case (with the labels facing inward), so they can instantly tell which cards are available for use (the ones with the labels visible) and which ones are full. The next time you're shooting in a fast-paced environment (like a wedding shoot or a sporting event), you'll be glad you adopted this system.

Which Brand of Camera Should You Buy?

A lot of folks struggle with this one, especially when they're moving from a point-and-shoot camera to a DSLR. Which brand should you buy? Canon? Sony? Nikon? Pentax? Olympus? This choice is made tougher by the fact that they all make great DSLRs. All of them. However, I have two great ways to make sure you choose the right one (and although they may sound a bit silly, they work better for matching you to your camera than an on-line dating service does for finding your soul mate). Method #1: Choose the camera brand your photography buddy uses. That's right—if they use Canon gear, you should use Canon gear, too, because it will make your life infinitely easier, less stressful, and you'll learn your camera faster. Here's why: (a) now you have someone to call when you can't figure something out; (b) they can show you how to use your camera long after you've left the camera store and chances are they've already run into, and solved, all the roadblocks you're about to run into; and lastly, (c) you can swap (borrow) lenses, filters, flashes, batteries, the whole nine yards. When you're out on a shoot with friends, there's nothing worse than asking, "Anybody got a spare battery?" and everybody does, but not for your brand. Trust me, buy what your friends use. It just makes life easier. Method #2: Go to a real camera store and hold each of the brands you're considering in your hands. Fire a few shots on each, navigate through the menus, change the f-stop, change the shutter speed, and load a memory card. One of those is just going to feel "right" in your hands (just like each guitar has its own feel, or each golf club—one will just feel right). That's the one.

Chapter Nine
Taking Travel & City Life Shots Like a Pro
Tips for Travel Photography

Ya know what there's not a whole lot of? Professional travel photographers. Ya know why? It's because there are not a whole lot of travel magazines. I mean there's *Condé Nast Traveler*, and *National Geographic Traveler* (one of my personal favorites), and *Travel + Leisure*, and well…I'm sure there are a couple more, but the thing is, there's not like a whole bunch of them. But just because the market's tight for jobs in the professional travel photographer market, that doesn't mean we don't want to take travel and city life shots like we're trying to compete, right? Well, that's what this chapter is all about—tips on beating the living crap out of a couple of those pro travel photographers, so they're in the hospital for a while so we can snag some of their assignments. It's the law of the jungle, and shooting in the jungle sounds like fun, except for the fact that some smug pro travel photographer already has the gig. Or did he just fall (was pushed?) off the side of a mountain in Trinidad and all his expensive gear went right along with him? What a shame. I wonder who'll cover that assignment to shoot the sand dunes in Namibia? Hey, what the heck—I'll do it (see, that's the spirit behind this chapter—jumping in and taking over when one of your photographic comrades has a series of unexplained accidents while shooting on location). Hey look, I'm obviously kidding here, and I'm not actually recommending on any level that you learn the techniques in this chapter so you'll be ready for a last-minute pro assignment, but hey—accidents do happen, right?

How to Be Ready for "The Shot"

Nikon *Canon*

When you're shooting urban (city) or travel photography, you're looking for "the shot." My buddy Dave calls it "the money shot." You know, that shot where you turn the corner and something fascinating, amazing, or [insert your own adjective here] happens and you just happen to be there with a camera to record it. It happened to me in Barcelona when I walked by an alley and saw a man sitting in the dead center of the alley, facing the alley wall, reading a book. It was an incredibly compelling photo (so much so that many people have asked me if it was posed). So, how do you stay ready to catch a photo that just appears on the scene (or maybe drives by in a car)? You shoot in a mode that lets you concentrate on one thing—getting the shot. That's right, when you're walking the city streets, you shoot in program mode. I know, I know, this goes against all sacred rules of professional photography, except the one that says getting the shot is more important than the mode you shoot it in. So, switch your digital camera's mode dial to program(med) mode (which sets both the aperture and shutter speed for you, without popping up the annoying on-camera flash every two seconds like auto mode does) and get the shot. Now, if you get to a scene that isn't changing for a few minutes, you can always switch back to aperture priority (or manual) mode and take creative control of your shot, but for quickly getting the shot as you roam through the city, there's no more practical mode than program. *Note:* Nikon's program mode has a feature called Flexible Program Mode, which lets you change either the shutter speed or aperture setting while the camera automatically changes the opposite setting to keep the same exposure. If you don't touch either dial, it does all the work for you. Sweet!

Shoot Kids and Old People. It Can't Miss

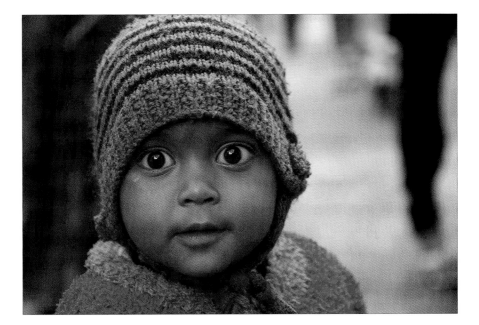

The next time you pick up a travel magazine, take a look at what's in the photos they publish. I can save you the trouble. Their travel photos have two main people themes: old people and children. Now, when I say old people, I don't mean people in their late 50s. I mean really old people, and by that I specifically mean old, wrinkly, craggy-looking women whose skin looks like shoe leather, and old, hobbly, crusty men with canes, wearing hats that haven't been washed since the Korean War. As for kids, the younger the better (but skip the babies). As long as you shoot them on uncomplicated, simple backgrounds, kids make incredibly compelling additions to your urban and travel pics (that's why the magazines love them). Also, if you get either age group to pose for you, make sure you spend some time talking with them before you start shooting—it can go a long way toward loosening them up, which will give you more natural looking poses and expressions (plus, they'll probably let you shoot longer after you've built up a little rapport).

WHAT NOT TO SHOOT

Okay, so kids and old people are "in." What's out? Crowd shots. They're just about useless (you won't even put 'em in your own travel album). Shoot an empty street first thing in the morning, or shoot two people together, but skip the crowds.

Hire a Model (It's Cheaper Than You'd Think)

LOCATION: EIFFEL TOWER, PARIS, FRANCE

How do the pros get those amazing shots of people in exotic locales? One of their tricks is to hire a local model (especially if they're shooting to sell the photos to a stock photo agency). Now, before you turn the page because you think hiring a model is out of your budget, it's usually cheaper than you'd think (well, unless you were thinking it's really, really cheap). Here's a real world example: I hired a professional model recently for a shoot out in New Mexico, and the going rate was $15 per hour, plus I had to provide her prints from the shoot for her portfolio. Some models new to the business will work for free in exchange for you making prints for their portfolio (the term for this in the business is TFP, which stands for "Time For Prints," [they are trading their time for your prints]), so ask your prospective model if they do TFP. If they look at you and ask, "Does that mean Tampa Free Press?" you should probably find another model. Two worldwide resources for finding working models online: www.modelmayhem.com and www.onemodelplace.com.

GET THAT MODEL RELEASE!

If you've hired a model, make absolutely certain that you get your model to sign a model release, which enables you to use those shots for commercial work. You can find some sample model releases online (I believe the PPA [Professional Photographers of America] has downloadable release forms available for its members), and having one could make all the difference in the world.

What Time to Shoot

LOCATION: GRAND CANAL, VENICE, ITALY

Many pros prefer to shoot urban and travel shots at dawn for a couple of reasons: (1) The light is perfect. That's right, the same golden, magical light that looks great for landscape shots looks great for shooting in the city, too. And (2) the streets are usually empty, so there's little distraction for your architecture shots, cathedral shots, or shots of charming little streets and alleys. You only have a limited time to shoot before the sun gets too light in the sky (and the lighting turns harsh) and the streets start to fill with traffic, so get set up before sunup and, of course, shoot on a tripod. Another great time to shoot is at dusk. The lighting will once again be golden, and the only major downside is that the streets won't be empty. There are still some decent opportunities to shoot urban and people shots during the day, because cities often have lots of open shade (sometimes courtesy of the tall buildings in downtown areas). So unlike the landscape photographer, you can often get away with shooting all day, especially if it's an overcast or cloudy day (remember, if the sky is gray, try to avoid including much sky in your photos). Afternoon is a perfect time to shoot charming doorways (in the shade), windows, kids playing in the park—pretty much anything you can find in decent open shade. So, to recap: The best time is probably morning. Second best is dusk, but you can still get away with shooting in open shade during the day, and there's often plenty of it, so fire away (so to speak).

Look for Bold, Vivid Colors

LOCATION: HAVANA, CUBA

One of the things to keep an eye out for when you're shooting urban and travel shots is the bold, vivid colors of the city. You'll often find brilliantly colored walls, doors (shots with a bold-color wall with a contrasting colored door), shops, signs, cars, and bikes. One of my favorite urban shots was of a bright red Vespa scooter parked directly behind a bright yellow Lotus sports car. It almost looked set up for me, and I took dozens of shots of it because the colors were just so vivid, and so perfectly matched. Keep your eyes peeled for brightly painted walls (especially wonderful if you find someone working in front of the wall, or waiting patiently for a bus with the colorful wall in the background, or a bright yellow car parked in front of a bright blue wall). If you're looking for these colorful combinations while you're out exploring, you'll be surprised at how often they'll reveal themselves to you. By the way, I know I'm beating a dead horse here, but these colors will look richer and have more depth in (you guessed it) great light, which generally occurs (you know it) around dawn and dusk. Just remember, the next best thing to those two is open shade.

Shooting Travel? Visit 500px.com First

If you're looking to find the shots everybody else misses (in other words, you don't want shots that are too touristy), before you leave on your trip visit 500px.com, click on Photos in the top left, and in their search field, type in the city or location where you're headed on your trip. You will find absolutely amazing shots, and often a fairly detailed description of where that scene is. (By the way, 500px is a site for serious photographers and a lot of the work there is really amazing, and shot in really amazing places, so it's my go-to resource for researching where to shoot when I'm going to take a trip.)

Don't Try to Capture It All: Shoot the Details

LOCATION: FORBIDDEN CITY, BEIJING, CHINA

I've heard a lot of photographers complain about the results of their urban shooting, and much of the time it's because they try to capture too much. What I mean by that is that they try to capture the entirety of a majestic building or the grandeur of a magnificent cathedral, but even with an ultra-wide-angle lens this is very, very hard to pull off. That's why the pros shoot details instead. For example, instead of shooting to capture the entire cathedral at Notre Dame in Paris, instead capture details that suggest the whole—shoot the doors, a window, a spire, a gargoyle, the pigeons gathered on the steps, or an interesting architectural element of the church, rather than trying to capture the entire structure at once. Let your photo suggest the height, or suggest the craftsmanship, and the mind's eye will fill in the blanks. By shooting just the details, you can engage in some very compelling storytelling, where a piece is often stronger than the whole. After all, if you want a photo of the entire cathedral, you can just buy one from the dozen or so gift shops just steps away. Instead, show your impression, your view, and your take on Notre Dame. Give this a try the next time you're out shooting in a city and see if you're not infinitely more pleased with your results.

The Best Shot May Be Just Three Feet Away

My good friend Bill Fortney said it best, "The biggest impediment to photographers getting great shots is the fact that they don't move. The best shot, the best view, and the best angle is sometimes just 3 feet from where they're standing, but they just don't move—they walk up, set up, and start shooting." It's so true (that's why I also made reference to this non-moving phenomenon in the landscape chapter). Once you find that fascinating detail, that vividly colored wall, that unique scene—walk around. Be on the lookout for other more interesting views of your subject and shoot it from there as well. Besides just moving left and right, you can present a different view by simply changing your shooting height: stand on a chair, squat down, lie on the ground and shoot up, climb up a flight of stairs and shoot down on the scene, etc. Remember, the best shot of your entire trip may be waiting there just 3 feet to your left (or 3 feet up). *Note:* The shot shown above is proof of this concept. It was taken in Morocco. Well, Disney's version of it anyway (at Disney's Epcot Center in Florida). If you were to walk 3 feet to the left (which is the shot I saw first), you'd see an outdoor courtyard full of park visitors eating dinner. But when I stepped 3 feet to the right, it hid the baskets of food and Coca-Cola cups and gave me this more authentic-looking view. By the way, that orange light through the open window is coming from a Disney gift shop. Another few feet to the right, and you'd see some stuffed Mickey Mouse dolls.

Shoot the Signs. You'll Thank Yourself Later

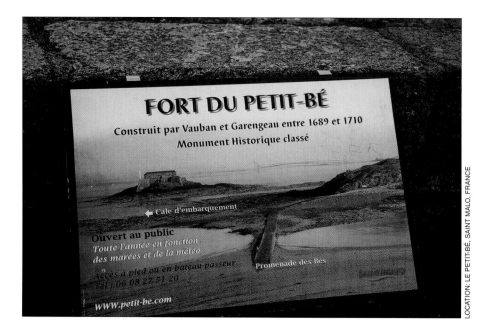

LOCATION: LE PETIT-BÉ, SAINT MALO, FRANCE

Want to save yourself from a lot of headaches? When you're out shooting a cathedral, or a stadium, or a building, etc., take one extra shot—shoot the sign. That's right, later on you may be scrambling to find out the name of that amazing church you shot, and without a lot of research, you may be out of luck. That is, unless you took a shot of the sign that has the name of the church (or building, bridge, etc.). This has saved me on more than one occasion, and if you ever wind up selling the photos, you will absolutely need this info (stock agencies generally won't accept "Pretty Church in Cologne" as a saleable name for an image). Shoot the sign and you'll thank yourself later.

TRIPOD WISDOM

When it comes to tripods, it's like my buddy Bill Fortney says, "There are two types of tripods: those that are easy to carry and good ones." Even with the advent of carbon fiber, if your tripod feels really lightweight, it's a lightweight. Spend the extra money and get a kick-butt tripod—you'll never regret it.

Showing Movement in the City

LOCATION: PARIS, FRANCE

If you want to show the hustle and bustle of a busy city, there's a simple trick that will do just that—slow down your shutter speed and let the people and traffic create motion trails within your image. It's easy (as long as you've got a tripod, which is absolutely required for this effect)—just switch your camera's mode to shutter priority and set the shutter speed at either 1/16, 1/8, or 1/4 of a second (you can go longer if you have low enough light that it doesn't blow the highlights out in your photo). Then press the shutter button, stand back, and in less than a second the motion of the city will reveal itself as the buildings, statues, lights, and signs stay still, but everything else has motion trails around it. If you're shooting at night, you can really have a blast with motion. Try to find a high vantage point (like from a hotel room window, or on a bridge, etc.) where you have a good view of traffic. Then put your camera on a tripod (again, an absolute must for this effect to work), go to shutter priority mode, set your exposure to 30 seconds, and take a shot. Thirty seconds later, you'll see long laser-like streaks of red lines (taillights and brake lights) and white lines (from the headlights), and you'll have an amazingly cool image that most folks won't get.

For Maximum Impact, Look for Simplicity

The single thing that probably kills more properly exposed city life photographs than anything else is clutter—all the distracting background items, foreground items, and just general stuff that gets in the way. So, one of the big secrets to creating powerful and dramatic urban and travel shots is to strive for simplicity. Look for simplicity in your backgrounds, in your people shots, in your architectural elements, in every aspect— the simpler the surroundings, the more powerful the impact. Go out shooting with that very goal in mind. Look for the absence of distraction. Look for the absence of clutter and noise, watch for distracting elements that sneak into the top and sides of your frame, and create some photos that have great impact, not because of what they have, but because of what they don't have—lots of junk.

The Monopod Scam

Now, a lot of places simply won't let you set up a tripod indoors (for example, try to set up a tripod in someplace like Grand Central Station. You can count the seconds before security arrives). However, here's the weird thing: while many places have a strict policy on tripods, they don't have a policy on monopods (a one-legged version of a tripod, often used for long-lens sports photography. Although they're not quite as stable as a good tripod, they're way more stable than hand-holding). So, the scam is this: if they say anything to you about shooting on a monopod, you can always counter with, "Hey, this isn't a tripod." It often stops them dead in their tracks. One reason they let you get away with a monopod is simply because they don't take up much space, and since there are no extended legs, there's nothing really for anyone to trip on (a concern for many building interiors, museums, etc.). So, if you know the indoor environment you're planning to shoot doesn't allow tripods, see if you can pull the old monopod scam. My guess is— you'll float right by 'em.

What to Do When It Has Been "Shot to Death"

So, you're standing in front of the Eiffel Tower (or the Lincoln Memorial, or the Golden Gate Bridge, etc.—any touristy landmark that's been shot to death). You know you have to shoot it (if you go to Paris and don't come back with at least one shot of the Eiffel Tower, friends and family members may beat you within an inch of your life with their bare hands), but you know it has been shot to death. There are a million postcards with the shot you're about to take. So what do you do to show your touristy landmark in a different way? Of course, the obvious thing (you'll find in every photography book) is to shoot it from a different angle. Frankly, I'd like to see an angle of the Eiffel Tower that hasn't been shot. But since, in many cases, that angle just doesn't exist, what do you do next? Try this: Shoot the landmark in weather it's not normally seen in. That's right— shoot it when nobody else would want to shoot it. Shoot it in a storm, shoot it when it's covered in snow, shoot it when a storm is clearing, shoot it when the sky is just plain weird. Since the landmark doesn't change, shoot it when its surroundings are changing to get that shot that you just don't see every day. Here's another idea: try shooting it from a difficult place to shoot from (in other words, shoot it from some view or vantage point that would be too much bother for most folks to consider. Find that "pain in the butt" viewpoint, and chances are you'll pretty much be shooting it there alone). Hey, it's worth a shot. (Get it? Worth a shot? Ah, forget it.)

Including the Moon and Keeping Detail

SCOTT KELBY AND ©ISTOCKPHOTO/DAVID LENTZ

This sounds like it would be easy—a nighttime scene with a crisp detailed moon in the sky in the background, but most people wind up with a totally overexposed bright white circle, rather than the detailed moon shot they were hoping for. That's because it's just about impossible to get both the nighttime scene (which takes a long exposure) and a detailed shot of the moon (which takes a very short exposure because it's actually quite bright) in the same shot. So, what photographers have been doing for years is creating multiple exposures (two images captured in the same frame). Now, there are some digital cameras today that let you create double exposures, but it's just as easy to take two sepa-rate photos—one of the nighttime scene (a barn, in this case), one of the moon—and combine them later in Photoshop. First, start with your nighttime scene. Use a wide-angle lens (maybe an 18mm or 24mm), put your camera on a tripod (an absolute must), set your camera to aperture priority mode, choose f/11 as your f-stop, and your camera will choose the shutter speed for you (which may be as little as 20 or 30 seconds or as long as several minutes, depending on how dark the scene is), then take the nighttime scene shot. Now switch to your longest telephoto (or zoom) lens (ideally 200mm or more). Switch to full manual mode, and set your aperture to f/11 and your shutter speed to 1/250 of a second. Zoom in as tight as you can get on the moon, so there's nothing but black sky and moon in your shot (this is critical—no clouds, buildings, etc.), then take the shot. Now add the moon to your nighttime scene in Photoshop (visit **kelbytraining.com/books/moon** to see my step-by-step Photoshop tutorial on how to do this).

Shooting Fireworks

©ISTOCKPHOTO/MISTIKAS

This is another one that throws a lot of people (one of my best friends, who didn't get a single crisp fireworks shot on the Fourth of July, made me include this tip just for him and the thousands of other digital shooters that share his pain). For starters, you'll need to shoot fireworks with your camera on a tripod, because you're going to need a slow enough shutter speed to capture the falling light trails, which is what you're really after. Also, this is where using a cable release really pays off, because you'll need to see the rocket's trajectory to know when to push the shutter button—if you're looking in the viewfinder instead, it will be more of a hit or miss proposition. Next, use a zoom lens (ideally a 200mm or more) so you can get in tight and capture just the fireworks themselves. If you want fireworks and the background (like fireworks over Cinderella's Castle at Disney World), then use a wider lens. Now, I recommend shooting in full manual mode, because you just set two settings and you're good to go: (1) set the shutter speed to 4 seconds, and (2) set the aperture to f/11. Fire a test shot and look in the LCD monitor to see if you like the results. If it overexposes, lower the shutter speed to 3 seconds, then check the results again. *Tip:* If your camera has bulb mode (where the shutter stays open as long as you hold the shutter release button down), this works great—hold the shutter button down when the rocket bursts, then release when the light trails start to fade. (By the way, most Canon and Nikon digital SLRs have bulb mode.) The rest is timing—because now you've got the exposure and sharpness covered.

If You Have a Laptop, Take It With You

You know what will drive you crazy on vacation? Visiting some amazing location, taking what you know are some really awesome shots, and then having to wait nine days until you get home to start editing and sharing the images. If you take your laptop, you have an editing studio with you wherever you go, and the other bonus is that you have a place to back up each day's shoots. What I generally do is back up my images onto my laptop after I return to my hotel after a day of shooting, and then I connect an inexpensive hard drive and copy those backups to another drive (now I have two copies of my photos from that day, so now I can erase my memory cards and go back out shooting tomorrow, knowing that I have two copies of my images, in two separate locations). After dinner, I usually open those images from the day and do a little bit of editing, so I can email them to friends or post them on Facebook, Twitter, etc. Lastly, I take one extra step: I upload only my final images (in JPEG format) to Dropbox (or any cloud-based service you like). That way, no matter what happens, my final images are safely stored off-site. One more thing: What if you either don't have a laptop or don't feel it's practical to bring one? In that case, bring a tablet and download Snapseed from Nik Software (now owned by Google). It's absolutely amazing for editing images, it's perfect for travel photos, and did I mention it's free? Well, it is, and it's awesome! Anyway, there are three morals to this story: (1) If you think it will drive you a little nuts to wait until you return from your trip to edit and/or share your images, bring your laptop. (2) If you can't go that route, bring a tablet and get Snapseed. (3) Back up your images on-site and, ideally, off-site, as well. You'll thank me.

Want a Rooftop Shot of the City? Try This

LOCATION: PARIS, FRANCE

If you walk into an office building or high-rise hotel and ask them if it's okay if you shoot some photographs from their roof, what are the chances they'll say, "Sure, no problem"? Pretty slim, right? It's because they really have nothing to gain from letting some stranger up on their roof (it's all downside for them, right?). Yet, you see shots from rooftops and from rooftop lounges or restaurants quite often, so what's the trick? The trick is this: when you book your hotel accommodations for your trip, try to find a high-rise hotel with a great view, and now you're no longer "some stranger." You're a hotel guest, and they have plenty to gain from making you happy (after all, that's their job). Start with the concierge. Tell them you're a serious photographer (not a commercial photographer—that might close the door for good) and that you'd love to take a shot from their [rooftop bar when it's closed, roof of the hotel, maybe the balcony of the Presidential Suite if it's available]. The concierge genuinely wants to help (and they might get a nice tip from you, right?), so they'll often bend over backward to get you access to some high vista where you can make your shot. If that doesn't work, introduce yourself to the hotel manager (who also wants to make you happy) as one of his "guests." If he can't let you on the roof, ask if there is some other high view in the hotel that might make a great city shot (the concierge may have already tipped you off as to what to ask for), but the bottom line is this: they want to say, "Yes" because you're a guest. If you're just a stranger walking in off the street asking for favors, they want to say no, and seem to have little trouble doing so.

Getting "Nearly Tourist-Free" Shots

LOCATION: PARIS OPERA HOUSE, PARIS, FRANCE

When you look at the photo above, taken during the middle of the day at the Paris Opera House while it was very busy, you might be wondering what the trick is to get a shot like this where you have very few tourists in the scene (well, if you look closely, down at the far end of the hall, there are a few tourists, but not enough to "kill" the shot). The trick is actually very easy, but it's kind of a pain to actually do it. The trick is patience. That's right—I stood there for 10 or so minutes hoping that there would be a break in the seemingly non-stop parade of tourists walking down the beautiful hall, and worse yet, walking directly in front of me, because immediately to my left was an open door to the balcony overlooking the busy street below (I took a few shots from that same balcony a little later, but the light was harsh and ugly, so they're pretty much hidden from public view until the end of time). Anyway, I just stood there, back a few feet, waiting for my chance and, sure enough, my patience paid off and suddenly I had about a 20-second opportunity where no one was walking in front of me, and no one was in the middle or front of the hall. So, I quickly fired off a few shots and got the one you see above. I actually use this trick quite a bit (see page 217 where I did this in Disneyland and it worked like a charm).

SHUTTER SPEED: 1/250 SEC   F-STOP: F/2.8   ISO: 1000   FOCAL LENGTH: 14MM | PHOTOGRAPHER: SCOTT KELBY

Chapter Ten

How to Print Like a Pro and Other Cool Stuff

After All, It's All About the Print!

This is a great chapter to read if you're a doctor, because you're going to want a great printer, and you're going to want big prints (at least 13x19", right?), and that means you're probably going to need to spend some money, and nobody spends money like doctors. Ya know why? It's because people always get sick or get hurt. Why just the other day this photographer was in Trinidad shooting and the next thing you know he tumbles down this hillside and winds up in the hospital (I know that last sentence made it sound like he finally stopped tumbling when he hit the wall of the hospital, but that was misleading—he actually was stopped by hitting a large llama grazing at the bottom of the hill, but luckily it was a pretty sharp llama, and she was able to summon an ambulance for him, but not before the llama put all his camera gear on eBay. Hey, I said she was pretty sharp). Anyway, who do you think is going to show up at the hospital to help this unfortunate accident victim? That's right—a doctor. And is this doctor going to fix this photographer for free? I doubt it. The doctor is going to get paid handsomely from the insurance carrier that covers the travel photographer. So what's this doctor going to do with the money? He's going to go on eBay and get a great deal on some camera gear. He'll probably save thousands. Now, what's he going to do with the savings? Buy a 13x19" printer. See, this is the wonder of market-driven economies and why we should all sell our camera equipment and go to medical school, because within a few years we'll all be able to buy some really nice gear.

The Advantages of Shooting in RAW

Most professionals today agree that RAW gives you three big advantages over JPEG-quality images: (1) It provides the highest possible image quality—RAW photos are not compressed (JPEG files are compressed to a smaller file size by throwing away some of the original data). (2) RAW files are a higher quality in general, and have a larger dynamic range, so they're more forgiving if you have to adjust the file because you didn't nail the proper exposure. (3) When you shoot in JPEG, your camera applies sharpening, contrast, color correction, and all sorts of stuff (called "processing") to make your images look good. When you switch your camera to shoot in RAW, it turns all that stuff (sharpening, contrast, and so on) off and you get the raw, unprocessed image just as the camera took it. Now you get to process the image yourself, adding contrast and sharpening and all that stuff (usually in Camera Raw [a part of Photoshop], or in Lightroom, or Apple's Aperture, or whichever RAW processor you choose). The idea is that you can process your images better than your camera's built-in automation (and I agree), but you can experiment without ever damaging the original RAW file.

THE DOWNSIDES OF SHOOTING IN RAW

There are really only two: (1) RAW files are larger in size, so you'll fit about 1/2 as many (or less) on your memory card, and (2) since RAW files don't have any sharpening or contrast or other in-camera stuff applied, they don't look as good as JPEG images do straight out of the camera.

How to Process RAW Photos in Photoshop

Adobe Photoshop (and Photoshop Elements) includes a RAW processor called Adobe Camera Raw (or ACR, for short). If you shoot in the RAW format, when you double-click on a RAW image on your computer, it will open that image in Camera Raw (if you use Lightroom instead, Camera Raw is built-in there, too—it's the Develop module. The same sliders and controls as ACR, in the same order, too!). Camera Raw lets you adjust everything from your image's white balance to exposure (and even fix lens problems) very quickly and easily. This is all done before you enter regular Photoshop for retouching and finishing touches. And, best of all, changes you make in Camera Raw never change your original RAW photo, so you can experiment and create new images anytime from your original RAW file (think of it as your digital negative). You can also process RAW files in Apple's Aperture, or even iPhoto.

WHERE TO LEARN MORE ABOUT RAW

If you want to learn more about processing your RAW photos (and you don't mind me subtly mentioning three of my bestselling books ever), try these: *The Adobe Photoshop Book for Digital Photographers*, where I did an entire section on processing RAW images step by step. If you use Photoshop Elements, try *The Photoshop Elements Book for Digital Photographers* (which I co-authored with Matt Kloskowski). Or, if you use Lightroom instead, I've still got ya covered with *The Adobe Photoshop Lightroom Book for Digital Photographers*. See how subtle that was? No? Oh, come on, that was totally subtle (wink).

Compare Your LCD to Your Computer Monitor

Once you're done with your latest photo shoot, go ahead and download the images from your memory card onto your computer and open them in whatever software package you use to view and organize your photos (I use Lightroom, which is a software application from Adobe specially designed from the ground up just for photographers. You can download a free 30-day trial version at adobe.com/lightroom). Now, once you've got your photos open on your computer, grab your camera and start comparing how the photos on your camera's LCD monitor look compared to the photos you're now seeing on your computer screen. Is it a pretty close match? Is your camera's LCD darker or lighter than what you see onscreen? This will give you a quick idea of how close your digital camera's LCD monitor is to what the image will look like once its on your computer (where you'll ultimately be editing your photos). This can be a big help when you're out shooting. For example, if you learn that your LCD makes everything look cooler (bluer) than it is on your computer screen, then you know you don't have to worry about adding a warming filter to your lens to warm up your photos—they're actually already warm enough. If the LCD is brighter than your computer screen, most cameras these days let you lower the brightness of the LCD screen, so it more closely matches how it will look when you edit your images on your computer. Try this and you'll be amazed at how knowing how "true" your LCD actually is can help you and your photography.

Organizing Your Photos with Lightroom

Although I use Photoshop for all the serious retouching and high-end tweaking of my photographic work, I use Lightroom for managing and organizing my thousands of digital photos, processing my RAW photos, creating onscreen slide shows, printing out multi-photo layouts, and even creating custom photo books. It is available for both Macintosh and Windows users, and only costs a fraction of what Photoshop costs (currently $149). Now, it certainly doesn't replace Photoshop, because it doesn't really allow for much serious retouching (like removing wrinkles, or reshaping facial features, or any one of a hundred things we can do in Photoshop to make people look their very best), nor does it create the amazing special effects, or photo composites, or layer adjustments, or the myriad of other things that only Photoshop can do, but then Lightroom isn't supposed to do all those things. Its strength is organizing, viewing, and editing RAW, JPEG, and TIFF files, and printing them, and it does that pretty brilliantly I might add. If you get serious about this whole digital photography thing (and if you bought this book, you're getting serious), I recommend you check out Lightroom—especially because if you actually go and buy it, I get a cash kickback from Adobe. I'm kidding of course, but I wish I weren't.

How Many More Megapixels Do You Need?

4 megapixel = 8x10"

5 megapixel = 11x14"

6 megapixel = 13x19"

8 megapixel = 16x20"

10–12 megapixel = 24x36"

36 megapixel = 30x40" and up

There's a ton of confusion (also known as marketing hype) around megapixels, and many people believe that megapixels have to do with image quality—the higher the number of megapixels, the better the quality, right? Unfortunately, that's not true. So, if you were using that as an excuse to buy a new camera, that's not going to float with me (although your spouse may buy that line). Here's what megapixels really mean: how large can I print my final photograph? That's it. If you're not going to print anything larger than 8x10", then a 5-megapixel camera is absolutely all you need. In fact, it's really more than you need, but I don't think you can even find a DSLR that's only 5 megapixels anymore (heck, our cell phone cameras are more than 5 megapixels these days). Anyway, if you want to routinely print 13x19" color prints, then you only need a 6-megapixel camera, so if yours is more megapixels (and you know, and I know, it is), then you're already set (I know, this is hard to swallow after years of thinking you needed more megapixels). So, what are today's 36-megapixel and up cameras for? Suckers. (Okay, not really, but you knew I was going to say that.) Actually, those high-megapixel cameras are for pros who need to print giant-sized images (think 30x40" and larger). If that's not you, then a 6-megapixel camera is all most people will really ever need, so put away your checkbook. Hey, don't blame me. I'm trying to save you some money, so you can buy some decent lenses and a fancy tripod.

Printing Lab-Quality 8x10s

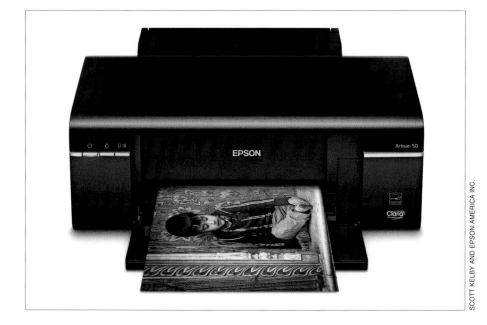

SCOTT KELBY AND EPSON AMERICA INC.

At some point, after putting all these techniques to use, you're going to want prints, and today many pro photographers create their own prints. Personally, I only use Epson printers, and about every other pro I know uses Epson printers as well, because they've become the standard for professional quality color and black-and-white inkjet printing. Now, before I start making recommendations as to which Epson printer to buy, I want you to know up front that the only reason I'm telling you this is because it's exactly what I'd tell any friend who asked. I don't get a kickback or cut from Epson. They have no idea I'm telling you this, so if you tell them, "Hey, Scott said I should buy an Epson," they'll say something along the lines of, "Scott who?" I personally have three Epson printers, and I love them dearly for three main reasons:

(1) They work pretty flawlessly most of the time, but if I do run into a bump along the way, they have live 24-hour tech support, which is actually quite good.

(2) They not only sell the printers, but the paper as well, and I love their paper.

(3) The output is absolutely stunning. The quality prints that come out of my Epson printers still amaze me.

For printing borderless 4x6s, 5x7s, and 8x10s, try the Epson Artisan 50 Inkjet Printer. The street price is around $150 (if that sounds pretty cheap, it is, but don't get too excited— you'll make up for it buying ink and photo-quality paper).

Printing Lab-Quality 13x19s

SCOTT KELBY AND EPSON AMERICA INC.

A popular print size with serious photographers is the 13x19" large print, and the Epson Stylus Photo R3000 is the king of this realm (it's the update to my beloved R2880—Epson tweaks their printers every year or so with the latest technology). Its color output is really stunning, but where the R3000 really kills is when you make black-and-white prints (it has a built-in advanced black and white mode). You'll lose your mind. Plus, the R3000 uses Epson's UltraChrome K3 archival-quality inks, so your prints are going to last longer than you will by a long shot. Of course, besides the 13x19" prints, it also does all of the smaller sizes, and you can print to roll paper, as well (for printing lots of prints on an overnight run—ideal for small studios). This is as in love with a printer as I've ever become. It costs around $790, which, for what it does, is a bargain.

Printing 17x22s—The Pros' Choice

SCOTT KELBY AND EPSON AMERICA INC.

Pros who sell their prints know that the bigger the print, the bigger the paycheck, and maybe that's why so many favor Epson's Stylus Pro 3880 large-print format printer, which makes prints on cut sheets up to 17x22" (or 17" by whatever if you use roll paper). For years, I've been a little miffed that Epson doesn't make a cut sheet in the classic 16x20" size, so I bought my 16x20 sheets from Red River Paper. I've finally gotten over it and now I just print on 17x22s, which fit digital file dimensions better anyway. Now that my rant is out of the way, this is one seriously killer printer (I think it's the best one Epson's ever made), and better yet, I just checked B&H Photo and they had it for $899, which is an insanely low price for a printer like this. If you're ready for a pro-quality photo printer, this is the one!

Which Paper Should You Print On?

If you're getting an Epson printer, then you definitely want to print on Epson paper. Epson paper not only works best on Epson printers, sometimes it's the only paper that will work (for example, one time when I was in a bind, I tried some HP paper. It didn't work at all—the paper went through the printer and ink came out, but it looked like… well, let's just say it didn't work and leave it at that). So, which papers do I recommend? Here they are:

Epson Velvet Fine Art Paper: This is a cotton paper with a matte coating that looks like watercolor paper and has a wonderful texture that gives your photos almost a painted feel. Clients love the feel of this paper and it's usually the first thing they notice.

Epson Ultra Premium Photo Paper Luster: This is probably my all-around favorite paper (and a favorite with many pros) because, although it definitely has a sheen to it, it does so without being overly glossy. It's that perfect paper between glossy and matte.

Epson Exhibition Fiber Paper: This is real pro-quality, high-end paper, with a true pro-quality look and a pro-quality price to match. This is about as good as it gets—use it for prints you're going to hang in a gallery or sell.

All of these papers are available directly from Epson.com, but I also often find these at my local Staples or Office Depot in sizes up to 13x19".

What Determines Which Paper You Use?

PREMIUM LUSTER

VELVET FINE ART

So, how do you know which paper to use? Believe it or not, there's an easy way—the paper you choose to print on is determined by one thing: the subject matter of your photo.

For example, if you're printing things of a softer nature, like flowers, birds, landscapes, waterfalls, or any type of image where you want a softer feel, try a textured paper like Epson's Velvet Fine Art Paper (provided you are printing to an Epson printer), which works wonderfully well for these types of images. This is your choice any time you want that "artsy" feel to your photography, and it also works well when your photo isn't tack sharp. Try it for black-and-white photography, too (especially on Epson's R3000), when you want extra texture and depth.

For serious portrait work, architecture, city life, travel, and finely detailed landscape shots, try Epson's Ultra Premium Photo Paper Luster. Anything with lots of detail looks great on this paper, and it really makes your colors vivid. So, when the shot has lots of detail and sharpness, lots of color, and you need it to "pop," this is the ticket for sharp, crisp prints.

Epson's Exhibition Fiber Paper is a great choice for landscape or cityscape black-and-white photos on the R3000 or the 3880 (this paper was designed expressly for printers that use Epson's Ultrachrome K3 inks), and it's one of the few fiber papers that print both color and black-and-white prints equally as well. When you see one of your landscape shots printed on this paper, you'll momentarily black out. I am not kidding.

Getting Your Monitor to Match Your Printer

Color management (the art of getting your color inkjet prints to match what you see on your monitor) has gotten dramatically easier in recent years, but the key to getting a color management system to work is getting your monitor color calibrated. A few years ago, this was a costly and time-consuming process usually only undertaken by paid consultants, but now anybody can do it because (1) it's very affordable now, and (2) it pretty much does all the calibrating work automatically while you just sit there and munch on a donut (you don't have to eat a donut, but it doesn't hurt). I use Datacolor's Spyder4ELITE hardware color calibrator, because it's absolutely simple to use, it's affordable, and a lot of the pros I know have moved over to it. It sells for around $249, and that's pretty much all that stands in the way of having your monitor match your prints. Well, that and downloading the free color profiles for the paper you're printing on (more on that on the next page).

Download the Color Profiles for Your Paper

If you buy Epson papers (or any of the major name-brand professional inkjet papers), you'll definitely want to go to Epson's (or your paper manufacturer's) website, go to their downloads page for your particular inkjet printer, and download their free color profiles for the exact paper you'll be printing to. Once you install these free color profiles (they install with just a double-click), when you go to Photoshop (or Lightroom, or Elements) to print your photo, you can choose the exact printer and paper combination you'll be printing to. This gives you the best possible results (and color fidelity) for your particular paper and printer. The pros do this every time and it makes a huge difference in the quality of their prints.

TIP FOR MORE PREDICTABLE COLOR

Your printer has a color management system, and Photoshop has one, too. Having two color management systems going at the same time is a guaranteed recipe for bad color. So, if you're printing from Photoshop, you should definitely turn off the color management system for your printer and use Photoshop's instead (in other words, let Photoshop determine the right colors).

Selling Your Photos as "Stock" Online

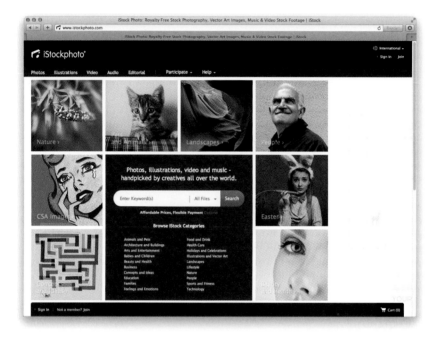

Selling photos to a stock agency is a dream of many photographers (pros included), but generally only the best of the best get this opportunity. Until now. Now you can start selling royalty-free stock photography today thanks to iStockphoto, which is a community of photographers all around the world who sell their photos online as stock (which means you give the rights to other people to buy, download, and use your photos in brochures, ads, wetbsites, flyers, and other collateral material graphic designers and web designers create for their clients). The great thing is anybody that follows their guidelines can upload their own photos and start selling them right away as part of iStockphoto's huge database of images. Now, you only get paid on how many people actually buy your photo, and since prices vary based on a buyer's subscription, and you get from 15%–25% (depending on how many people download your image), you're going to need to move a lot of photos to make this a business. But let me tell you this, there are photographers who make their living (and their Porsche payments) strictly from what they sell on iStockphoto.com, because iStockphoto is used by about a bazillion people around the world. Needless to say, the better quality your work is, and the more popular the subjects are, the more your images will get downloaded. How popular is iStockphoto? Well, Getty Images, one of the world's leading and most respected providers of high-quality stock images, bought them out—if that gives you any idea.

A Quick Peek at My Gear

For those interested in what kind of photo gear I use, here's a quick look: my main camera is a Nikon D4 and my backup camera body is a Nikon D3S. My go-to lens (if I have to have just one) is a Nikon 70–200mm f/2.8 VR II zoom lens (I use it for everything from portraits to my second lens when shooting sports).

For travel, I like to use just one lens (less is more for travel), and that's a Nikon 28–300mm f/3.5–f/5.6 VR lens. For landscapes, it's a Nikon 14–24mm f/2.8 super-wide-angle lens. I also use a Sigma 15mm f/2.8 fisheye lens for when I want an extreme-wide-angle for special effects type shots. You can't use it every day, but use it sparingly and it's really effective. I have a few other lenses (like a Nikon 85mm f/1.4 and a Nikon 24–70mm f/2.8), but those are the ones I use day-in/day-out (for sports, I have some long glass: a Nikon 300mm f/2.8 VR II, a Nikon 400mm f/2.8 VR II, and a Nikon 200-400mm f/4 VR).

I use two Nikon SB-910 hot shoe flashes and a Nikon TC-14E II 1.4x teleconverter to make my long lenses even longer. I use a collapsible Hoodman HoodLoupe, so I can see my LCD screen clearly when I'm shooting outside, and two Gitzo tripods (one for travel; one for everything else) with a BH-55 (and a smaller BH-40) Really Right Stuff ballhead (the mother of all ballheads, if you ask me). I have Lexar 600x and 1000x CompactFlash memory cards (you can never have enough), and I move all this gear in a Think Tank Photo Airport International V 2.0 Rolling Camera Bag (it's awesome!). You can see all my latest gear, with photos and links, at scottkelby.com/gear.

There Are Three Other Books in This Series

I hope this book has ignited your passion to learn more about photography, and if that's the case, I want to let you know that the book you're holding is Part 1 of what is (so far) a four-part series. I didn't plan it that way, but so many folks wrote me and asked, "When are you doing a part 2?" that I did Part 2. It did really well, so my publisher asked, "When are you doing a part 3?" and then I emailed myself a note asking, "When are you doing a part 4?" I am now concerned that I might send myself a tweet asking, "Will there be a part 5?" Probably, but only when I come up with enough kick-butt tips to fill an entire book—sometime in the year 2525, if man is still alive. (Okay, did anyone catch that vague reference to the song "In the Year 2525?" You did? Nice! Okay, bonus question: What's the name of the artists? Don't feel bad; nobody knows this one. It's by Zager and Evans.) Anyway, each part builds on the previous book, so you started with the right one by starting here with Part 1. You should read Part 2 next—don't jump ahead to Part 3 or Part 4. Here's what's in the other books in this series:

Part 2: It includes chapters on hot-shoe flash, studio lighting basics, shooting macro, more on everything from travel to landscapes to portraits, and more photo recipes.

Part 3: There are chapters on shooting outdoors, composition, product photography, lenses, and lots more on portraits, hot-shoe and studio flash, and sports.

Part 4: Lots more on lighting, chapters on shooting HDR and shooting DSLR video, plus more travel, portraits, shooting with natural light, sports, and lots more.

I hope you'll continue your photographic journey with me through this series. There's always the possibility the jokes will get better in Parts 2, 3 & 4 (Spoiler Alert: They don't).

Learn More with Me Each Week
on *The Grid*

Every Wednesday at 4:00 p.m. EST, I co-host (with photographer and Photoshop Guy Matt Kloskowski) a free, weekly photography talk show called *The Grid*. We talk about the week's hot topics in the photography community, and once a month we do a very popular episode called "Blind Photo Critiques," where you can send us five images for critique on the show. They're called "Blind Photo Critiques" because we don't reveal your name on-air, so we can be really honest and helpful to the person sending in the images. If you want "a hug," post your images on Flickr, and people will line up to tell you you've reinvented a photography genre, even if it's just a photo of your cat, Mr. Whiskers, playing with an empty juice box. Here, we actually tell you the truth (good or bad) and do it in a way that helps people learn about photography. Photographers from around the world tell us they learn a tremendous amount from it (in fact, the Light Stalking website included us in their list of "5 Incredible Online Communities to Get Genuine Feedback on Your Photography"). We also have famous in-studio guests, like Joe McNally, Cliff Mautner, Joel Grimes, Moose Peterson, Glyn Dewis, Lindsay Adler, Dave Black, and more. It's fast-paced, informative, sometimes controversial, often enlightening, and always a lot of laughs and fun. It airs live at **kelbytv.com/thegrid**, and we take your questions live on-air during the show. See you on *The Grid*!

WANT TO LEARN EVEN MORE?

I also produce a free weekly show called *Photography Tips and Tricks* ("Photo TNT" for short), hosted by RC Concepcion and Larry Becker. It's packed full of short little quick tips to help you make better photos—kinda like this book. You can catch it live (or we rebroadcast episodes free starting the next day) over at **kelbytv.com/photographytnt/**.

SHUTTER SPEED: 1/8000 SEC   F-STOP: F/2.8   ISO: 160   FOCAL LENGTH: 400mm   PHOTOGRAPHER: SCOTT KELBY

Chapter Eleven
Ten Things I Wish Someone Had Told Me
When I First Started Out in Photography

So, why don't pro photographers tell you about these things when you're "on the way up"? It's actually very simple, but you need to know the back story to understand how, historically, this has all worked. For as long as I can remember, there has been a "Secret Society of Photographers Who Have Taken a Blood Oath to Never Share Their Hard-Earned Secrets with Outsiders" (known as the SSOPWHTABOTNSTH-ESWO, for short), and this cartel of working pros (supposedly funded by an "unofficial" government agency, or Pentax) controls the flow of information, much like the ICANN controls the distribution of top-level web domains. Anyway, the sacred brothers (as they're called) of the SSOPWHTABOTNSTH-ESWO controlled the flow of photographic techniques for many years by only sharing them with other sacred brothers during a ritualistic "sharing of the mastery" ceremony held once at year in a hidden cave (which some claim is in Dunwoody, Georgia, just outside Atlanta). Anyway, what finally broke this chain of religious-like secrecy was actually a clerical error—a typo, if you will. When they were updating their official letterhead and business cards back in 2006, an intern working on the design apparently typed in their name as "SSOPWHTABOTTH-ESWO," accidentally leaving off two critical letters, "NS," which was the "Never Share" part of their name. As things tend to go in secret societies like this, the members felt this was actually an edict from the governing body (the Parliamentary Order of Professionals, a group which regular members are forbidden to ever refer to by their acronym), and so members began to share these once secret techniques openly and freely, and that's how we got to where we are today. Or, it could be that those pros are just afraid that if other people learn this stuff they'll wind up losing wedding jobs to them. It's hard to say.

#1: Buying a More Expensive Camera Doesn't Necessarily Mean Better Photos

If you bought a new DSLR camera in the past year or two, even an entry-level model, it already takes better quality photos right out of the box than the high-end pro models did just a few years ago. The quality of the sensors in today's entry-level digital cameras is truly amazing and, whether it's a Nikon, Canon, Sony, Pentax, etc., they all make great quality photos. For example, if you went out at dawn to a beautiful landscape location, set up a tripod, and took 10 shots with an entry-level camera, like the Canon Rebel T4i (I found a body online for $499), then took the same shots, in the same location, with the high-end Canon 5D Mark III (around $2,600), printed all 20 images, and mixed them up, you wouldn't be able to tell which camera took which images. They'd be that close in quality. So, if they both take such great shots, why would anyone ever need a high-end pro camera? Well, it's *not* because they take better photos; it's because they have more features. It's kinda like buying a car. You can buy a Toyota Camry from around $22,000 up to around $30,000. They're all Camrys (great cars), but you buy the $30K model because it has more features—heated seats, a back-up camera, a bigger engine, a security system, more speakers, and so on. But, when you're on the highway going 60 mph, the results are the same. So, how can you get better photos out of the camera you already have? Learn your camera inside and out—all the features, all the menus, and what all the buttons do. That way, using your camera becomes automatic and you can stop worrying about all the buttons and dials and start focusing on making great pictures, which is really about two things: what you aim your camera at and how you aim it.

#2: You Need to Sharpen After the Fact

There are lots of things you can do to help really sharpen photos, and obviously I thought it was so important that I started this book with a whole chapter just about sharpness. But, if there is one single trick that really takes a sharp shot to one that's tack sharp, it's sharpening after the fact on your computer. It doesn't matter whether you use Photoshop, Photoshop Elements (the "light" version of Photoshop that really isn't very light), Apple's Aperture, or Adobe's Lightroom, you need to sharpen every single photo to get the look the pros have. Think about this: with all the money we spend on tripods, and cable releases, and really sharp lenses, the reality is that as long as the shot is pretty sharp coming out of the camera, the $99 you spend on a program like Photoshop Elements will have the most impact on you getting a truly sharp photo (heck, I just did a quick Google search and found Elements for $65—that's a small price to pay to have all your photos from here on out jump to the next level of sharpness). By the way, whether you buy Photoshop Elements for $65 or the full version of Photoshop for around $700, the sharpen filter we use, called the Unsharp Mask filter, works exactly the same in both. To use it, go under the Filter menu, under Sharpen, and choose Unsharp Mask. Back on page 18 in Chapter 1, I gave you the settings I use day-in, day-out for people, cityscapes, urban photography, or travel, general everyday use, super-sharpening (for sports photos, landscapes, stuff with lots of details), and for images I've already made smaller and lower resolution, so I can post them on the web. Try them out and see if this sharpening doesn't make as big of a, or bigger, difference than all the rest.

#3: The Pros Take Lots of Bad Photos

You just don't see them, because one of the traits of a real pro is that they only show their very best work. I know a lot of folks think that these pros walk up to a scene, take one amazing shot, and then walk away and do it again someplace else—every time they press the shutter button, they create yet another amazing shot. I can tell you, for certain, that's just not how it works (if it was that way, the photographer's workday would be all of five minutes long, right?). I've worked and taught alongside some of the most famous photographers in the world today and they'd be the first ones to tell you that it often takes hundreds of shots of the same subject to come away with that one amazing shot (the only one that anyone will see). But, when we shoot, we see *all* our shots (the good ones and bad ones), so we start to compare *all* our shots to the pros' highlight reels, and it bums us out. Remember: we're not judged as photographers by the bad shots we take; we're judged by the ones we share. Take a cue from the pros—only share your best shots and just know that pros simply don't nail every shot. So, don't compare all your shots to the pros' cream of the crop. By the way, if I shoot 200 or 300 shots and I come away with five or six really good ones in there, I'm thrilled. Sometimes I get a few more than that; sometimes I literally walk away with none, which is disappointing, but it happens. If that happens to you, don't let it get you down—chances are that at the next shoot you'll make up for it. One more thing: every once in a while something amazing happens right in front of us and we raise our camera, shoot, and capture something magical. It happens to both amateurs and pros and it's called "getting lucky." Thankfully, it happens more often than you'd think.

#4: Learn Exposure Compensation

If you take a shot and you look at it on the back of your camera and it just looks awful (it's way too dark, way too bright, your subject is in shadows, etc.), do you know exactly which controls on your camera will fix it? If not, the next most important thing for you to learn is exposure compensation. I cover it back on page 74, but a lot of people will skip over that page because the phrase "exposure compensation" doesn't mean anything to them at that point. I wish it had a better name, because I think it's probably one of the most important camera techniques to learn when you're starting out. It helps you overcome two big problems: (1) your camera's built-in light meter is really good, but sometimes it's wrong and you know it's wrong, but you're not sure how to fix it; and (2) it helps you retain the detail in your photos, primarily in the brightest parts of your image. If you and I were out shooting and you asked me what one thing you needed to understand about your camera itself to really take better shots, learning exposure compensation would be it. Learning this is what will turn more of your messed up shots into prints you'll want to hang on your wall. Turn to page 74 right now and learn it. You can always come back to this chapter later (yes, it's that important).

#5: Don't Worry About Manual Mode

Good news: you can be a great photographer, and make amazing images, and live a long, happy life all without ever having to learn to shoot in manual mode. I know a lot of new photographers worry that the reason their photos don't look like they want them to is because they're not shooting in manual mode. But, trust me, manual mode isn't some magical mode that transforms everyday photos into gallery pieces—it's just another shooting mode on your camera like the rest. And, ultimately, what makes magical photos is, say it with me, "what you aim your camera at and how you aim it." It's not which mode you shoot in. I think the reason some of us get sucked into thinking it's the magical unicorn of modes is that you'll sometimes read in an online forum some photographer bragging that he "only shoots in manual mode" (like he's earned some special honor). But, again, trust me, it's just another exposure mode on your camera, so you can scratch that one off your worry list. Now, I don't want you to think that I'm saying you shouldn't learn manual mode, or that manual mode is bad (I actually recommend it for shooting in a photo studio with strobes), but I don't want you to think it's this big hill that one day you're going to have to climb to get to photography nirvana. In the list of things we have to worry about in our quest to become better photographers, you can move this one way, way down your list.

#6: Today You Should Probably Shoot Wide

Where do most of our images wind up being seen today? On the web, right? I mean, we still make some prints from time to time (you do make prints, right?), but really, in today's world, you'd have to admit that for most of us, the web is where most folks will see our images. If that's the case for you, then I hope you take this advice I got a few years ago: shoot wide. By wide I mean shoot horizontal (landscape) shots rather than tall, vertical shots. Here are two reasons why: (1) The bigger your images appear, the more impact they have, right? Right! So, when you shoot tall shots and put them on the web, they usually wind up looking like small thumbnails because that's the way most websites, portfolio sites, and social media sites are designed. Your image will have a lot of empty space on either side of it, and in the middle, there's your little picture. However, if you shoot wide, you'll be able to make your images much larger on the web and they'll have that much more impact. (2) It's usually much easier to crop a wide image so it looks like a tall image, than it is to try to crop a tall image so it looks like a wide image (give it a try and you'll instantly see what I mean). So, I know there's an old saying that goes, "When do you shoot a tall image? Right after you've shot a wide version of it," but there's a reason that's an "old" saying. It used to apply because all our images used to be prints, and they all had the same impact because you could just rotate the print. Today, things have changed and we need to change our thinking (and our shooting strategy), too!

#7: Nothing Has Impact Like a Print

If you want to really make an impression on people, make a print. I know it sounds simple, but a printed piece, especially today, is one of the most powerful, impactful things you can do for your photography, and the bigger the print, the more powerful the impact (I personally think the impact size starts at 13x19", but if you can go bigger, like 17x22", it really adds impact. This is a case where bigger is better). So, why do prints have such an impact these days? (1) Prints are real. The rest of the time we're looking at images inside a glass screen on a computer. We can't hold them. We can't touch them. They're "inside" a box of some sort. When you make a print, your image is no longer a bunch of 1s and 0s and a bunch of digital code. It's real. (2) When you make a print, watch the person's hands right after you hand them the print. They start feeling the paper. Touch is one of our five senses, and when you add touch to your visual sense, your image connects with the viewer on a different level. (3) There is a certain legitimacy to having prints of your work. It says something about you, about how serious you take your work, and it's an investment in your photographic journey. (4) Prints open doors. If you want to shoot in a particular location (let's say it's a restaurant interior), and you take a large print in to show the restaurant owner the type of work you do, my guess is they'll welcome you to shoot in their restaurant. It tacitly says, "I'm legit—it's okay to let me do this." Believe me, it works wonders. Lastly, (5) prints make an amazing gift. Think of it this way: How much impact does it have when you email an image to a friend? Now, make a nice print, sign it, roll it in a tube, and mail it to them the old fashioned way. You'll be amazed at the reaction you get. There's power in the print. Try it once, and you'll see.

#8: Ignore Your Histogram

I know that headline above just made someone's head explode, but remember, these are things I'd tell a personal friend (and things I wish somebody had told me), and one of those things would be to ignore the histogram on the back of your camera. I know that people desperately want a tangible, technical measure of the age-old question, "Is this a good photo?" But, I can promise you the answer isn't found there. I remember being one of the guest speakers at a photography workshop and, during my presentation, the subject of histograms came up. Standing in the back of the room were some of the other instructors (literally, some of the best in the business—Joe McNally, Vincent Versace, Laurie Excell, and Moose Peterson). I mentioned I didn't use histograms, and then I asked those famous photography instructors if they ever used the histogram on the back of their camera. They yelled back: "Nope," "Never," "Not me," and "Not a chance!" What is it that these pros know that so many people arguing endlessly on the web don't know? They know that great photos don't come from looking at a graph. They know that great photos aren't about the technical stuff (even though so many photographers desperately wish that it was, because people can learn technical stuff—it's much harder to develop an "eye" and a heart for photography). Getting a good exposure with today's digital cameras just isn't that hard. In fact, it's simple, because today's cameras are so advanced that you almost have to work hard to get a bad exposure. So, stop worrying about the graph and start worrying about what you aim your camera at, and how you aim it. That's where great photos come from.

#9: Figure Out What Type of Photographer You Are

You should try shooting all sorts of stuff—from food to landscapes, from portraits to sports, from products to travel, and everything in between. When you're just starting out, shoot everything! And once you've done that, sit down and figure out what kind of photographer you really want to be and work on that. The first step is to take a good look at the stuff you've been shooting and ask yourself, "Which one of these do I seem to have a knack for?" Or, "Which shots have people told me I have a knack for?" Chances are there is something you shot that you particularly felt you had a knack for—you just kind of knew what to do. Okay, that's step one (and it might be more than one thing—you might feel like you have a knack for travel, sports, and natural light portraits, and that's okay). The next step is to ask yourself, "Which one of these do I really enjoy shooting?" This is really important, because this is what you should be focusing on. There's no sense in getting really good at product photography when what you really want to be is a natural light portrait photographer. But, few photographers, even more experienced ones, really sit down and think this through—they just shoot what comes their way. And, while they may wind up being competent at shooting a lot of different things, I'm guessing being *competent* isn't your goal (it's like getting a C+ in class). Finding out who you are as a photographer allows you to focus your learning, your energy, and your time in the right direction. When you start to get good at what you really enjoy, this is when the magic happens.

#10: Do What It Takes to Get the Photos You Want

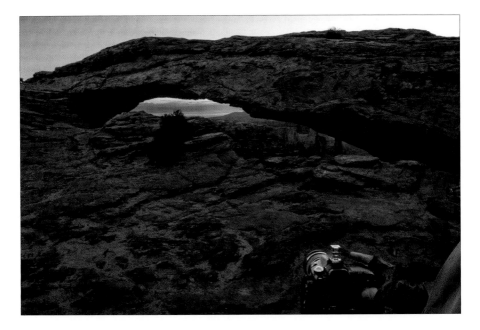

Look, somebody has to tell you this (I wish it wasn't me, but since we're here together, here goes): great photos aren't around your house. One day, they might be, but chances are, you're going to have to venture out, perhaps quite far, to make the type of photos you want to make. For example, if you decide you want to take great landscape photos, chances are (unless you live in Page, Arizona, or Moab, Utah), you're not going to be able to make great landscape photos in the city where you live. You're going to have to go someplace where great landscape photos are made. I know that takes time and it costs money, but if you want amazing landscape photos, you'd better start by standing in front of an amazing landscape, preferably at dawn. That's the other part. If you do spend the money and make the trip, don't sleep in and shoot at 9:00 a.m. You need to be in place, ready to shoot, at least 30 minutes before sunrise—more like 4:45 a.m. This is what I mean when I say, "Do what it takes to get the photos you want." When you see amazing landscape photos, someone did just that. They paid for the trip. They learned the settings. They bought (borrowed, or rented) the right equipment. They got up at dawn (maybe two mornings in a row at the same location. Maybe more). They did what it took to get the type of shot they wanted. But shouldn't you practice a lot before you make that trip? That trip is the practice (and this won't be your only practice trip). If you want to shoot people, find interesting looking or extremely photogenic people, and then either learn to light them or find amazing light. If great photos were easy, everybody would have them. Making great photos takes more than a great camera. Do whatever it takes to make the shot or you'll wind up with a lifetime of shots you're disappointed with.

#11: You Need a Portfolio

You're probably thinking, "Wait, this is #11. I thought you said there would be just 10 things?" I know, but 11 things just sounds kind of weenie, so consider this one a bonus thing. Okay, back to the portfolio. It doesn't matter if you have an online one or a printed portfolio. The most important part at this point is that you have one. Why is this so important? It's because you probably have literally thousands of photos on your computer, so what you really have is a big pile of photos that doesn't really tell you much, besides that you've taken a bunch of photos. The reason you need a portfolio of your best work is so you know where you are, right now, as a photographer. When you compile your best photos, you'll get a real sense for where you are on your journey and only then can you decide what you need to learn or do next. Okay, so how many photos should be in your portfolio? Start with just 24 of your best photos and compile them into a portfolio. I don't mean put them in folder on your computer—you need to post them somewhere online (yes, you have to post them). You don't have to pay a bunch, as there are lots of places to get an online portfolio for free or next to nothing (try 500px.com or www.squarespace .com, which are both very cool and affordable). If you don't think you can narrow things down to just 24 images, ask another photographer who you feel can give you an un-biased opinion to help. If you're serious about growing as a photographer, this is an important step (a bigger one than it sounds).

#12: Stop Reading Books About Photography

Now you're thinking, "Really? There's a number 12?" Well, this was going to be a blank page, because of the way books are printed, so I thought I'd toss in another bonus one, and although the headline sounds kind of negative (well, certainly from my book publisher's point of view), it actually isn't. But, let's switch gears for a moment. Have you ever read *Golf Digest* magazine? Terrific magazine, full of great articles on everything from how to improve your swing to "bunker shots made simple." I always learn a thing or two reading *Golf Digest*, which is great because I love golf. I'm just not very good at it. When I play a round with my brother Jeff, I don't score very well. I do hit a few nice drives, sink a nice putt or two, and every once in a while I even make a simple bunker shot. I've taken golf lessons, I have a pretty decent set of clubs, and thanks to *Golf Digest*, I pretty much know what to do, which is why it's so frustrating that when I play a round, I don't do nearly as well as I should. But, at least I know why. I don't practice. Taking lessons, reading *Golf Digest*, and watching the Golf Channel teach me about golf, but it's not practice. I need to take what I've read, watched, and been taught, and actually go practice those techniques. I need to hit the driving range regularly. I need to practice my short game. And, I need to practice actually getting out of bunkers (and not just reading about how to do it). Photography is the same way. If you want to get better, reading will pretty much show you what to do, but that's not doing it. That's reading about it. You need to practice. You need to shoot regularly with the single intent of practicing the things you've read about. I really do appreciate that you bought this book, and I hope it gives you some great ideas about what to work on, but now put down the book. It's practice time.

Chapter Twelve

Photo Recipes to Help You Get "The Shot"

The Simple Ingredients That Make It All Come Together

Hey, it's the end of the book, and now is as good a time as any to let you in on a secret. There's really no way in hell we're going to get those really magical shots (like you see in magazines such as *Outdoor Photographer* or *Shutterbug*). That's because when we get out to that prime shooting location at the crack of dawn to hopefully capture one of these once-in-a-lifetime shots, carrying so much gear that our chiropractors are on speed dial, we'll soon find that it's too late—there are already a dozen or so photographers set up there waiting for that magical light, too. Since they were there first, the only spot left on that tiny plateau is behind them, and every shot you take is going to have some, if not all, of their camera gear fully in your frame, ruining any possible chance of you getting "the shot." But this chapter is all about recipes for getting the shot, and I've got a special recipe for this very situation. Just as the golden light appears over the horizon, you quietly slide your foot inside one of their tripod legs, then quickly pull your foot back, toppling over their entire rig, and as their thousands of dollars of gear begins to crash violently to the ground, you deftly press the cable release on your camera and capture that amazing vista as the sound of broken glass echoes off the canyon walls. Ahh, that, my friends, is the magical sound of you getting "the shot." If you hear the faint sound of sobbing in the distance, it all becomes that much sweeter. Enjoy.

The Recipe for Getting This Type of Shot

Characteristics of this type of shot: A sweeping landscape with beautiful overall light and some areas lit brighter than others.

(1) This type of beautiful light doesn't happen at 2:00 p.m. You have to get up early and be in place, ready to shoot, 30 minutes before the sun comes up.

(2) To get a big, sweeping feel to your image, you'll want to use a "big, sweeping feel" type of f-stop, something like f/22, which is perfect for landscape shots like this.

(3) Right around sunrise, the light is very low and since you're shooting at a slow f-stop, like f/22, you'll need to be on a tripod, and you'll need a cable release (or wireless shutter release) to reduce the chance of any movement of your camera.

(4) Since you'll be on a tripod, you can shoot at the lowest native ISO for your camera (usually 100 for Canon and Sony cameras, and 200 for most Nikons, although some of the newer ones are 100 ISO, as well. Check the manual for your camera).

(5) For landscape shots like this, use the widest wide-angle lens you have. If you're using a full-frame camera, something like a 14mm or 16mm would be ideal. If you're shooting a cropped-sensor camera, something like a 12mm would be ideal.

(6) For a warmer look overall, set your white balance to Cloudy.

(7) This particular shot was taken right at sunrise, which is why some of the mountains are still in the shade and some have some light peeking through. The red glow on the arch (that's Mesa Arch in Moab, Utah) appears right before and during sunrise.

The Recipe for Getting This Type of Shot

Characteristics of this type of shot: A "beauty style" shot with soft, punchy light that eliminates most shadows on the face.

(1) This is a two-light shoot: The main light is a studio strobe (flash) with a 17" beauty dish attachment that's directly in front of the subject (to soften the punchy light from a beauty dish, put a diffusion sock over it), up about 2 feet above her face, aiming down at her at a 45° angle. (*Note:* If you don't have a beauty dish, you can use a small softbox instead.) The other light is a small 24" square softbox down at her waist level, aiming up at her at a 45° angle.

(2) Position the camera height right at eye level and, to keep everything in focus from front to back, you'll need to use an f-stop that holds details (like f/11) and a long enough lens (like a 200mm) to give nice perspective. You're in the studio, so use the lowest native ISO you can (100 or 200 ISO max).

(3) Position your subject about 8 to 10 feet in front of a white seamless paper background. Don't put any light on the background, and your white seamless paper will be light gray, like you see here.

(4) If you only have one strobe, use that as the main light up top, then have your subject hold a reflector flat at their chest level, as high as possible without being seen in the frame, to reflect the light from the top strobe back up onto their face to reduce any shadows.

The Recipe for Getting This Type of Shot

Characteristics of this type of shot: Still water and interesting shades of blue and pink come together for this travel shot taken in Jaipur, Rajasthan, India.

(1) Soft, beautiful light like this only happens twice a day—at sunrise and sunset— and this shot was taken after sunset. The fact that there is mirror-like water was total luck.

(2) Since this is taken in the low light of dusk, it has to be taken on a tripod with a cable release or the shutter speed will fall so low that the image will be blurry and out of focus.

(3) Since you're shooting on a tripod, you can use the lowest, cleanest ISO for your camera (probably 100 or 200 ISO).

(4) The color comes from experimenting with the camera's white balance setting. Try a different setting (like Fluorescent or Tungsten), take a shot, and then look at the LCD monitor on the back of your camera to see how it looks to you. You're not looking for accuracy here, you're looking to create art—something beautiful—so try different ones out and see which one really creates stunning color.

(5) The other key to getting a shot like this is composition. By putting the palace in the bottom third of the frame (rather than the boring dead center of the image), it creates more visual interest, a more dynamic image, and draws your eye right to the subject.

The Recipe for Getting This Type of Shot

Characteristics of this type of shot: An aggressive-looking car detail shot (only showing part of the car—in this case, the front), lit with soft, even lighting.

(1) This shot is actually much easier than it looks, since it only uses one single light: a studio flash with a long, thin (14x35") softbox called a strip bank. It's surprisingly affordable for the wonderful light it creates (the one I use costs around $175) and since it's long and thin, the light it delivers is long and thin.

(2) The big trick to this is getting the background and sides to fall off to solid black, even though this was taken indoors with lots of lights on. The trick is the f-stop. Shooting at f/22 makes the light fall off (end) very quickly, so the flash only really lights just where you're aiming it.

(3) In this case, I have the light on a boom stand directly over the front of the car, aiming straight down at the hood (you can see a reflection of the softbox right below the Lamborghini logo on the hood).

(4) To get the aggressive look to the image, I am literally lying down on the floor. This really low perspective makes the car look bigger and badder (not that it needs it).

(5) Since I'm using a flash, it will pretty much freeze any minor movement by my camera, so I don't have to worry about setting up a tripod 6" off the ground. I used my elbows to steady my camera nevertheless. The hardest part of all of this is finding a friend with a really cool car. A big thanks to automotive photographer Tim Wallace for teaching me this car detail shooting technique and for letting me share it here with you.

The Recipe for Getting This Type of Shot

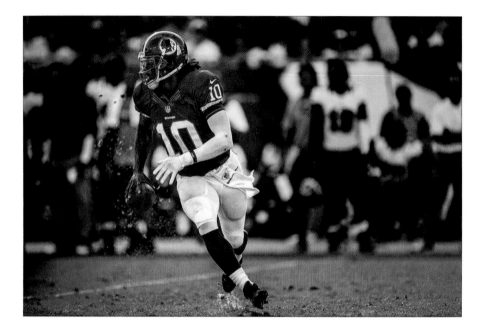

Characteristics of this type of shot: Sports photo, freezing the action and keeping the athlete in focus while the background is soft and out of focus.

(1) To get a tight-in shot like this, you'll need a very long lens, ideally a 400mm f/2.8 lens or a 300mm lens with a 1.4x teleconverter to get you in closer. If this seems like a crazy-expensive proposition, turn back to page 92 for a refresher.

(2) To get the out-of-focus background (which you want, as it creates separation of the player from the background), you need to shoot at the widest possible aperture your lens will allow (meaning, shoot at the lowest number your lens will go. Ideally f/2.8, but if your lens won't go that low, then f/4. If your lens will only go down to f/5.6, you're not going to get the type of out-of-focus background and separation you see here, which is why these fast lenses—ones that shoot at f/2.8 or f/4—are ideal for sports). During a game, I shoot in aperture priority mode and I won't change the f-stop even once—it will always be f/2.8 (and the camera will pick the shutter speed for me).

(3) Your shutter speed needs to be at least 1/1000 of a second or faster to freeze action in sports. During a daylight game like this, with you shooting at f/2.8, it will not be a problem (you'll probably see shutter speeds more like 1/4000 or higher). However, if part of the field winds up in shadow later in the day, you might have to raise your ISO to get your shutter speed back up to 1/1000 of a second.

(4) Lastly, to shoot a moving athlete like this and not lose the focus, switch your camera to AI Servo Mode (Canon) or Continuous Focus mode (Nikon and Sony). That way, the focus tracks and moves with your athlete as he/she moves during the action.

The Recipe for Getting This Type of Shot

Characteristics of this type of shot: A nighttime shot of a building lit with neon lights (this is Flo's V8 Cafe in Cars Land at Disney California Adventure Park).

(1) There are just three things you need to make a shot like this: The first is patience. I had to wait quite a while until there was a 5-second break between streaming crowds of tourists walking right in front of the cafe. This also took a lot of patience for my wife and kids (luckily, there was a gift shop nearby).

(2) The second thing you need is a tripod to steady your camera in low light. Unfortunately, I didn't have a tripod with me, so I had to find something to steady my camera because the shutter was going to be open for a couple of seconds (if I handheld that, it would be out of focus for certain). I tried leaning my camera on a garbage can right across the way from Flo's. I also tried setting it on the ground and using a self-timer. I tried setting it on a railing and a few other different locations, but to get the perspective you see here, I actually wound up setting it on the seat of a park bench.

(3) The third thing is to shoot in manual mode. If you shoot in aperture priority mode, it's probably going to overexpose the shot (not always, mind you, but enough times to where when I shoot nighttime shots, I switch to manual mode). Start by taking one shot in program mode, then note the settings it used. Now switch to manual mode, enter those settings as your starting place, and then if the shot looks too bright, raise your f-stop by one stop (like from f/5.6 to f/8) or higher until the sky gets nice and black.

The Recipe for Getting This Type of Shot

Characteristics of this type of shot: Soft, beautiful light with your background out of focus so there's lots of separation between your subject and the background.

(1) The first step, way before the shoot, is to go to a bridal store and buy a very, very long veil. Years ago, I heard a top pro wedding photographer say, "Give me a really long veil, and I'll give you magic!" So that's the first step (and what I used here).

(2) Put your camera in aperture priority mode so you get to choose the f-stop you want, and in this case you want to shoot with the lowest numbered f-stop your lens will allow (the lower the better, so f/1.8, f/2, or f/2.8 would be ideal). This gives you that out-of-focus background. Well, it pretty much does, but not without the next step.

(3) Use a long lens (like a 200mm lens) and zoom in on your bride. Zooming in (like I did for this shot), combined with the f/2.8 f-stop is what gives you that magical, soft, out-of-focus background. If you shoot at f/2.8, but with a wide-angle lens or zoomed way out, the background will all be in focus and you won't get this look.

(4) Shoot at the cleanest ISO your camera will allow (probably 100 or 200 ISO).

(5) Wait until the sun goes behind a cloud. That way, the cloud acts as a giant softbox and softens and spreads the sunlight so you don't have harsh shadows. Then, try to position your subject so the sunlight that does come through the clouds hits mostly on one side of her face (in this case, the left side in the photo above).

(6) Set the focus on your subject's eye that's closest to the camera, because if her eyes aren't in focus, the shot goes in the trash.

The Recipe for Getting This Type of Shot

Characteristics of this type of shot: A soft beautiful gradient of light wrapping around a classic P-51 Mustang.

(1) Beautiful light like this, with that beautiful gradient of color in the sky, happens only twice a day—at dawn or at dusk—and this shot was taken at dusk, with the plane sitting on the ramp at an airshow.

(2) Since this is taken at dusk in low light, it has to be taken on a tripod with a cable release or the shutter speed will fall so low that the image will be blurry and out of focus.

(3) Since you're shooting on a tripod, you can use the lowest, cleanest ISO for your camera (probably 100 or 200 ISO).

(4) To get the perspective you see here, you'll need to lower the tripod way down (I took this shot with my tripod so low I had to shoot on my knees. Glad I remembered to take gel-filled knee pads with me, since I figured I'd wind up shooting down low like this on the airfield's tarmac). However, the main reason I shot down low like this was to avoid seeing all the distracting stuff behind the plane, like other planes, airshow vendors, and an ugly trailer. By shooting up at the plane, all you see is sky.

(5) To capture as much of the plane as possible, and still be close enough for the shot to have impact, you'll need to shoot with a wide-angle lens (this was shot at 24mm with a 24–105mm f/4 lens). Since you're shooting on a tripod, this lens doesn't have to be a fast lens (in fact, I shot it at f/8, so everything would be in focus).

The Recipe for Getting This Type of Shot

Characteristics of this type of shot: Popular "blown-out" look with tons of light, and the image is converted into a high-contrast black and white.

(1) This is a natural-light shot made by positioning the bride and groom about 6 feet from a window in the church (you move them 6 feet back, so the light is soft and beautiful). The window is yellow stained glass, which means the light from it will be yellow, and if the light is yellow, the bride and groom will look very yellow, so I knew when I was taking the photo that I would have to convert this image to black and white (that's an old trick: if the color looks way off, convert the image to black and white).

(2) Position yourself so you're aiming into the window (if the bride and groom stepped away, I'd have a great shot of the empty window), but then use a long lens to zoom in tight. I used a 70–200mm lens all the way out at 200mm. Notice how tight in I am— the top of his head is cut off, which is perfectly fine (and very common). Zooming in tight like this makes the photo feel more intimate.

(3) The light from the window is so bright the photo is already kind of blown out, but you can make it more blown out in Photoshop (or Elements, or Lightroom) by dragging Camera Raw's (or the Develop module's) Highlights slider way over to the right to accentuate the effect.

(4) Lastly, convert the image to black and white (using one of the programs above). To create the high-contrast look, drag the Camera Raw (Develop module) Contrast slider way over to the right.

The Recipe for Getting This Type of Shot

Characteristics of this type of shot: A food shot, cropping in tight with lots of detail, while the background falls off to being out-of-focus very quickly.

(1) The first step to a shot like this happens before you're seated at your table. Ask to either be seated outside (if possible) or near the window. The reason is the challenge of shooting food—you need light. Nice, natural light looks wonderful for food shots, so if you can sit near a window, or outside, you're halfway there. However, to keep the plates looking white (instead of tinted blue), make sure you change your camera's white balance to Cloudy or Shade (try both and see which one looks better).

(2) The other key to great-looking food shots is to zoom in really tight on the food. For example, if you have an 18–200mm lens, zoom all the way in to 200mm. Don't try to show the whole plate, just show part of it. To do this, you'll probably have to stand up behind your chair for a moment, then shoot from a little lower angle (don't stand up straight and shoot down on your food—crouch down to lower your angle).

(3) To get the soft, out-of-focus background, shoot in aperture priority mode at the lowest number f-stop your lens will allow (in this case, it was only f/5.6, but because I was zoomed in so tight, it still creates that out-of-focus background). If my lens would have gone to f/4 or f/2.8, I could have made it even more shallow and out-of-focus.

(4) To create some energy in food shots like this, I normally tilt the camera to the right or to the left (as seen here).

The Recipe for Getting This Type of Shot

Characteristics of this type of shot: A concert shot with multi-colored lighting.

(1) You can't (and shouldn't) use a flash for concert or event photography, so you don't have to worry about that. One key to a shot like this is to use the lowest possible f-stop your lens will allow (ideally, f/2.8 or f/4) to help separate the musician from the background by making the background go out of focus. In fact, the depth of field here is so shallow that the arm on the left is in focus and the arm on the right is out of focus.

(2) For a close-up shot like this, you'll need a zoom lens to zoom in tight (this was taken with a 70–200mm lens at 200mm).

(3) The real challenge in getting a shot like this is freezing the motion of the musicians on stage, so the shot is in focus. That means keeping an eye on your shutter speed. If it falls below 1/60 of a second, your shot will definitely be out of focus. If you're shooting a big major touring act, most times light will not be a problem, because there will be a ton of it. However, in some cases (like with the shot above), the light is low. Here, there were only four lights total for the whole night, so I had to shoot at (wait for it…wait for it…) 8,000 ISO to get to a shutter speed of just 1/100 of a second. If this happens to you, you'll need to use the noise reduction software in Camera Raw (in Photoshop or Elements, or the Develop module in Lightroom) to reduce the amount of visible noise that you see when shooting at that high an ISO. Go to the Detail tab (panel) and drag the Luminance slider to the right until the noise starts to disappear (stop as soon as it's gone, or your image will get blurry).

The Recipe for Getting This Type of Shot

Characteristics of this type of shot: A "beauty style" shot with soft light against a white background.

(1) Unlike the beauty shot I showed at the beginning of this chapter, this is just a one-light shoot, but it has a lot in common with the first shot—this one is just easier. The one light is a single studio strobe (flash) with a 17" beauty dish attachment that's directly in front of the subject, with a $20 diffusion sock over the front of the beauty dish to soften and diffuse the light. It's positioned about 2 feet above her head, aiming back at her at a 45° angle. (*Note:* If you don't have a beauty dish, you can use a small softbox instead.)

(2) Have your subject (or, ideally, a friend) hold a white reflector up at waist level, tilted back toward your subject to fill in any shadows under her eyes and her face. If you need the light to be brighter, have your subject hold the reflector up a little higher.

(3) Since you're using studio lighting, you'll want to shoot in manual mode so you can set the shutter speed and then forget it. Set it to 1/125 of a second. To keep everything in focus, set your aperture to f/11, and use a long lens (like a 200mm) to give a nice perspective. Also, use the lowest native ISO you can (like 100 or 200 ISO max).

(4) Position your subject fairly close to the white seamless paper background, so your front light spills over onto the background to help make it white (instead of gray). However, you shouldn't see any shadows casting on the background. If you do, move your subject farther away from the background.

The Recipe for Getting This Type of Shot

Characteristics of this type of shot: A travel shot taken with soft light, capturing a moment and capturing it in focus (which is the challenge).

(1) When you're shooting travel photos and you're not in bright, direct sunlight (this shot is taken on an overcast day and the subjects are under a tree), chances are the photo is going to be blurry because your shutter speed falls too low to keep everything in focus.

(2) The trick for having these types of shots in focus is to set your camera to a high ISO (this was shot at 1,600 ISO). By shooting at a high ISO like this, it raises your shutter speed high enough to freeze most movement (from your subjects, or from camera shake on your part). That way, you don't miss a quiet moment like this (by the way, I bought one of the crêpes she's making [in the Luxembourg Gardens in Paris], and it was insane!).

(3) If you look closely at the image, the edges all the way around the photo are darkened, and that is done using the Camera Raw software in either Photoshop or Elements, or the Develop module in Lightroom. You do it by going to the Effects tab (panel), under the Post Crop Vignetting section, and then dragging the Amount slider to the left. The farther you drag it, the more it darkens the edges. By default, it darkens just the outside edges, but if you want it to darken a little farther in toward the center of your photo, drag the Midpoint slider to the left, too.

The Recipe for Getting This Type of Shot

Characteristics of this type of shot: A brightly lit set of wedding rings with a mirror-like reflection.

(1) The trick here is simply to place the rings on a piano, so you get a natural reflection from the black, highly polished wood. If there's not a piano where the wedding reception is being held, try placing them on the hood of a black car (ideally, one that's not out in the direct sun. But, if that's your only choice, have a friend or assistant hold a white handkerchief between the sun and the rings to soften and diffuse the light).

(2) The lighting is just light coming in from a nearby window. In this case, the piano was located about 6 feet from a nearby window, so the light wasn't very bright. To keep the shutter open long enough to make it look like it's perfectly lit, you have to shoot this on a tripod or it would be crazy-blurry.

(3) To have the rings appear this large in the photo and with this much detail, you'll need to use a macro (close-up) lens. That way, you can position your lens really, really close to the rings (just a few inches away)—being that close makes them appear really large (this shot was taken with a 105mm macro).

(4) Because macro lenses have such an incredibly shallow depth of field (which means if you're not really careful, just the front of the first ring will be in focus, and then the other ring, and basically everything else, will be totally out of focus), you need to choose an f-stop that offers as much depth as possible (like f/22). That lets you keep most of the rings in sharp focus.

Index

Dfine 2.0 plugin for, 41
flash used for, 41–43
formal portraits, 45–53, 218
high vantage point for, 57
ISO settings for, 38
lenses for, 39, 40, 218, 220
lighting conditions for, 38, 41–44, 218, 220
low-light situations for, 38–39
memory cards for, 59, 60, 152
number of shots for, 59
outdoor shots, 43, 53, 218
popular format for, 47
posing people for, 48
reception photos, 54
ring photos, 225
soft light for, 41–42
white balance for, 61
wide-angle lens for, 58
Westcott collapsible reflector, 127
Westcott Micro Apollo Softbox, 41
white backgrounds
flower photography and, 31
portrait photography and, 116, 213, 223
white balance
Auto White Balance, 61, 132
avoiding problems with, 132
experimenting with, 214
indoor sports and, 97
JPEG format and, 61
panoramas and, 84
presets for, 61
RAW format and, 61, 97, 132
sunrises/sunsets and, 72
wedding photos and, 61
wide-angle lenses
airplane photography and, 219
landscape photography and, 88, 212
moon included in photos using, 173
polarizing filters and, 77
sports photography and, 93
wedding photography and, 58
wind, shooting flowers in, 34
window light
indoor portraits using, 124
wedding shots using, 44, 220
Woods, Tiger, 3

Z

Ziser, David, 125
zoom button, 17
zoom lenses
close-up lens added to, 26, 27
concert shots and, 222
fireworks shots and, 174
flower photography and, 25
landscape photography and, 88
moon included in photos using, 173
portrait photography and, 114
quality considerations, 15
sports photography and, 93, 94
zooming the LCD monitor, 17, 147

The Digital Photography

The step-by-step secrets for how to
make your photos look like the pros'!

Book

Scott Kelby

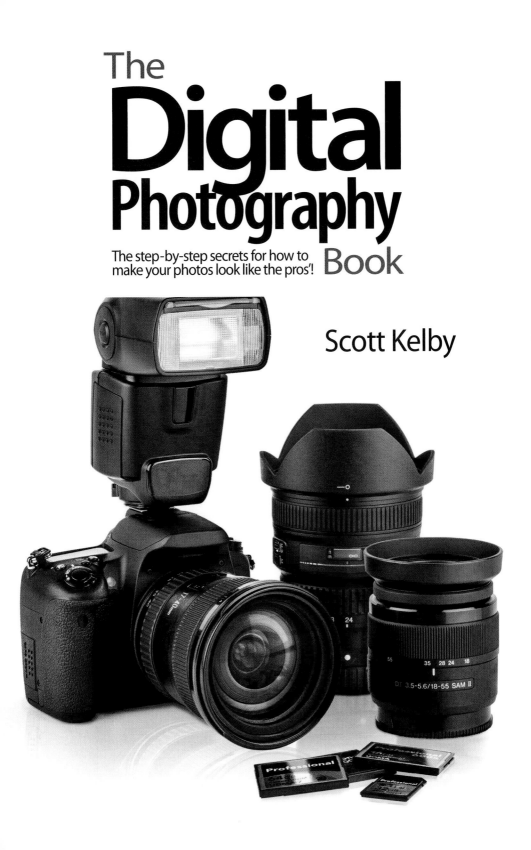

The Digital Photography Book, part 2

The Digital Photography Book, part 2 Team

CREATIVE DIRECTOR
Felix Nelson

ART DIRECTOR
Jessica Maldonado

TECHNICAL EDITORS
Kim Doty
Cindy Snyder

EDITORIAL CONSULTANTS
David Hobby
David Ziser
Steve Dantzig

PRODUCTION MANAGER
Dave Damstra

PHOTOGRAPHY
Scott Kelby

STUDIO AND
PRODUCTION SHOTS
Brad Moore

PUBLISHED BY

Peachpit Press

©2014 Scott Kelby

Composed in Myriad Pro (Adobe Systems Incorporated) and LCD (Esselte) by Kelby Media Group Inc.

Trademarks
All terms mentioned in this book that are known to be trademarks or service marks have been appropriately capitalized. Peachpit Press cannot attest to the accuracy of this information. Use of a term in the book should not be regarded as affecting the validity of any trademark or service mark.

Photoshop, Elements, and Lightroom are registered trademarks of Adobe Systems, Inc.
Nikon is a registered trademark of Nikon Corporation.
Canon is a registered trademark of Canon Inc.
Sony is a registered trademark of Sony Corporation.

Warning and Disclaimer
This book is designed to provide information about digital photography. Every effort has been made to make this book as complete and as accurate as possible, but no warranty of fitness is implied.

The information is provided on an as-is basis. The author and Peachpit Press shall have neither the liability nor responsibility to any person or entity with respect to any loss or damages arising from the information contained in this book or from the use of the discs or programs that may accompany it.

ISBN 13: 978-0-321-94854-0

ISBN 10:   0-321-94854-8

15 14 13 12 11 10 9 8 7 6 5 4 3 2 1

Printed and bound in the United States of America

www.peachpit.com
www.kelbytraining.com

*This book is dedicated to the memory of
Lakeland High School Band Director William C. Miller.
His job was to teach us music, but the things he taught us
about life changed us, challenged us, and improved us
in ways he could never imagine. I feel very
fortunate to have been one of his students.*

Acknowledgments

Although only one name appears on the spine of this book, it takes a team of dedicated and talented people to pull a project like this together. I'm not only delighted to be working with them, but I also get the honor and privilege of thanking them here.

To my amazing wife Kalebra: I don't know how you do it, but each year you somehow get more beautiful, more compassionate, more generous, more fun, and you get me to fall even more madly in love with you than the year before (and so far, you've done this 24 years in a row)! They don't make words to express how I feel about you, and how thankful and blessed I am to have you as my wife, but since all I have here are words—thank you for making me the luckiest man in the world.

To my wonderful, crazy, fun-filled, son Jordan: When I wrote the first version of this book, I wrote that you were the coolest little boy any dad could ever ask for. Now that you're 16 years old, and you're 6'1" and 220 lbs. of muscle (my brother calls you "The Wall"), you're not a little boy by any means, but you definitely still are the coolest! Although I know you don't read these acknowledgments, it means so much to me that I can write it, just to tell you how proud I am of you, how thrilled I am to be your dad, and what a great big brother you've become to your little sister. Your mom and I were truly blessed the day you were born.

To my beautiful daughter Kira: You are a little clone of your mom, and that's the best compliment I could ever give you. You have your mom's sweet nature, her beautiful smile, and like her, you always have a song in your heart. You're already starting to realize that your mom is someone incredibly special, and take it from Dad, you're in for a really fun, exciting, hug-filled, and adventure-filled life. I'm so proud to be your dad.

To my big brother Jeff: A lot of younger brothers look up to their older brother because, well…they're older. But I look up to you because you've been much more than a brother to me. It's like you've been my "other dad" in the way you always looked out for me, gave me wise and thoughtful council, and always put me first—just like Dad put us first. Your boundless generosity, kindness, positive attitude, and humility have been an inspiration to me my entire life, and I'm just so honored to be your brother and lifelong friend.

To my friend and fellow photographer Brad Moore: My personal thanks for shooting most of the product shots for this book and for working as first assistant on many of the shots I took throughout it. You're absolutely invaluable and an awful lot of fun.

To my in-house team at Kelby Media Group: You make coming into work an awful lot of fun for me, and each time I walk in the door, I can feel that infectious buzz of creativity you put out that makes me enjoy what we do so much. I'm still amazed to this day at how we all come together to hit our often impossible deadlines, and as always, you do it with class, poise, and a can-do attitude that is truly inspiring. You guys rock!

To my Editor Kim Doty: It broke Kim's heart that she wasn't able to work on the original, first edition of this book, but she had a pretty good excuse with that whole "I'm having a baby" thing. Kim, it's wonderful to have you back for this second edition (though, **Cindy Snyder** did a really great job pinch-hitting for you while you were out), and to have both you and Cindy working with me on this edition is really a treat.

To Jessica Maldonado (a.k.a. Photoshop Girl): I can't thank you enough for all your hard work on the cover, and on the look of this and all my books. I love the way you design, and all the clever little things you add to everything you do. You're incredibly talented, a joy to work with, and I feel very, very fortunate to have you on my team.

To my friend and Creative Director Felix Nelson: You're the glue that keeps this whole thing together, and not only could I not do this without you—I wouldn't want to. Keep doin' that Felix thing you do!

To my best buddy Dave Moser: Besides being the driving force behind all our books, I just want you to know how touched and honored I was that you chose me to be the Best Man at your wedding. It meant more than you know.

To my dear friend and business partner Jean A. Kendra: Thanks for putting up with me all these years, and for your support for all my crazy ideas. It really means a lot.

To my Executive Assistant Susan Hageanon: Thanks so much for managing my schedule, so I can find the time to write these books, and also for keeping a lot of plates in the air while I'm doing it. I know I don't make it easy, but you sure do! Thanks so much!

To Ted Waitt, my awesome Editor at Peachpit Press: There's nothing like having a serious photographer as your editor, and while you're a kick-butt editor, you're an even better friend.

To my publisher Nancy Aldrich-Ruenzel, marketing mavericks Scott Cowlin and Sara Jane Todd (SJ), and the incredibly dedicated team at Peachpit Press: It's a real honor to get to work with people who really just want to make great books.

To David Ziser, David Hobby, and Steve Dantzig who acted as tech editors on the original edition of this book, in three very important chapters: the wedding photography chapter, the off-camera flash chapter, and the studio chapter, respectively. I asked for your help because I knew you were the best, and the book is far better because of your input, suggestions, and ideas. I am so very grateful to you all.

To all the talented and gifted photographers who've taught me so much over the years: Moose Peterson, Joe McNally, Bill Fortney, George Lepp, Anne Cahill, Vincent Versace, David Ziser, Jim DiVitale, Cliff Mautner, Dave Black, Helene Glassman, and Monte Zucker.

To my mentors John Graden, Jack Lee, Dave Gales, Judy Farmer, and Douglas Poole: Your wisdom and whip-cracking have helped me immeasurably throughout my life, and I will always be in your debt, and grateful for your friendship and guidance.

Most importantly, I want to thank God, and His Son Jesus Christ, for leading me to the woman of my dreams, for blessing us with such amazing children, for allowing me to make a living doing something I truly love, for always being there when I need Him, for blessing me with a wonderful, fulfilling, and happy life, and such a warm, loving family to share it with.

Other Books by Scott Kelby

Professional Portrait Retouching Techniques for Photographers Using Photoshop

The Digital Photography Book, parts 1, 2, 3 & 4

Light It, Shoot It, Retouch It: Learn Step by Step How to Go from Empty Studio to Finished Image

The Adobe Photoshop Book for Digital Photographers

The Photoshop Elements Book for Digital Photographers

The Adobe Photoshop Lightroom Book for Digital Photographers

The iPhone Book

It's a Jesus Thing: The Book for Wanna Be-lievers

Photo Recipes Live: Behind the Scenes: Your Guide to Today's Most Popular Lighting Techniques, parts 1 & 2

About the Author

Scott is Editor, Publisher, and co-founder of *Photoshop User* magazine, is Publisher of *Light It!* and *Lightroom* digital magazines, and is co-host of the weekly webcasts *The Grid* (a photography talk show) and *Photoshop User TV*.

He is President of the National Association of Photoshop Professionals (NAPP), the trade association for Adobe® Photoshop® users, and he's President of the software training, education, and publishing firm Kelby Media Group.

Scott is a photographer, designer, and an award-winning author of more than 50 books, including *The Digital Photography Book*, parts 1, 2, 3, & 4, *The Adobe Photoshop Book for Digital Photographers*, *Professional Portrait Retouching Techniques for Photographers Using Photoshop*, *The Adobe Photoshop Lightroom Book for Digital Photographers*, *Light It, Shoot It, Retouch It: Learn Step by Step How to Go from Empty Studio to Finished Image*, and *The iPhone Book*. His book, *The Digital Photography Book*, part 1, is now the top-selling book on digital photography ever.

For the past three years, Scott has been honored with the distinction of being the world's #1 best-selling author of books on photography. His books have been translated into dozens of different languages, including Chinese, Russian, Spanish, Korean, Polish, Taiwanese, French, German, Italian, Japanese, Dutch, Swedish, Turkish, and Portuguese, among others.

Scott is Training Director for the Adobe Photoshop Seminar Tour, and Conference Technical Chair for the Photoshop World Conference & Expo. He's featured in a series of online courses (from KelbyTraining.com), and has been training photographers and Adobe Photoshop users since 1993. He is also the founder of Scott Kelby's Annual Worldwide Photowalk, the largest global social event for photographers, which brings tens of thousands of photographers together on one day each year to shoot in over a thousand cities worldwide.

For more information on Scott, visit him at:

His daily blog: **http://scottkelby.com**
Twitter: **@scottkelby**
Facebook: **www.facebook.com/skelby**
Google+: **Scottgplus.com**

Chapter One   *1*

Using Flash Like a Pro

*If You Hate the Way Photos Look with Flash,
You're Not Alone*

Chapter Five

Shooting Weddings Like a Pro
How to Get Professional Results from Your Next Shoot

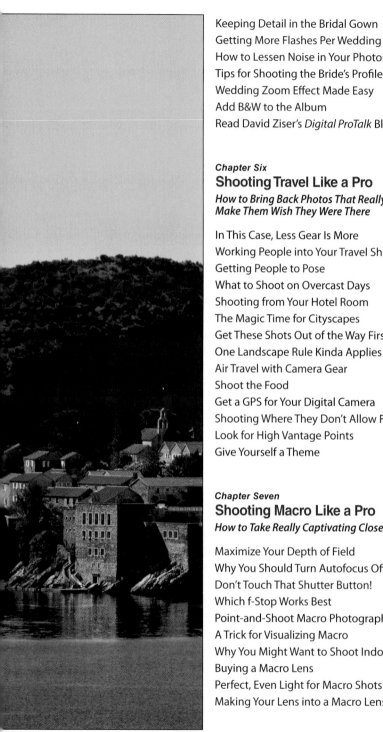

Chapter Six 157

Shooting Travel Like a Pro

*How to Bring Back Photos That Really
Make Them Wish They Were There*

Chapter Seven 173

Shooting Macro Like a Pro

How to Take Really Captivating Close-Up Photos

SHUTTER SPEED: 1/15 SEC   F-STOP: F/9   ISO: 100   FOCAL LENGTH: 55mm | PHOTOGRAPHER: SCOTT KELBY

Chapter One
Using Flash
Like a Pro

If You Hate the Way Photos Look with Flash, You're Not Alone

If you've taken a photo with your camera's pop-up flash, you're probably wondering how camera manufacturers list pop-up flash as a feature and keep a straight face. It's probably because the term "pop-up flash" is actually a marketing phrase dreamed up by a high-powered PR agency, because its original, more descriptive, and more accurate name is actually "the ugly-maker." You'd usually have to go to the Driver's License Bureau to experience this quality of photographic light, but luckily for us, it's just one simple push of a button, and—BAM—harsh, unflattering, annoying, blinding light fires right into your subject's face. Seriously, does it get any better than that? Actually, it does. You just have to get your flash off your camera. Now, the first time you actually use pop-up flash and you see the quality of light it creates (and by "quality" I mean "a total lack thereof"), you'll be tempted to do just that—rip that tiny little flash right off the top of your camera (I'm not the only one who did that, right?). I have to figure that camera manufacturers include a pop-up flash on most camera models to do one thing and one thing only: spur sales of dedicated off-camera flash units (which are actually fantastic). Because as soon as you see the results from your pop-up flash, you think, "There has just got to be something better than this!" or maybe "I must be doing something wrong," or "My camera must be broken," or "This camera must have been stolen from the Driver's License Bureau." Anyway, this chapter is for people who figured there must be something better, and if someone would just show them how to use it, they could love flash again (not pop-up flash, mind you, but off-camera flash, which is a gas, gas, gas!).

10 Things You'll Wish You Had Known…

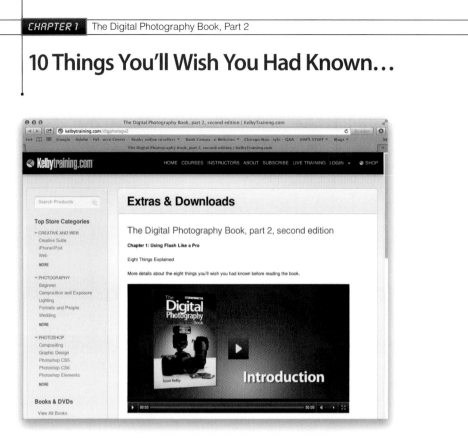

Okay, there aren't really 10, there are just eight, but "Eight Things" sounded kinda lame.

(1) **First, go right now to http://kelbytraining.com/books/digphotogv2** and watch the short video I made to explain these points in more detail. It's short, it's quick, and it will help you read this book in half the time (that "half the time" thing is marketing hype, but you'll get a lot out of the video, so head over there first. I'll make it worth your while).

(2) **Here's how this book works:** Basically, it's you and me together at a shoot, and I'm giving you the same tips, the same advice, and sharing the same techniques I've learned over the years from some of the top working pros. When I'm with a friend, I skip all the technical stuff, so for example, if you turned to me and said, "Hey Scott, I want the light to look really soft and flattering. How far back should I put this softbox?" I wouldn't give you a lecture about lighting ratios or flash modifiers. In real life, I'd just turn to you and say, "Move it in as close as you can to your subject without it actually showing up in the shot. The closer you get, the softer and more wrapping the light gets." I'd tell you short and right to the point. Like that. So that's what I do.

(3) **Sometimes you have to buy stuff.** This is not a book to sell you stuff, but before you move forward, understand that to get pro results, sometimes you have to use some accessories that the pros use. I don't get a kickback or promo fee from any companies whose products I recommend. I'm just giving you the exact same advice I'd give a friend.

...Before Reading This Book!

(4) We don't all have budgets like the pros, so wherever possible I break my suggestions down into three categories:

 If you see this symbol, it means this is gear for people on a tight budget.

 If you see this symbol, it means photography is your passion, and you're willing to spend a bit more to have some pretty nice gear.

 If you see this symbol, it means this gear is for people who don't really have a budget, like doctors, lawyers, venture capitalists, pro ball players, U.S. senators, etc.

To make this stuff easier to find, I've put up a webpage with links to all this gear, and you can find it at **http://kelbytraining.com/books/vol2gear**.

(5) If you're shooting with an Olympus or a Sigma digital camera, don't let it throw you that a Nikon, Canon, or Sony camera is pictured. Since most people are shooting with a Nikon, Canon, or Sony, I usually show one of them, but don't sweat it if you're not—most of the techniques in this book apply to any digital SLR camera, and many of the point-and-shoot digital cameras, as well.

Here Are Those Last Three Things

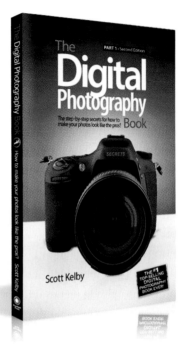

(6) The intro page at the beginning of each chapter is designed to give you a quick mental break, and honestly, they have little to do with the chapter. In fact, they have little to do with anything, but writing these off-the-wall chapter intros is kind of a tradition of mine (I do this in all my books), but if you're one of those really "serious" types, you can skip them because they'll just get on your nerves.

(7) This is part 2 of *The Digital Photography Book* **and it picks up where the last book left off** (so it's not an update of that book, it's new stuff that people who bought the first book asked me to write about next). If you didn't buy part 1, now would be a really good time to do that (just think of it as a "prequel." Hey, it worked for George Lucas).

(8) Keep this in mind: This is a "show me how to do it" book. I'm telling you these tips just like I'd tell a shooting buddy, and that means, oftentimes, it's just which button to push, which setting to change, where to put the light, and not a whole lot of reasons why. I figure that once you start getting amazing results from your camera, you'll go out and buy one of those "tell me all about it" digital camera or lighting books. Okay, it's almost time to get to work. I do truly hope this book ignites your passion for photography by helping you get the kind of results you always hoped you'd get from your digital photography. Now pack up your gear, it's time to head out for our first shoot.

Pop-Up Flash: Use It as a Weapon

The pop-up flash built into your digital camera is designed to do one thing: give you the flattest, harshest, most unflattering light modern-day man has ever created. If you have a grudge against someone, shoot them with your camera's pop-up flash and it will even the score. Here are just some of the reasons why you want to avoid using that flash at all costs: (1) The face of the pop-up flash itself (where the light comes out) is very, very tiny and the smaller the light source, the harsher the light it produces. (2) Since the flash is positioned right above your camera's lens, you get the same quality of light and angle that a coal miner gets from the light mounted on the front of his helmet. (3) Using a pop-up flash is almost a 100% guarantee that your subject will have red eye, because the flash is mounted so close to, and directly above, the lens. (4) Because the flash hits your subject straight on, right square in the face, your subject tends to look very flat and lack dimension all around. (5) You have little control over the light, where it goes, or how it lands. It's like a lighting grenade. These are the reasons why so many people are so disappointed with how their shots look using their camera's flash, and it's exactly why using your pop-up flash should be absolutely, positively a last resort and only done in the most desperate of situations (okay, actually it can do a somewhat decent job if you're shooting outdoors, your subject has the sun behind them, and you need a little bit of light so they're not just a silhouette. Then, maybe, but other than that…). So, what should you use instead? That's on the next page.

The Advantages of a Dedicated Flash

If you want to get pro-quality results from using flash, you're going to need to get a dedicated flash unit (like the one shown above or the ones listed below). What makes these dedicated flashes so great is:

(a) You can aim the flash in different directions (a pop-up flash just blasts straight ahead);

(b) You can angle the flash upward (this is huge—you'll see why later in this chapter);

(c) You can take this flash off your camera to create directional light;

(d) Even when mounted on your camera, because it's higher, you'll get less red eye;

(e) You get control, a more powerful flash, and most importantly, a better quality of light.

Best of all—today's dedicated flashes do almost all the work for you. Here are some I like:

Scott's Gear Finder

Yongnuo YN-560 II Flash (around $62)

Nikon SB-700 Flash (around $327) or Canon 320EX (around $209)

Nikon SB-910 (around $547) or Canon 600EX-RT (around $499)

If You Don't Already Own a Dedicated Flash

Nikon and Canon both make really great, pro-quality dedicated flashes (we call them "hot shoe flashes" because they're designed to sit in the hot shoe flash mount on top of DSLR cameras). But, if you're just getting into this and you're not sure you want to plunk down a few hundred bucks for a Nikon or Canon entry-level flash, you might want to consider a Yongnuo YN-560 II flash for around $62. These inexpensive flashes look and feel pretty much like a Canon 600EX-RT flash, for about $437 less (in fact, if I handed you one and you didn't look closely, you'd just assume it was the Canon 600EX-RT flash). They actually work well and do a pretty darn good job (after all, any flash unit just creates a "bright flash of white light." It's really what you do with that bright flash of light— how you aim it, how you soften the light from the flash, and so on—that determines how your light will actually look on your subject). By buying a Yongnuo for just $62, you're fully in the flash game without risking a big chunk of change right up front, and if you eventually fall in love with hot shoe flash, then you can go buy a fancy Nikon or Canon flash.

The Pro Look: Get It Off-Camera & Soften It

There are really just four things you need to do to get professional-looking images using a dedicated flash, and the two that are the most essential are: (1) you've got to get that flash off the top of your camera, so you can place it where it's much more flattering for your subjects (which you'll learn next, and there are a number of ways to do just that), and (2) you've got to find a way to soften and diffuse the light from the flash to make it beautiful. Otherwise, these flashes create really bright, really harsh, really unflattering light (and there are a number of ways to do that, as well, and we'll cover those in a bit). So, just so you know going in, these are the two hurdles we're going to focus on, because they pretty much are the key to great-looking flash images. So, if you keep that in mind (and don't overthink everything), the whole hot shoe flash thing becomes pretty easy and fun. Remember: Our goal is to get it off the top of the camera, and then make it soft and beautiful. That's what the rest of this chapter is about.

Get Your Flash Off Your Camera, Method #1

As I just mentioned, one of the best things you can do to get better results from your dedicated flash is to literally get it off the camera. That way, you can create directional light—light that comes from the side of your subject or above (or both)—rather than the flat, straight-on light you get when your flash is mounted on your camera. Directional light is much more flattering, more professional looking, and it adds dimension and depth to your photos. There are three ways to get your flash off your camera, and we'll cover the first one here, which is to use a flash sync cord. One end plugs into the flash; the other end connects to the sync terminal on your camera or slides into its hot shoe flash mount. Easy enough. Prices vary for the cord. It's not pretty. It's not elegant (and you'll probably trip over it at some point, if it's a long one), but it beats the heck out of having the flash on top of your camera. Although you're about to learn the two other ways to get your flash off-camera, it doesn't matter which method you choose, because getting that dedicated flash unit off-camera is one of the big steps to getting pro-quality results, and is all that's standing between you and more professional-looking directional light.

Using Pop-Up Flash Wirelessly (#2)

If your DSLR camera has a built-in pop-up flash, you can configure that pop-up flash so it doesn't light your subject, but instead sends out a dim, mini pre-flash that fires your big dedicated flash wirelessly (and you don't have to worry about your flash sync cord breaking or getting lost. In fact, you don't have to worry about dealing with cables at all). However, for this to work, the dedicated flash has to be able to "see" the mini pre-flash from your pop-up flash (that's why this type of wireless flash triggering is called "line of sight"—if the dedicated flash can't see the light from the pop-up flash, it won't fire). This won't ever be a problem until the one time where you really, really need it to fire, which is why there is a second way to fire your flash wirelessly (on the next page).

Using a Wireless Triggering System (#3)

You can consistently fire your wireless flash using a wireless triggering system (these work the best and, of course, they're the most expensive). There are two parts to this: (1) a wireless flash transmitter (which sits in your camera's hot shoe flash socket on top of your camera) and (2) a wireless receiver that attaches to a small socket on your dedicated flash itself with a very small utility cable (only a few inches long). This used to be a very expensive proposition, but today you can buy a decent set (both a transmitter and a receiver) for around $60. That's a steal. Just a few years ago, it was more like $400. What's great about these is they're *not* line of sight. These are real radio transmitters, so you can put them wherever you need them, even a few hundred feet away, and they'll still fire every time. The downside: you change the power of the flash by walking over to the flash and turning the power up/down (although there are some transmitters that will let you change power from the transceiver itself).

Scott's Gear Finder

Cactus Wireless Flash Transceiver V5 Duo (around $60—includes both parts)

PocketWizard PlusX Transceiver (around $99 each—you need two)

PocketWizard Plus III Transceiver (around $149 each—you need two)

Going Wireless (Nikon), Part I

If your Nikon camera has a built-in pop-up flash, you can make a Nikon SB-700, SB-900, or SB-910 flash go wireless in two easy steps: (1) On the back of your Nikon flash unit, just turn the ON/OFF switch to Remote and your flash is now wireless. (See? At least step one is really easy.) The second step is on the next page (because it kinda needs its own page).

Note: If you have a higher-end Nikon pro camera, they don't come with a built-in pop-up flash, so you have to buy something to trigger your other flash. So, what will work? Well, you could buy another Nikon flash, which you can use to trigger your first Nikon flash (as if it was a pop-up flash), or you can buy a Nikon SU-800 Wireless Speedlight Commander Unit for around $250, which despite its fancy name is still line of sight [sigh]. They both work, but they're both kinda expensive (well, in comparison to a pop-up flash anyway, which is free as long as your camera has one).

GOING WIRELESS WITH AN OLDER NIKON SB-600 OR SB-800 FLASH

Press-and-hold the Zoom and – (minus sign) buttons until the Custom Settings menu appears. You should see the word "OFF" and a squiggly line with an arrow beneath it. Press the Mode button to turn the wireless function On, then press the ON/OFF button, and your flash is now wireless.

Going Wireless (Nikon), Part II

Okay, here's what we need to set up on the camera itself:

(1) First, pop up your camera's built-in pop-up flash (it actually triggers the wireless flash, so if you don't have your built-in flash popped up, it won't work) by pressing the little flash symbol button near the flash.

(2) Now, you need to switch your camera's pop-up flash into Commander mode, so instead of firing its flash, it only sends a small light pulse to your wireless off-camera flash unit to trigger it. To do this, press the Menu button on the back of your camera, go to the Custom Settings menu, and choose Bracketing/Flash. When the Bracketing/Flash menu appears, choose Built-in Flash, then choose Commander Mode. Highlight the Built-in Flash field, and use the dial on the back of your camera to toggle the setting until it reads just "--" (as shown above), which means the pop-up flash is off (except for that little light pulse, of course).

(3) Now when you fire your shutter, as long as your flash unit's sensor can see the little light pulse (it's that small red circle on the side), it will fire when you press the shutter button. You control the brightness of your wireless flash from this same menu—just scroll down to Group A and over to the last field on the right. To lower the bright-ness (power output), use a negative number (like –1.0, as shown above, for one stop less power) or a positive number to make the flash brighter. I've put together a short video clip just to show how to set this all up at **http://kelbytraining.com/books/digphotogv2**.

Going Wireless (Canon), Part I

With Canon flashes, to go wireless you'll need either of the following:

(1) A Canon Speedlite Transmitter ST-E2 (around $220 at B&H Photo) or ST-E3-RT for radio transmission (around $287), which sit right on your camera's hot shoe, and not only trigger the wireless flash, but let you control its brightness (power output), which is a key part of this process.

(2) You can use another Canon Speedlite flash (like a second 600EX-RT, which does line of sight or radio transmission) as your transmitter. This second flash sits on the hot shoe on top of your camera, doing basically the same job that the Speedlite Transmitter does, which is to send a tiny light pulse or radio signal from your camera to the wireless flash unit to tell it when to flash, and it lets you control the brightness of the wireless flash, as well.

Either way, the process is pretty similar: If you're using the transmitter, it's already set up as your wireless controller, and it has no flash of its own to turn off, so just put it into your camera's hot shoe and it's ready to go—you can jump over to the next page and pick up there. If you're using a Canon 600EX-RT, press the wireless button on the back of the flash until you see the radio transmission icon or optical transmission icon and Master. Now go to Part 2 on the next page. (*Note:* If you're using an older flash, like the 580EX II Speedlite, put it in your camera's hot shoe, then hold the Zoom button on the back of the flash until the display starts flashing. Then turn the Select dial until the screen reads Master and press the center Select button.)

Going Wireless (Canon), Part II

Now that you have a master flash mounted on your camera's hot shoe, you have to set up the other flash (the one you want to be wireless). (1) If you're using a Canon 600EX-RT, press the wireless button on the back of the flash until you see the radio transmission icon or optical transmission icon and Slave. (*Note:* If you're using an older Canon flash, like the 580EX II Speedlite, hold the Zoom button on the back of the flash until the display starts flashing. Then turn the Select dial until the screen reads Slave and press the center Select button.) Now, to recap: The flash unit on top of your camera is set to be the master unit (the controller), and the other flash is set to be the wireless unit (the slave). (2) Turn off the flash on the master unit so it just emits a pulse of light or radio signal, which triggers the wireless flash (you don't actually want it to light your subject). To do this, press function button 4 on the back of the flash to display Menu 2. Then press function button 1 until you see the Master Flash Firing OFF icon. I've put together a video to show you exactly how this all is done, and you can watch it at **http://kelbytraining.com/books/digphotogv2**.

IF YOUR WIRELESS FLASH DOESN'T FIRE

If your wireless flash isn't firing, make sure your master unit and slave unit are both on the same channel (or wireless radio ID). If not, press function button 4 to display Menu 3, then press function button 1 to set the channel or function button 2 to set the radio ID, and turn the Select dial.

"Drag the Shutter" to See More Background

Like I mentioned, there are four big things the pros do to get beautiful quality light (and professional-looking images) from their dedicated flash units. One, you've already learned, is getting the flash off the camera so you can create directional light. The second is to set up your flash so it blends in with the available light already in the room, so the background behind your subjects looks natural. Without using this technique, you'll get what everybody else gets—the background behind your subjects turns black, they look harsh, and the shot will look pretty awful, which is why most people hate flash shots. The technique is called "dragging the shutter," and what you're doing is slowing down your camera's shutter speed so it allows in the existing light, then your flash fires to light your subject. Although this sounds complicated, it's incredibly simple. First, set your camera to shoot in program mode. Then, aim at your subject and hold the shutter button down halfway, so your camera takes a meter reading of the scene. Look in your viewfinder and see the f-stop and shutter speed your camera chose to properly expose your subject, and remember those two numbers. Now, switch to manual mode and dial in those same two numbers. If the camera showed a shutter speed of $^1/_{60}$ of a second, to drag the shutter you'd need to use a slower shutter speed, right? So try lowering the shutter speed to $^1/_{15}$ of a second and take the shot. Don't worry—your subject won't be blurry, because when the flash fires it will freeze your subject. You'll be amazed at what just lowering the shutter speed like this will do to the quality of your flash photos.

How to Soften the Light from Your Flash

Okay, so you've used all the tricks we've covered so far, and your flash photos are already looking better—but there's still a problem. The light is still harsh because the flash itself is very small, and the smaller the light source, the harsher the light. So, to get softer, more flattering light, you need to make your light source larger, right? Right! There are a number of different tricks for doing this, and each pro does it differently, but I will tell you this— they all do it. They all use tricks to soften and diffuse the light from their flash (it's the third thing [and second most essential one] to do to get professional-looking light from your dedicated flash). Probably the quickest and easiest way to soften the light from your flash is to snap a diffusion dome cap over the end of your flash (like the one shown above), which softens and diffuses your light. Considering how small and light it is, it does a pretty decent job. Once this cap is on, you aim your flash head upward at a 45° angle and it takes care of the rest. If you're a Nikon user and buy a Nikon SB-910 flash, it comes with the dif-fusion dome you see above right in the box (if you've lost your SW-13H dome, you can buy a replacement from B&H Photo). If you have a Canon flash, you can buy a diffusion dome separately, and the one I recommend is the Sto-Fen Omni-Bounce, which does a great job and is a favorite with pro wedding and event photographers (it sells for around $10 at B&H Photo). One thing to note: Adding this diffusion dome works great indoors, but outdoors where there's really nothing much for the light to bounce off of, it doesn't do much at all. Hey, I thought you should know.

Make It Softer Light by Bouncing It

Another popular way to soften the quality of your light is to bounce your light off a ceiling. This does three wonderful things: (1) When your small, direct flash of light hits the large ceiling, it spreads out big time, so the quality of the light that falls back onto your subject is much wider and much softer. It immediately takes the harshness out of your flash, and gives you better quality light. (2) Because the light is now coming from above, it's no longer that one-dimensional, straight-on flash—now it's directional flash, which creates nice shadows and lots of dimension for your subject's face, and as a bonus (3) it keeps you from having harsh shadows on the wall behind your subject. Because the light is coming from above (down from the ceiling), the shadows appear on the floor behind your subject, not on the wall behind them. Plus, because the light is softer, the shadows are softer, too. So, if this bouncing off the ceiling technique is so great, why don't we use it all the time? Well, there are a number of reasons: (1) There's not always a ceiling you can bounce off. Sometimes you're outdoors, or (2) the ceiling is too high to bounce off of (like in a church). If the ceiling is much higher than about 10 feet, the bounce trick really doesn't work be-cause the light has too far to travel up and back, and your subject doesn't get properly lit. Of course there's also (3) the fact that light picks up the color of what it hits, so if the ceiling is yellowish, your light becomes yellowish, and your subject will now appear (come on, say it with me) yellowish! However, if it's an 8' or 9' white ceiling, you're set.

Putting That Nice Twinkle of Light in the Eyes

If you're using bounce flash and you want to add a little bit of life and sparkle into your subject's eyes, then simply pull out and raise the little white bounce card that's tucked into your flash head (well, at least it is if you're using a Nikon or Canon flash), as shown above. When you put that little white bounce card up, it redirects just enough of that light heading toward the ceiling back onto your subject to add a nice little catch light in their eyes, and the bonus is this also often removes some of the shadows that appear under their eyes. The key to making this work is that your flash head is aiming up at a 45° angle and the card is fully extended.

WHAT TO DO IF YOU DON'T HAVE A BOUNCE CARD OR YOURS BREAKS

If your bounce card is broken, or if your flash doesn't have a bounce card (hey, it's possible), then try this: use your hand. That's right—shoot with your camera in one hand, and then put your other hand up at the same position and angle a bounce card would be. It will send some of that light forward (like a bounce card), and because light picks up the color of whatever it reflects off of, your light will be nice and warm (thanks to your skin tone).

Softbox-Quality Softening from Your Flash

If you want to take this whole softening thing to the next level (quality-wise), you could buy a small softbox that mounts over your flash, but the problem is they're small, so the light doesn't spread and soften all that much. So, one really easy way to spread and soften your light is to shoot your flash directly through a large diffusion panel. These panels are made of white translucent stretched fabric (usually round or square with rounded corners like the one you see above), and they spread and diffuse the light from your flash. Since they're just fabric, they're super-lightweight—they're designed to collapse down into a very small, flat size, so they're easy to take with you (they come with a small, flat carrying pouch)—and best of all, they're a bargain! You can get a Westcott 30" 5-in-1 Reflector (the same one I use), which includes a 30" diffuser, for around $30 (plus, now you have a great reflector, as well. Actually, you'll have four reflectors—more on them later). To use this diffuser, have an assistant (or a friend, spouse, etc.) hold the panel about 1 foot or more in front of your flash. That way, when the tiny light from the flash hits the panel, it causes the light to spread out dramatically, which gives you much softer, smoother, more flattering light. If you don't have an assistant or a friend nearby, you can clamp your diffuser on a second light stand using a Manfrotto 275 Mini Clip Clamp for around $14.50. If you want to invest in a pro-quality diffusion panel, check out Lastolite's 30" TriGrip Diffuser, One Stop (with a built-in handle) for around $70.

Tip for Shooting Through a Diffuser

If you're shooting your flash through a diffuser (like the Westcott diffuser I just mentioned), here's a tip: position the diffuser as close to your subject as possible without it actually being seen in the photo. This gives you the best quality wraparound light that is the softest and most flattering (think "closer is better"). Then position your flash so it's aimed at your subject, but still firing through the diffuser (set it at least 1 foot back from the diffuser, or even farther if you'd like softer, smoother light, but just know that the farther away you move the flash, the lower the power the light will become, so if you move it far away, you'll have to increase the power of the flash).

WHERE TO LEARN MORE ABOUT OFF-CAMERA FLASH

If this chapter ignites your passion for off-camera flash, and you want to take things to the next level, you'll definitely want to check out Strobist, which is the #1 site on the web for flash enthusiasts (both amateurs and pros). It's run by David Hobby, a tremendous photographer and teacher who has built an entire worldwide community of flash users, and there's really nothing like it anywhere on the web. Highly recommended (you'll find it at www.strobist.blogspot.com).

Why You Might Want a Stand for Your Flash

Most of us don't have the luxury of having an assistant to hold and position our wireless flash for us, so we either wind up holding the flash in our left hand (so our right hand is still free to press the shutter button), or we put our flash on a lightweight light stand and position it where we'd like it. You can buy a standard light stand, like the 8' Impact Air-Cushioned Light Stand, for around $33. You'll also need a flash shoe mount (less than $25 from B&H Photo), which lets you mount your flash on a light stand like the Impact. This mount has a little plastic hot shoe on it, and your flash slides right into that hot shoe to hold your flash securely on top of the light stand. That flash shoe mount is surely the inexpensive route, but the downside is they don't all allow you to angle your flash head downward—only upward, and that's why the Justin Clamp, while more expensive, is really the way to go (see the next page for more on this). So, once you've got your flash on this light stand, where do you put it? There's no single right answer, but I'll give you a good starting point—put it to the left, and in front, of your camera, up about a foot or so higher than your subject. That way, if you have your flash mounted on a Justin Clamp, you can aim the flash head back down at your subject, so the light is more like studio light (or window light) and helps to create that all-important directional light.

Mounting Flashes Anywhere

If you're going to wind up attaching your flash to something other than a light stand (heck, this works great even if you're using a light stand), I recommend picking up a Manfrotto 175F Justin Spring Clamp with Flash Shoe (better known as simply a "Justin Clamp"). This is just the handiest little gizmo and you'll love it for two reasons: (1) Your flash slides into a little plastic hot shoe on the top of the clamp, and that clamp is con-nected to a miniature ballhead that lets you easily and instantly position your flash in any direction or at any angle. So, instead of moving the light stand every time you want to change the angle of the flash, you just move that little ballhead. (2) It has a large clamp on one end, so if setting up a light stand isn't practical (or isn't allowed), you can clamp it onto just about anything, from a railing, to a tree branch, to a ceiling tile. These sell for around $61 (at B&H Photo, anyway), and it's one of those accessories that once you use it, you'll never go anywhere without it.

Rear Sync Rocks (& Why You Should Use It)

There's a setting on your camera that will help you get better-quality photos using flash. In fact, your flash shots will get so much better that you'll wonder why this feature isn't turned on by default (but it's not—you'll have to go and turn it on yourself). It's called Rear Sync, and what it basically does is changes when the flash actually fires. Usually, your flash fires the moment you press the shutter button, right? So it does freeze any action in the scene, but it also generally makes everything solid black behind your subject (like you see in most snapshots). Changing to Rear Sync makes the flash fire at the end of the exposure (rather than the beginning), which lets the camera expose for the natural background light in the room first, and then at the very last second, it fires the flash to freeze your subject. Now your background isn't black—instead, it has color, depth, and detail (as seen above right), and this gives you a much more professional look all the way around. In the example above, the shot on the left is using the normal default flash setting (notice how dark the background is, and how washed out the flash makes him look). For the shot on the right, I only changed one single thing—I switched the flash to Rear Sync. Give it a try and you'll see what I mean (just remember to keep the camera still when shooting in Rear Sync mode, because the shutter stays open longer—enough to expose for the background. This can create some cool effects if your subject is moving while your shutter is open, or it can create some irritating effects if they're moving and you don't want them to).

The Fourth Secret to Pro Flash Results

The fourth of the four pro flash tricks is one you can use to make your flash look like natural light. In fact, this trick works so well that if you do it right, most folks won't be able to tell that you used a flash at all—you'll just have glorious-looking, soft, natural light whenever and wherever you want it. Your goal is to create light from your flash that matches, and blends in with, the current lighting in the scene (the ambient light) and doesn't overpower it. Here's the trick: don't change your f-stop or shutter speed—instead, just lower the power output of the flash until it matches the available light. To do that, first get the flash off the camera for directional light, and diffuse the light, then take a test shot. Chances are your flash will overpower the existing light. Now, go to your flash unit itself, lower the flash output power by one stop, and take another test shot. Look at the LCD panel on the back of your camera, and see if the light from your flash still looks obvious—like light from a flash. If it does, lower the power of your flash another ½ stop and shoot another test shot. Keep doing this (lowering the power and shooting a test shot) until you're getting just enough flash to light your subject, and nothing more. That way, it looks real, directional, and natural, instead of looking like flash (like the shot above, lit with one flash). It might take you five or six test shots to dial in the right amount of power, but that's the beauty of digital cameras: it doesn't cost anything to do test shots—as many as you need—until you strike that perfect balance between ambient (existing) light and the light from your flash.

Using Gels (& Why You Need Them)

The light from your flash is always the same color—white. It's nice, bright, white light, which is great in most circumstances, but what if you're doing a portrait of someone in an office, or you're shooting in a locker room, or in a meeting room? Well, that's a problem, because the color of the light from your flash won't match the color of the lighting in the room, which is exactly why some flashes (like the Nikon SB-910) actually come with pre-cut gels that slide right onto the flash to let you change the color of your flash's light, so it matches the rest of the lighting in the room. (*Note:* If you have an older Canon flash or your flash doesn't come with gels, you can buy a large sheet of Rosco CTO gel for around $6.50 from B&H Photo. You'll have to cut it down in size so it fits over your flash head, but at least you'll have a huge supply of them, whereas Nikon only gives you one. Or, check out Rosco's Strobist 55-Piece Filter Kit, which comes with 55 pre-cut gels, for around $18.50.) Amateurs don't worry about this because they're going to just overpower the light in the room, right? But since you now know the pro tricks of how to balance the light from your flash with the ambient light already existing in the room, you'll need to do this next step, but believe me, for the 20 seconds it takes to slide that gel into place, it's worth it. You'd use a yellow gel for balancing your flash color with incandescent light (the standard light found in homes), and a green gel for balancing the light if you're shooting under fluorescent lights, like the ones found in most office interiors (Rosco makes those, too). Just pop that tiny gel inside your diffusion dome, or tape it to your flash with some gaffer's tape, and you're ready to go!

Using Gels to Get That *SI* Look

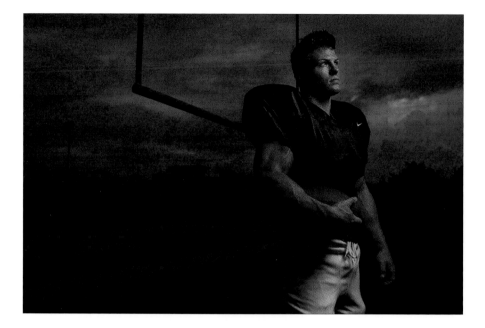

There's a very cool trick you can do using just a yellow gel that I learned from *Sports Illustrated* photographer Dave Black when he and I were teaching a class out in San Francisco. When you try it, you'll see it has that *SI* look you see in a lot of outdoor sports portraits. It actually requires you to do two things: (1) First, you set the white balance on your camera to Tungsten (it's one of your camera's built-in white balance presets, and it makes your whole photo look very blue—well, at least it does if you're shooting outdoors), then (2) pop a yellow gel onto your flash (see the tip on the previous page to find out if you already have them or where to get them). That's it. Now, you want to shoot this near dusk, so the background sky is dark and moody. The Tungsten white balance setting makes the sky look moody and blue, but the yellow light (from the gel on your flash) hits your subject with a warm light. It's a very clever combo that is easy to achieve, and lots of pros are using this style today because, well…it's really cool (no pun intended, but I wish it had been).

If You Have to Use Pop-Up Flash, Do This

If you can't get around it, and you are in a situation where you must use your camera's pop-up flash, then at least do these two things: (1) set your flash to Rear Sync first, so you'll pick up some of the ambient light in the room (we covered this back on page 24), and (2) do something—anything—to soften the harshness of the flash, and that can be as simple as shooting your pop-up flash through a white table napkin or cutting a rectangle-shaped diffuser out of the side of a plastic jug of milk and shooting through that. If you know in advance that you might have to shoot with your pop-up flash, then check out LumiQuest's Soft Screen (shown above), which is designed to fit over your pop-up flash to spread and diffuse the light. Luckily, it's very inexpensive (around $12), and well…if you have to use pop-up flash, this will at least make it bearable.

TWO TIPS FOR GETTING BETTER RESULTS FROM YOUR POP-UP FLASH

Another thing that will help you get better-looking images from your pop-up flash is to reduce the flash's brightness (lower its power) or lower your flash exposure (using flash exposure compensation). Most DSLRs have a setting where you can lower the brightness of the flash, and that helps to not blow out your subject with harsh white light. You might also try taping a small warming gel (like a ¼-cut CTO gel from B&H Photo) over your flash and leaving it there all the time. This gives the cold flash a much warmer, more pleasing look. Thanks to flash guru David Hobby for sharing these tips.

Using a Second Flash

If you want to add a second wireless flash (maybe you want to use it as a hair light, or to light the background, or…whatever), it's easy. When your first flash fires, it automatically triggers the second flash so they both fire at exactly the same time. Let's say you want to add a flash to light your subject's hair. First, position the flash behind your subject, but off to the right (if you're holding your other flash in your left hand while you're shooting or have it positioned to the left), as shown here. This is a perfect time to use one of those Justin Clamps I mentioned earlier, so you can clamp your second wireless flash to anything nearby, or you can position your second flash on a light stand—just make sure you don't see the stand, or the flash unit itself, when you look through your camera's viewfinder. Set your second flash to wireless mode (look back on page 12 for Nikon flashes or page 14 for Canon flashes). Best of all, you can control the brightness of this second flash wirelessly from on your camera (see the next page[s] to find out how).

Controlling a Second Flash (Nikon)

You will want to be able to control the brightness of each flash individually, so that way if the second flash is too bright, you can lower it without affecting the first flash or you can turn it off altogether. However, you want to be able to do all this right from your camera itself—without running around behind your subject, or running from flash unit to flash unit. On a higher-end Nikon camera, here's how it's done: On the back of the flash, set this second flash to Group B. That's all you do on the flash itself. Now, you control the brightness of each flash by pressing the Menu button on the back of your camera, going to the Custom Settings menu, and choosing Bracketing/Flash. When the Bracketing/Flash menu appears, choose Built-in Flash, then scroll down and choose Commander Mode. Your first flash (the one you hold in your left hand, or near you on a light stand) is in Group A. You set your second flash to Group B, so the brightness control for your second flash is found in the Comp field to the far right of Group B. Scroll over to that field, and to lower the brightness by one stop, dial in –1.0 (as shown above). Now shoot a test shot, and if that second flash appears too bright, try lowering it to –1.3 and shoot another test shot, etc., until it looks right. To turn if off altogether, toggle over to the Mode field, and change the setting until it reads "--" which turns off your second flash. To control the brightness of your main off-camera flash, it's controlled the same way, but in Group A. Just remember, for all of this to work, you have to have your pop-up flash up, because it triggers the flash (or you can use an SU-800 transmitter if your camera doesn't have pop-up flash).

Controlling a Second Flash (Canon)

External flash func. setting

Master flash	Enable
Channel	3 ch
Firing Group	A:B C
Group A output	1/4 . . 1/2 . . 1/1
Group B output	1/8 . . 1/4 . . 1/2
Group C output	1/16 . . 1/8 . . 1/4

INFO. Clear flash settings

To add a second Canon Speedlite flash (one you'll use for a hair light or to light the background), press the Wireless button on the back of the flash until you see the radio transmission icon or optical transmission icon and Slave. Now your first wireless flash and this second flash will fire simultaneously, which is good, but you want to be able to control the brightness of each flash individually, right from your camera (so you're not running back behind your subject just to lower the brightness of the second flash. After all, what's the good of wireless if you have to keep running over to the flash every time you need to make a small change, eh?). To do that, you'll want to assign this second flash to a separate control group (Group B). To assign the second flash to Group B, while Menu 1 is showing, press function button 3 on the back of your Speedlite, and then select Group B. Now you can put this flash into place (behind the subject), and do a test shot. Both flashes should fire, but if the second flash (the one behind your subject) is too bright, then press the Menu button on the back of your camera, go to Shooting Menu 1, choose Flash Control, then choose External Flash Function Setting. Under Flash Mode, choose Manual Flash, then scroll down to Group B Output and set the ratio to 1/2 (one stop less bright), then do a test shot. If the second flash still looks too bright (when you look at the shot in your LCD monitor), then lower the brightness to 1/4 or 1/8 and shoot another test shot, and keep this up until the second flash looks balanced. If you want to control the brightness of the first flash, make sure it's on Group A, and it's controlled the same way.

How Far Back Can You Stand Using Flash?

So, how far back can you stand from your subjects and still get pro-quality results from your flash? Well, if you're using a flash with a diffusion dome, or you're bouncing your flash, or you're using some type of diffuser to soften the light (and you should be), as a general rule, you really don't want to stand farther than about 10 feet back from your subjects. Unfortunately, any farther than that and your dedicated flash won't have enough power to get the right amount of light all the way over to your subjects to light them properly.

How to Stand Back Even Farther

If you absolutely need to stand back more than 10 feet from your subject, then you can use this trick to extend the power and range of your flash: just raise your camera's ISO setting (making the camera more sensitive to light). So, if you're shooting at 100 ISO (it's always our goal to shoot at the lowest possible ISO—more on this later), then if you increase your ISO to 200, you effectively double the power (and range) of your flash. So, if you need to be 20 feet back, try increasing your camera's ISO to 200 or 400, and that should do the trick. Okay, well, there is one more thing you can try: if you don't want to raise your ISO and you have to be back farther than 10 feet from your subject, then you'll need to (gasp!) remove the diffuser cap from your flash, so your light has more power and reach (personally, I'd raise the ISO, but hey—that's just me).

HOW TO GET MORE POWER FROM YOUR FLASH AT LONG DISTANCES

If you find yourself having to shoot pretty far back (maybe you do a lot of large group shots), you might want to buy another diffusion dome cap and cut out a little section of the top so some of that light reaches a bit farther.

Controlling Your Light to Add Drama

If you want to add some serious drama and interest to your flash images, one of the quickest ways to get there is to limit the amount and shape of the light that hits your subject. By lighting only part of your subject, it puts part of your subject into the shadows, and although this is a fairly common technique using full-blown studio lighting, ExpoImaging has come up with their own inexpensive, lightweight light modifiers for hot shoe flashes like the Nikon SB-910 and Canon 600EX-RT. They're called Rogue FlashBenders and they've got a 10" positionable reflector you can shape into a snoot (as seen above) that acts like a funnel for light—concentrating it in just one area. It fits right over your flash head and is secured with a little ring of velcro. The snoot sells for around $40 at B&H Photo.

Shooting Sunset Portraits with Flash

First, turn off your flash, then switch your camera to shutter priority mode (S), and dial in 1/125 of a second (a good, safe sync speed for our flash). Now, aim up at the sky (but not directly at the sun itself), and press-and-hold your shutter button halfway down, so your camera takes a meter reading of the sky. While that button is still held down, look in your viewfinder to see the f-stop your camera chose, and remember that number (in the example above, it read f/5.6, so remember that f-stop). Now, switch your camera to manual mode, dial in 1/125 of a second for your shutter speed, and dial in that f-stop your camera chose in shutter priority mode (which, in this case, was f/5.6). Next, position your subject so the sun is behind them. Your job is to turn your subject into a silhouette against the sky. Luckily this is pretty easy—just raise the f-stop by a stop or two (our f-stop was f/5.6, so we'll raise it to f/8) and take a test shot. If your subject isn't a silhouette yet, raise it another stop to f/11, and take another test shot. Usually that'll do it, but you might have to go as high as f/16 (or any one of those fractional f-stops in-between, like f/13). When you choose a darker f-stop, the sky will get much darker and richer, which is great. Once your subject is a silhouette against a beautiful, dark, rich-colored sky, turn your flash on (switch your flash to Manual mode and choose a low power setting, like 1/4 power), and take a test shot. If the flash is too bright, try lowering the power to 1/8 power, then take another test shot. If the flash isn't bright enough, raise the power to 1/2. Don't change the camera settings—they're set just right—instead lower (or raise, as the case may be) the power (brightness) of your flash to get a realistic mix between the sky and your subject. That's the recipe for portraits at sunset.

Chapter Two

Building a Studio from Scratch

It's Much Easier and Less Expensive Than You'd Think

It used to be that only full-time working professionals could afford to put together a studio, but these days the prices of studio gear have come down so much, and the equipment is so much easier to use, that anyone (well, anyone with a platinum American Express card) can now build a studio of their own. Of course, I'm joking, you don't have to have a platinum card (a gold card will do just fine). Actually, the main reason why building a studio from scratch is within most folks' reach today is that you can do so much with just one light. In fact, nearly this entire chapter is to show you how to get professional results using just one light. Now, in the studio we don't always refer to lights as simply "lights," because then people would know what they do (we call them "strobes," because it sounds much cooler). Studio photography is intentionally shrouded in mystery to make the process appear more complicated than it really is. In fact, there is a special committee, The Council for Creation of Complex-Sounding Studio Gear Names (the CCCSSGN, for short), whose charter is to create confusing insider lingo to throw beginners off track. For example, when we talk about the color of light, we don't use the term "indoor lighting." Nope, people would realize what that is, because they've been indoors before. Instead, we assign a color temperature measured in Kelvin, so to throw beginners off, we might say to one another, "It looks like that strobe is throwing 5500 Kelvin." And the other person might say, "It looks a bit warmer to me. More like 5900," then the other person might say, "Ya know, you might be right—it is more like 5900 Kelvin." It's amazing that either of these people ever get a date. Anyway, this chapter is designed to cut through the Kelvin and show you the light.

Studio Backgrounds

One of the least expensive, and most popular, studio backgrounds is seamless paper. This paper comes in long rolls, and the two most popular widths are just over 4 feet wide (53") and nearly 9 feet wide (107"). The nice things about seamless paper are: (1) It's cheap. A 53-inch-wide white roll that's 12 yards long goes for around $25 (at B&H Photo), and if you want the 9-foot-wide roll, it's only around $40. (2) It's seamless. There's no visible seam where the paper folds as it reaches the floor (or a tabletop), so the background looks continuous. (3) The stands to support seamless paper backgrounds are pretty cheap, too. For example, the Savage Economy Background Stand Support System, which supports both the 53" and 107" rolls, only costs around $75. That ain't bad. And, (4) this paper comes in a wide variety of colors, from solid white to solid black, to blue, green, and everything in between (hey, that rhymes). If you're building your first studio, this is a great way to start, because you can get your background and the supports to hold it up for around $100.

SO WHICH SHOULD I GET, THE 53" OR THE 107" SEAMLESS?

If you're planning on shooting products on a table, or strictly just head-and-shoulder shots of people, you can get away with the 53" width. If you need to see more of your subjects, go with the 107".

Using Studio Flash (Called Strobes)

A lot of people are intimidated by studio lighting, thinking it's complicated or too technical for them, but in reality, most studio lights are just bigger versions of the hot shoe
flash you're already used to using off-camera (in fact, they are flashes, but in the industry
they're usually called "studio strobes" or just "strobes"). The main differences between
hot shoe flashes (like a Nikon Speedlight or a Canon Speedlite) and studio strobes are:
(1) studio strobes usually plug into the wall rather than running on batteries; (2) studio
strobes are much more powerful (they put out a lot more light) than the hot shoe flashes;
(3) they have a modeling light (more on this on page 43); (4) they're designed to have
lighting accessories, like softboxes, attached right to the front of them; and, (5) since
they're designed to be mounted on top of a light stand, they have a light stand mount
right on the bottom of the strobe itself (to mount a hot shoe flash on a light stand, you
usually will need some sort of separate adapter or swivel head).

Scott's Gear Finder

AlienBees B400 (around $225)

Elinchrom Style BRX 500 Monolight ($675)

Elinchrom Digital Style RX 1200 1200ws Monolight ($1400)

Softening Harsh Studio Strobes

So, if the light from your regular off-camera flash is harsh, imagine how harsh the light will be from a brighter, more powerful flash (your studio strobe). Right, it's harsh city. To diffuse that light and make it softer, you have to make the light that comes from your strobe larger, because the rule is: the larger the light source, the softer the light. So, we have to put something big between our studio strobe and our subject to spread and soften that light, and for that I recommend a softbox. They're aptly named because they soften the light from your strobe big time, and they are very popular with professional studio photographers (in fact, it's the softening device of choice for most top pros). They fit right over your studio strobe (they have a hole in one end) and your flash fires through the white diffusion material at the large end of the softbox. This spreads the light, so when it hits your subject, it's a bigger source of light, and that means it's a much more flattering, softer light. But this softer light isn't just for lighting people—even if your subject is a product, you still want nice, soft shadows throughout your image, and a softbox is your key to getting just that.

Why I Prefer Softboxes to Umbrellas

Besides softboxes, another way to spread and soften your light is to use a lighting umbrella. Surprisingly, you don't generally put the umbrella between your strobe and the subject (although you could). Instead, you turn the strobe so it's aiming 180° away from your subject—in the opposite direction. Then you put the umbrella in front of the flash (strobe) itself, so that your strobe fires into the underside of the umbrella. When the light hits the umbrella, it spreads out and travels back in the opposite direction, back toward your subject. Because the light spreads out when it hits that umbrella, the light from your strobe is much softer. So, why don't I like, or recommend, using an umbrella? It's because with a softbox your light is pretty much contained within a box—it doesn't spill out, so your light is more directional. You aim it in a direction and it pretty much goes right there. But with an umbrella, you have less control over what happens once the light leaves your umbrella. I think of it more like a lighting grenade—you throw it in the general direction of what you're trying to light, and it'll probably light it. So, while an umbrella does take the harsh light from your strobe and create soft, pretty light from it, it kind of goes everywhere. Whereas, a softbox is more contained, more directional, and you can add other accessories to narrow the throw of your softbox light even more.

What a Speed Ring Does (& Why You Need It)

So, you need: (1) a strobe, (2) a light stand to hold it up, (3) a softbox to spread and soften the light, and (4) you're also gonna need a speed ring. A speed ring is generally made of a light metal, and has four holes on the edge where you insert the ends of the four thin metal poles on each corner of your softbox. Once you insert those poles into the speed ring, it gives your softbox its form (it creates the shape of a box), and then you attach this whole rig (the speed ring with your softbox attached) to your strobe. I use an Elinchrom Rotalux softbox, which has an Elinchrom speed ring built right in, with an Elinchrom BRX 500. However, most softboxes don't come with a speed ring built in, so if you have to order one, make sure you order one designed to fit your brand of strobe. By the way, most speed rings are rotating (meaning you can rotate the softbox from tall to wide while it's mounted on the strobe), and if that's important to you (and I would think it would be), then make sure the one you have or order does rotate.

Using a Modeling Light

Usually, when you're shooting in a studio environment, the only lights you want to light your subject are the studio strobes themselves. Otherwise, the other lights in the room can affect your exposure, so studios are generally pretty dark once the shooting starts. This creates a problem, because the autofocus on the camera needs some light to lock its focus onto. That's one reason why studio strobes usually come with a built-in modeling light, which is a fairly dim, continuous light that stays on between flashes to let your camera's autofocus do its thing. Another advantage of using a modeling light is that it gives you an idea where your shadows are going to fall on your subject (it's not exact, but it does give you an idea). I leave the modeling light on all the time during a shoot, but you'll find an on/off switch on the back of your strobe unit itself (or on a separate power pack or battery pack, if you're using one).

When you're talking about studio strobes, there are basically two kinds: (1) A monolight, which is what we've been talking about here in the book, is a self-contained unit (with the power pack, flash bulb, and power controls all in one) that plugs directly into a standard wall outlet, and (2) a flash head, which is just the flash itself, and all controls are in a separate power pack or battery pack, which you plug the flash head into.

Firing Your Studio Strobe

To get your strobe to fire when you press your camera's shutter button, you'll need to connect your strobe to your camera (either wirelessly or using a sync cord). If you go with a sync cord (it's way cheaper, around $10 for a 15' sync cord at B&H Photo), it's pretty straightforward: one end plugs into your camera's sync terminal, and the other end plugs into your strobe. That's it. Now when you press your shutter button, your studio strobe fires. That being said, I can't really recommend using a sync cord because, at some point, you or your subject will trip over it. Guaranteed. Somebody's going to trip over it and, at the very least, pull your whole lighting rig over (you'll know exactly when this happens because of the sound of shattering glass), or they'll pull over your camera rig (listen for the sound of lenses shattering), or both. At that moment, however much you saved by using a cheap sync cord will pale in comparison to the repair bill and/or attorney's fees (if your subject trips and falls) you'll be faced with next. So, I highly recommend using wireless to fire your strobes (it's easier than you'd think).

Firing Your Studio Strobe Wirelessly

Besides avoiding the potential for broken glass (well, broken everything actually), there's another thing using a wireless flash setup gives you—freedom. You're no longer tied (well, actually tethered) to your strobe. You're free to move around the studio, completely untethered, unencumbered, unfettered (insert your own "un" word here), without being on a leash (so to speak). Here's how it works: to start, you need two of these wireless devices—one sits on the top of your camera (in your camera's hot shoe) and transmits the wireless signal to the other wireless unit, which plugs into the sync input on your strobe. What I love about them is you just plug them in, turn them on, and they do their thing. There's no real configuring or messing around for this simple setup. Now when you press your shutter button, it instantly fires your strobe, even if it's across the room (even way across the room). The most popular wireless units are from a company called PocketWizard, and their new PocketWizard PlusX is a small, thin, lightweight model of simplicity that is incredibly reliable and very well made. They go for around $100 each (and you need two of them, so $200 for the set). They also make more expensive units with more features and stuff, but at this point, you don't need 'em). If you want a cheaper alternative, go with the Cactus Flash Transceiver V5 Duo. They're a bargain at around $60 for a set of two (so, $30 each), and they actually work really well. Perhaps they're not quite as rock-solid as the PocketWizard, and they may not have the 300+ foot range of a PocketWizard, but they're pretty darn reliable and about $140 cheaper.

Using Continuous Light Instead

A fast-growing alternative to studio strobes is continuous lights, and with these lights there is no "flash of light"—instead, the lights just stay on continuously. This makes studio lighting incredibly easy, because what you see is what you get. I use these continuous lights in my studio (I have three of them) and I took them on the road with my Adobe Photoshop Lightroom Live Tour, where they nearly created a sensation, because no matter what I tell you about them here in this book, it doesn't have the impact of seeing them used live. People just go nuts over them. The ones I use are Westcott Spiderlite TD6s (as shown above), which use daylight-balanced fluorescent light (since they're fluorescent, they produce hardly any heat—they stay nice and cool the entire time you're shooting with them, and your subjects stay cool, too). These lights are naturally softer than the studio strobes, but of course I still use them with a softbox attached, and the nice thing is the speed ring is built right into the light itself, so you don't have to buy a speed ring. Best of all—they're fairly inexpensive, and you can buy a kit, which includes a light stand, the Spiderlite TD6 fixture, a tilter bracket, and a 24x32" softbox, for around $830 at B&H Photo. Hard to beat. So, what's the downside with these lights? There's one: since there's no flash to freeze things, things need to be fairly still, because the fluorescent lights aren't as bright as the light from a strobe. So as long as your subjects don't move a whole bunch (for example, I wouldn't buy these for shooting toddlers or puppies), they're awesome.

Choosing the Size for Your Softbox

When you're trying to decide which size to choose for your softbox, there are a couple of considerations: the first being, what are you planning to shoot, and the second being, how soft do you want your light? We'll tackle the "What are you planning to shoot?" question first. If you're shooting product shots on a table, you can get away with a smaller softbox, like one that's 2x3', yet it would still be big enough to also work for head-and-shoulders portraits. If you're going to be shooting people, and doing more than just head-and-shoulder-type stuff, then you'll need to go with a larger softbox. I mentioned before that the larger the light source, the softer the light, so if you buy a very large softbox (like one that's 3x4'), you're going to get very soft light, and you're going to be able to light a larger area. I use three sizes in my studio: a 27x27", a 39x39" for people shots, and a 53" Elinchrom Midi-Octa (it's an octagonal-shaped softbox) when I want really, really, wonderfully soft wraparound light.

Scott's Gear Finder

Photoflex 2x3' (24x32") Litedome Softbox (around $113)

Chimera Pro II 3x4' Softbox (around $196)

Elinchrom 53" Midi-Octa Light Bank (around $315)

How a Light Meter Makes Your Studio Life Easier

COURTESY OF SEKONIC CORP.

Once you've got your lighting all set up, how will you know what f-stop to set your camera at to get a proper exposure? Of course, once you've had years of experience you can get pretty close, or you can go the trial and error route. But, what if there were a device that would actually tell you to "set your f-stop at this number," and then all you had to do was dial in that f-stop on your camera and your exposure would be right on the money? Well, that's what a light meter does. In fact, that's all a light meter does. You fire your strobe, the meter measures the light from the strobe, and it shows you on its screen what f-stop to use for a perfect exposure. Sounds like cheating, right? It kinda is.

Scott's Gear Finder

Gossen Digiflash Light Meter 2 (around $200)

Sekonic Litemaster Pro L-478D Light Meter (around $390)

Gossen DIGISKY Light Meter (around $470)

How to Use a Light Meter

Before you get started, there are three simple things you'll need to do before you measure the light from your flash: (1) Enter the ISO that your camera is set to into your light meter (so, if you're shooting at 100 ISO, you enter 100 ISO). (2) Enter the shutter speed you're going to be using (in a studio, I generally use $1/125$ of a second—a good, safe shutter speed for working with studio flash. So, go ahead and enter $1/125$ of a second). And, (3) make sure the round white plastic dome on the meter is extended (turn the wheel so it extends out). That's it—you're ready to put it to use. Most people aim the light meter at the light itself, but today's meters are actually designed so they work with that white plastic dome aiming back directly at your camera's lens. If you're metering a person for a portrait, position the meter directly under their chin, with the dome aiming back directly at the camera. Now, push the measurement button on the meter, and then fire the flash (if you're firing your flashes wirelessly, make sure you get a light meter that has a wireless trigger built right in, so when you push the measurement button, it fires the flash for you. Otherwise, you'll have to have your subject hold the meter under their chin and push the measurement button, so you can walk back to your camera to take a test shot which fires the flash). When the flash fires, it instantly tells you the exact f-stop you need to dial in on your camera for a perfect exposure. Go over to your camera, make sure you're in manual mode, set your f-stop to what it said (make sure your shutter speed is still set at $1/125$ of a second) and you've got it—perfect exposure. As long as you don't move the light or change the power of the flash, you can continue to use those settings. If anything does change, just take a new meter reading the same way and dial in your f-stop just like before.

How Many Lights Should You Use?

One. I am not kidding. The secret to lighting success is to keep it simple, and if you stick with just one light at this stage, your chances for success go up by about 1000%. Here's why: (1) You won't get into trouble with just one light. You'll set it up, you'll position it, you'll take a shot, it'll look great, and you'll be happy (think: less is more). In fact, it'll probably look so good that you'll want to add more lights. But, as soon as you start setting up more lights, the problems begin because, while one light is simple, two lights takes the complexity of getting overall good light up a big notch. Three lights is a total circus (at least until you really know what you're doing). So, do yourself a favor and get really good at just one light. (2) One light costs about half of what two lights cost, it takes about half the time to set up, and it weighs half as much. (3) With one light, you'll probably sidestep one of the biggest mistakes people new to studio lighting always tend to make, and that is to "overlight" everything. They use too many lights and make everything too bright. (4) You'll have a chance to really understand light because the whole process will be really simple. You'll get really, really good at using one light. You'll become a master of one light, and then you'll know exactly when you need to use a second light, and precisely why. This "stick with just one light" is some of the best advice in this chapter (heck, in this whole book), and if you do stick with it, it won't be long before you'll become known for your lighting. I know that sounds like a dream at this point, and it will stay a dream if you rush out and buy a three-light kit. Go with one.

The Least Expensive Extra Light

So, what do you do if you set up your one light and your subject's eyes look too dark, or if one side of their face is too dark, but I just told you not to use more than one light? Still don't buy that other light (not yet anyway). Instead, buy a reflector. They're cheap (about $30 for the Westcott reflector I use) and it's like having a second light but without the cost, complexity, size, weight, or electrical requirements. Here's how they work: When light hits a reflector, it bounces off it the way a billiard ball bounces off the rail cushion in a game of pool—it hits the reflector and changes direction. Your job is to direct that bounced light back toward your subject (well, back toward the part that needs more light). So, the idea is this: if one side of your subject's face is really dark, position the reflector so the light from your strobe hits it, and then bounces back onto that side of their face. Is it really that simple? Yup. You control how bright this bounced light is in two ways: (1) just like a real light, the closer the reflector is to your subject, the brighter it will be (so if it's too bright, move it farther away), and (2) the color you use affects how much light it bounces back—silver reflectors reflect a lot of light; white reflectors reflect much less (you can buy reflectors with white on one side, and silver on the other). So, if you just need a little light to fill in those shadows, use the white side. If you need a lot of light, use silver. Also, there are probably just two places you're really going to wind up placing this reflector in a studio: (1) right beside your subject, on the opposite side of the light to bounce light back toward the shadowy side of your subject, or (2) directly in front of your subject for headshots, to bounce light back into their eyes, usually around chest or waist level.

Adding a Hair Light

If you're thinking of adding a second light to your studio, it should probably be a hair light. A hair light is just another strobe, but it's generally aimed directly at your subject's hair (did I even have to say that?), which helps to separate your subject from the background and give your portraits a more professional look all around. For lighting hair these days, we generally use a tall, thin rectangular softbox called a strip bank, which helps keep the light more directional (and lights just the hair and/or shoulders, instead of spilling over everywhere). The strip bank size I use is 12x36". Also, I usually set the power on my strobe for the hair light so it's around one stop brighter than my front light, so the light from my front light doesn't overpower it.

Scott's Gear Finder

Westcott Strip Softbox 12x36" ($150)

Chimera 9x36" Super Pro Plus Strip ($183)

Westcott Strip Softbox 12x50" ($248)

Where to Position Your Hair Light

We used to position hair lights on a boom stand directly above our subjects, but honestly, that's kind of an outdated "old school" approach to hair lighting. Today, it's much more popular to use a strip bank behind and to the side of your subject instead. Generally, you position it on the opposite side of your front light (catty-corner to it), behind your subject, aiming back at their hair. As far as height goes, position it so about the top half of the softbox is above their head and then you angle it down slightly toward your subject. As far as how close/far to place this hair light from your subject, that's easy: if you want the light to be harder, move it farther away (6 to 8 feet); if you want it softer, get it as close as you can to your subject (without it being visible in the shot. I didn't really have to say that last part, did I?). One more advantage of not going "old school" with the boom stand right overhead: you don't need a boom stand. You can do this strip bank hair light using just a regular ol' light stand. Another victory for simplicity!

Testing Your Hair Light's Position

A trick for checking the position of your hair light, to make sure none of the light from it is spilling onto your subject's face, is to turn off your main strobe (your front light), so nothing but the hair light is turned on. Your subject should be in complete silhouette, with no light on their nose, cheeks, or face whatsoever. If you see any light now, you'll need to reposition your hair light (maybe move it back a little bit, or to the side), until you only see light on their head and shoulders—none on the face. By the way, this "turn off the front light" trick isn't just for hair lights—it's for any time you're using more than one light. By doing a test shot with just one light on at a time, you'll see exactly what each one is doing. If you turn them all on from the beginning, the lighting won't look good, but you won't have any idea why. So, always start with just one light (I always do any back lights first), and then add another light, one at a time. If something doesn't look right when you add another light, turn the other lights off, adjust the one that didn't look right, then turn them on again, one at a time.

Keeping Your Hair Light from Spilling

Probably the most popular accessory for hair lights is an egg crate grid. This is a fabric grid that Velcros (or slips, depending on the brand) over the front of your strip bank. It narrowly focuses the light from your hair light so it doesn't spill out the sides, and it really does a wonderful job of focusing your light just where you want it. They come in different sizes, and there's one to match the exact size and shape of your strip light. These used to be insanely expensive (literally, often more than the cost of the softbox itself, like the price was controlled by some sort of egg crate cartel), but a number of new sources now have them at really affordable prices (for example, instead of being $190 for a grid for 12x36" strip banks, you can get one from Denny Manufacturing [www.dennymfg.com] for around $40. Whew! That's better). Once you use one, you'll always use one, because for hair lights they're absolutely ideal.

Which Mode Should You Shoot In?

When it comes to shooting with studio strobes or flashes, this is the one time I would absolutely recommend that you shoot in manual mode. The reason is you need to set both the f-stop and shutter speed independently, and manual mode easily lets you do just that. Start by setting your shutter speed at ¹⁄₁₂₅ of a second (a good, safe speed that will sync your camera with your flash unit, no sweat). This shutter speed, in a studio, is a "set it and forget it" setting. Now all you have to worry about is setting your f-stop. So, set your shutter speed to ¹⁄₁₂₅ of a second, your f-stop to f/11 (great for studio portraits because everything will be in focus), and then take a shot and see how it looks on your camera's LCD monitor. If it's too dark/too bright, don't change the settings. Instead, just raise/lower your flash power until the lighting looks right to you. Of course, you could just use a light meter to tell you exactly which f-stop to use for the power setting you currently have on your flash (if you'd rather not mess with changing the power of your flash).

A "SHOW ME HOW TO DO IT" BOOK

This is a "show me how to do it" book. I'm telling you these tips just like I'd tell a shooting buddy, and that means, oftentimes, it's just which button to push, which setting to change, where to put the light, and not a whole lot of reasons why. I figure that once you start getting amazing results from your camera, you'll go out and buy one of those "tell me all about it" digital camera or lighting books.

Where to Position Your Main Light

There is no absolute "right" place to position your lights, so it really comes down to your personal preference about how you want the shadows to look on your subject. Shadows are what create depth and dimension on a person's face (and having soft shadows on your subject's face is usually very flattering), so I usually position my main light so it's at a 45° angle to the subject. So, for example, if your subject was standing at the center of a clock face, and the camera is straight in front of them at 6:00, then you'd place the light at around 7:30. This creates some nice soft shadows on the side of their face that's farthest away from the light (the side opposite the light). If you want more shadows on that side of their face, you'd move the light to around 8:00. Want more shadows? Move it to 8:30. Want that whole side of their face totally in shadow (often seen in dramatic portraits of men)? Put the light right beside them at 9:00. Okay, what if you actually want less shadows on that opposite side of their face—maybe just a hint of shadows? Then, move the light closer to the camera position—to around 7:00. If you move the light right in front of the subject, their whole face will be lit evenly with no shadows on the opposite side of their face. This is "flat lighting" and it usually looks okay on someone with really good skin. Okay, so which one of these positions is the "right" position? The one you choose—it's totally up to your personal preference (my preference has me positioning my light at between 7:30 and 8:00 most of the time).

How High to Position Your Main Light

If you were doing a shoot using natural light from the sun, where does the light come from? It comes from above us, right? When it's straight above us, it's really harsh midday sun, but later in the day, the sun is lower in the sky and it becomes softer and more flattering as it now comes down on us at an angle. We want to do the same thing with our studio lights—we want to mimic that soft, late afternoon position. That's why we position our light up high above our subject, and aiming down at them at an angle, so it creates a more flattering look to our light. So, in short, we place it above them, angled down at them. If they're standing, the center of the light is usually up a couple of feet higher than their eye level. If they're sitting, it's also usually a couple of feet up higher than their eye level. Easy enough.

SOMETIMES YOU HAVE TO BUY GEAR

Just so you know, I don't get a kickback, bonus, or promotional fee from any of the companies whose products I recommend. I'm just giving you the same advice I'd give a friend if we were out shooting (which is the theme behind this entire book). This is not a book to sell you stuff, but before you move forward, understand that to get pro results, sometimes you have to use (and that means buy) some of what the pros use.

How Close to Position Your Light

Once you know this rule, you'll know exactly how close (or far away) to position the light. The rule is actually very simple: the closer the light is to your subject, the softer the light is. That's it. Now that you know that rule, how far the light is positioned away from your subject is actually based on (wait for it…wait for it…) your subject. For example, if you're shooting a mother and daughter portrait, and you want the light to be really soft and beautiful, you'll position the light as close to them as possible (without actually seeing the softbox in the shot). If you're shooting a boxer, and you want the light on him to be hard and edgy, move the light back maybe 8 or 10 feet, and the shadows become much harder and edgier. The farther the light is away from him, the harder it will be. So, really, how close (or far) you position the light from your subject is based on how soft or hard you want the light to be. By the way, there's nothing to say you couldn't have soft, beautiful light on a boxer—it's actually a good look (I've done it myself). But, in the end, this is a call you make based on your subject and how soft or hard you want the light to be. Soft = close. Hard = far away. One thing to remember: when you move the light close to your subject, it gets brighter, so you might have to turn the power down. By the same token, if you move the light away from your subject for a harder look, the light gets darker (I know, duh!), so you'll have to turn the power of your flash up to compensate.

Using a Fan for Windblown Effects

If you're shooting portraits of women, this is going to sound silly at first, but you want to buy a fan. Not just a fan, a powerful, hurricane-force commercial fan that would put most of your lighting equipment in jeopardy if you were to ever turn it on to its highest possible setting (which I believe, on most fans, is marked "Category Five"). Anyway, a fan with a nice kick to it (like the Lasko 3520 20" Cyclone Pivoting Floor Fan, for around $35) creates a windblown hair effect that can add energy and excitement to your portraits (besides making the subject's hair look full and glamorous). The fan should be positioned on the ground, aiming upward at your subject, and once the fan is in place and turned on, there's not much else to do but shoot. If you really want to "blow people away," take a look at Buffalo Tools' 42" Industrial Fan (it sells for $366), which was designed for use in factories and sports arenas, and features high-performance, belt-driven motion with a two-speed capacitor and a thermal cut-off (whatever that means). In short, it's guaranteed to relocate anything in your studio that's not bolted to the foundation.

WANT TO IMPRESS THE FOLKS AT VOGUE? BUY THIS FAN!

If you get a huge, paying, fashion cover shot gig and you want to really impress your new clients, buy the only fan I've found that is made for shooting fashion—the Bowens Jet Stream 350 Wind Machine. With its 2500-rpm blast and a wireless remote, it'll be knocking your clients off their feet (and it should—it sells for around $1,300). B&H Photo has 'em in stock. What the heck—buy two!

Want Softer, More Even Light? Feather It!

If you're already using a large softbox (one that's around 36x48" or larger), and you want softer, more even light than it delivers, then you can use a technique called feathering, which puts your subject in the softest and most even light your softbox can deliver. Feathering just means that you turn the light away from your subject, so they are now lit by just the edges of the light. They won't be getting the full intensity of the light when you feather it, so you might have to adjust your exposure so it's not too dark (use a lower number f-stop on your lens—like f/4 or f/3.5, etc.—or better yet, use your light meter and it will tell you exactly which settings to use when feathering your light). This light out at the edges of your softbox is very even, very soft, and very flattering (since the light in the center of the softbox is usually brighter and less even), so when you really need that super-soft, even light—now you know where to get it. This technique looks great on portraits of young children, a mother/daughter shot, or when you want a very soft, glamorous look to your lighting.

What That Extra Panel in Your Softbox Does

When you buy your first softbox, it may come with a second, smaller diffusion panel, which you place inside the softbox (and then you place the larger outer diffusion panel on the inside edge of the softbox, to cover the front). That internal diffusion panel really serves one purpose: to try to even out the light, so you don't get a hot spot in the center of your light where the flash bulb is. This internal panel does make the light a tiny bit softer, but that's not its main job—it's to hide that hot spot. Of course, by adding this internal panel, your light has to pass through that diffusion material first, so you lose a little bit of light in the process. As a general rule, if I'm using continuous light (like the Westcott Spiderlites), I always take this extra internal diffusion panel out. That's because those daylight fluorescent bulbs are already soft (by their very nature), and the panel doesn't really soften them significantly, it just eats up light, so I especially want them out when using continuous lights, because I need all the brightness I can get. Other-wise, if I'm using strobes, I leave them in place.

Using a Pop-Up Collapsible Background

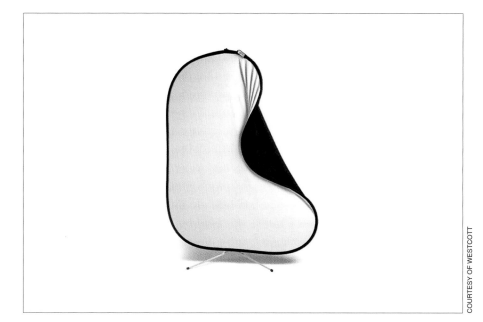

COURTESY OF WESTCOTT

Another quick and flexible studio background is a pop-up collapsible background that instantly folds up into a small, flat circle, but expands to be a full studio background in a matter of seconds. The one I use is a 6x7' Westcott Masterpiece 2-in-1 Collapsible Illumina-tor Background with white on one side and black on the other. It sells for around $220, and I also recommend buying the Illuminator stand to hold it up, which is another $90, but unless you can stand there and hold it up (or have somebody else hold it up), it's worth its weight in gold. So, with this background, anytime you want to shoot, you just open the round plastic case it comes in, pull it out, and it pops up, ready to go. You put it on the Illuminator background stand, and you're ready to go. Another advantage of this particular background (over the seamless paper route) is that it's very portable, lightweight, and you can set it up in literally seconds—by yourself. The only downside is it doesn't go all the way to the floor seamlessly, so it's fine for 3/4-body shots, but not full-body shots. One more thing: although I use the black/white version, these collapsible backgrounds come in all sorts of patterns, looks, sizes, and colors.

Keep Light from Hitting the Background

If you want to create a portrait with dramatic lighting, the key is to control where the light goes, so only a small portion of it actually hits your subject (and little or none winds up lighting the background). The problem is that even with a softbox (which is fairly directional compared to an umbrella), the light aiming back at your subject can spread too much, so we use black "flags" to block the light from hitting our background (or anything else we don't want it to hit). These flags are really just tall, or wide, black rectangular reflectors that absorb and block light, so you put one between your strobe (softbox) and the background, and voilá—it stops the light from spilling (as shown above). So, if you have more than one, you can really keep your light pretty much directed just where you want it by putting these black flags up to block any extra light. I use two Mathews 24x36" black flags (around $42 each). If you're not ready to plunk down that kind of change, you could always get two large black pieces of poster board or foam core, and that will do the trick.

Three Backgrounds for the Price of One

One of the advantages of shooting on a white background is that you can get three different looks from it, depending on how you light it. For example, if you put two bright strobes (or continuous lights, for that matter) aiming at the background behind your subject (or product), the background will look bright white. If you dim those lights, or remove one, then the background looks like a light gray. If you leave the background lights off altogether, your white background will now look medium gray. So, with white you get three separate looks: bright white, light gray, and medium gray—all based on whether, and how, you light the background.

Using Off-Camera Flash to Light Backgrounds

If you want to add a light to your background (aiming back at your seamless paper), but you don't want to go through the extra expense of adding a second studio strobe, if you have a standard off-camera flash (like a Nikon SB-910 or a Canon 600EX-RT), you're in luck. You can set either of these off-camera flashes to become wireless slave flashes, meaning that when your studio strobe fires to light your subject, it automatically triggers your off-camera flash to light your background. You only have to do two things to make this happen: (1) Put your flash on a light stand. (*Note:* If you have a Nikon SB-910 flash, it actually comes with wonderful little flash stand that lets you set your flash on the floor. Then you aim the head back up at your background, and this will work in a pinch.) So, the first thing (once again) is to put your flash on a light stand, and position it directly behind your subject so your subject's body hides the flash from view. Then, (2) set your off-camera flash to Slave, so it fires when it senses the light from your studio strobe. For example, on a Nikon SB-910, turn the ON/OFF switch to Remote, press the Menu button, scroll down to Wireless, and then choose SU-4 (as shown above). Press the OK button, then press the Menu button, and you're ready to go.

The Advantage of Shooting Tethered

You know that tiny LCD screen on the back of your camera? Yeah, that one. That little screen is what we use to make critical decisions about our photography (like "is this photo really tack sharp" or "are my subject's eyes both open"), but that screen (usually either 2½" or 3" in size) is actually smaller than the screen on our cell phones. I know—crazy, right? No wonder we misjudge sharpness and quality so often—that screen is absolutely tiny. That's why, if I'm shooting in a studio, I shoot tethered directly into my computer, so that way I see each image really large (at least at 8x10" size on my laptop, or larger on my desktop monitor) right as I take it. At this larger size, you can really see what's going on in your photo (and how your lighting looks), and you can make adjustments based on a much larger-sized image, which makes it hard to look at that tiny 2½" or 3" LCD display anymore. Tethering itself is actually very simple, just two steps: (1) Connect a USB cable from your camera's mini-USB port to your computer's USB port. (2) Now, you just need some tethering software. Luckily, Adobe's Photoshop Lightroom and Apple's Aperture already have tethering built right in. If you don't have Lightroom or Aperture and you're a Canon shooter, you already have the software you'll need—it's that EOS Utility software you got when you bought your camera (if you can't find it, you can download it for free from Canon's website). If you're a Nikon shooter on a Mac, go to www.sofortbildapp.com and download their excellent free tethering software. If you're a Nikon shooter on Windows, go to ControlMyNikon.com. If you're a Sony Alpha-series DLSR Shooter, you can use Sony's free Sony Camera Remote Control software.

Getting Super-Saturated Background Color

If you want some really vivid, punchy colors as your background, here's a recipe to get just that: Start on a background of black seamless paper (I know, it sounds weird that we start creating vivid colors with a black background, but believe it or not, this is the easiest way), and then position a light on the background. Now, for a background light you can use another one of the same strobes you already have (so, basically, you're going to need a second strobe if you want to light the background, or there's the trick you can pull to use your off-camera flash as a background light that we talked about a couple pages ago). Once you've got your black seamless paper in place and a second strobe (or off-camera flash) positioned behind your subject, aiming at the background, the trick is to put a vivid-colored gel (a translucent piece of plastic) over the front of your flash, and when your background flash fires, the color it produces is rich, vivid, and surprisingly colorful. You can get these gels (made by Lee or Rosco) from B&H Photo for around $6.50 for a 20x24" sheet (choose really vivid colors—reds, yellows, greens, etc.).

Lighting a White Background

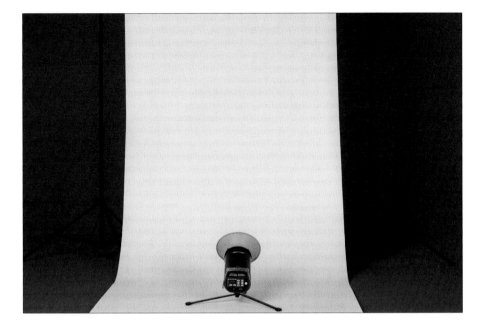

When you shoot on a white seamless-paper background, you'll probably be surprised to find out that most of the time it doesn't look white—it looks light gray. To get it to look solid white (that nice bright white you're used to seeing in portraits and product shots), you have to light the background. It doesn't take a bunch of lights—usually just one or two will do the trick, and they don't have to be very high-powered strobes either (see the off-camera trick a few pages back), so it's not a bad idea to buy a lower-powered, less expensive strobe just for lighting the background. But beyond just having a background light aimed at your white seamless background, there's a little trick you'll want to use to make sure that the light does make the background look that nice solid white, but without blowing out the background so much that the back light starts to wash out the edges of your subject (this happens more than you might think). The pros' trick to getting around this is (you guessed it) to use their light meter. They hold the meter up against the background, aim the white dome back toward the camera position, and check the reading. You want the background to be around one stop brighter than the light on your subject. So if your meter showed f/11 for your subject, you want the background to read one stop brighter (like f/16). You get that background brighter by increasing the power (brightness) of the strobe itself. Try increasing a bit, then recheck the background with your meter again, and keep adjusting the power of the background light until it reads that one stop (or slightly more) than your subject. That's the formula.

Which Color Reflector to Use

Outdoor   Studio   Both

Reflectors come in a variety of colors (white, black, silver, gold, etc.), and if you're wondering which color does what, well, here ya go:

- **Silver** reflects the most amount of light, and doesn't change the color of the studio light that hits it, so you see a lot of portrait pros using silver.

- **White** reflectors don't bounce nearly as much light, but they're still used in portraits because the reflected light is very soft and works both indoors and outdoors. White reflectors are also a good choice if you're doing product photography.

- **Gold** reflectors are for outdoor portraits to match the warm color of sunlight. They don't work well in a studio, because when the white light from your strobe hits the gold reflector, it becomes very yellow (so one side of your subject's face looks studio white, and the shadow side looks overly yellow).

- A **Black** reflector actually absorbs light, so it's used to cut reflections when you're shooting anything that's reflective, like glass, or jewelry, or tableware, or anything that's clear, etc.

For my studio portraits, I use a reflector that is silver on one side and white on the other, and I use the silver side around 80% of the time.

Where to Position a Reflector

Reflectors are a key part of a studio setup, because they keep you from having to set up a second light. Luckily, they're pretty inexpensive (the Westcott 30" Silver/White square reflector I use costs only around $40), but once you've got one, where do you put it? A reflector's job is to bounce some of the light from your main light (your flash) back into the shadowy areas of your subject, so you'll need to position it where it can do its job, right? One popular method is to place the reflector directly beside your subject (on the opposite side from your studio flash), then move it a bit forward so it extends a little in front of the subject, so it catches the light and fills in the shadows. Make sure that: (1) it is indeed in front of them a bit, and not right beside them, and (2) it's not positioned up higher than they are—it should be at their height. Another popular place to position a reflector for head shots is directly in front of your subject, usually right below your subject's head and shoulders, so the light bounces back to lighten the shadows on their face—in particular, the areas under their eyes and neck. You can have your subject hold the reflector flat in front of them, or you can position it on a reflector stand, or even lay it on the floor in front of them. Another popular position is to place it out in front, where you'd place a second light (on the opposite side from your studio strobe), so it bounces light back toward your subject. The key thing to remember with reflectors is: if the light isn't hitting the reflector fairly directly, it has nothing to bounce, so make sure that wherever you position it, the light from your strobe is hitting it directly.

Reflectors Without an Assistant

If you don't have an assistant to hold your reflector in the studio, you just need an inexpensive light stand and a cheap clamp. The light stand I use for this is a 6' model made by Impact (I got mine at B&H Photo for around $20), and it's great for holding a pretty decent size reflector (like the Westcott 30" 5-in-1 Reflector I mentioned in the Flash chapter). Then just attach the reflector to the light stand using a cheap 2" Pony clamp, like the 2" Adjustable Clamp Company Pony Spring "A" Clamp with Plastic Tips for around $3. This is incredibly handy to have around (and much less expensive than hiring an assistant to hold your reflector).

VISIT B&H PHOTO'S NEW YORK SUPERSTORE

If you're ever in New York City, make it a point to drop by the B&H Photo store. It is absolutely amazing. It's like Disneyland for photographers. I could spend a day there (and I have). Anyway, they're good people and are pretty much beloved throughout the photography community (and that's saying something).

Seeing the Light from Your Reflector

So, you're standing there holding a reflector. How do you know if it's really hitting your subject? Here's a quick trick for helping you position the angle of your reflector so you know the light is hitting where you want it to. Hold the reflector by its side and tilt it up and down a few times as you're facing your subject, and you'll see the reflected light move across their face. By tilting the reflector up and down a few times, you'll locate that "sweet spot"—where the light is hitting and fully bouncing from—and then you can tilt the reflector to right where you want it.

WHERE TO GO TO LEARN MORE ABOUT STUDIO LIGHTING

If this chapter gets you excited about what can be done with just one strobe (or one strobe and a hair light), and you want to learn more (and learn how and when to add more lights), then man did I write a book for you. It's called *Light It, Shoot It, Retouch It: Learn Step by Step How to Go from Empty Studio to Finished Image* and I go through a number of lighting setups from scratch, but without using diagrams. Instead, I use real photos, taken overhead, and from the front, the sides, and in back, so you can actually see exactly where everything goes. You'll totally dig it (but, of course, I would say that, right?). It's published by Peachpit Press.

Chapter Three

Shooting Portraits Like a Pro

More Tips to Make People Look Their Very Best

Getting professional-looking shots of people is harder than you might think, for one simple reason: the pros hire really good-looking models, and as you know, models are models for one simple reason—they forget to eat. I'm joking, of course. They're models because they photograph really, really well. So, what makes our job so hard is that we're not surrounded by fabulous-looking models who just happen to be standing around not eating. Nope, we usually wind up shooting portraits of our friends, many of whom (on a looks scale) fall somewhere between Mr. Bean and Jabba the Hut. This is why our job, as portrait photographers, is actually substantially more challenging than that of a seasoned professional—we've got to make magic from some seriously un-model-like people. This is precisely why we're often so disappointed with our portraits (when it's really not our fault). So, in this chapter, we'll look at two proven strategies to get better, more professional-looking portraits every time, including: (1) how to make friends with better-looking people (it helps if you're rich), and (2) learning to control your light and pose your subjects so that no one gets a really good look at them. The key to this is to use dramatic light, and by "dramatic light" I mean—virtually none at all. The less you light these "un-model-like" subjects, the better your final images will be. In fact, think silhouette or long distance night photography, where your subjects are 100 to 200 yards away—anybody looks good from that distance (that's why long distance relationships work so well). Anyway, what this chapter will give you is a strategy for photographing people, and a list of places where good-looking people hang out and wear jeans that cost more than the gross national product of Luxembourg.

Don't Leave Too Much Headroom

When your average person takes a snapshot of someone, they almost always leave way too much space above their subject's head (as you see on the left here) because they almost always put their subject's eyes in the center of the frame. It's a classic mistake most amateurs make, but luckily it's one that's really easy to fix. Just don't do that—don't leave too much space. If you remember my portrait composition tip from part 1 of this book (position your subject's eyes at the top one-third of the frame), then you'll usually avoid this "too much headroom" problem altogether.

Great f-Stop for On-Location Portraits

In a photo studio, our goal is usually to make everything in focus, so we use high-numbered f-stops like f/11. However, if you're shooting on location or outdoors, now we have a new goal: make the background soft and out of focus, so our subject stands out from the background, creating some separation (this makes for a much more professional look on location). There are just two things you need to do to make this happen: (1) Shoot wide open (meaning, use the lowest number f-stop your lens will allow, so if your lowest number is f/4, use that. If it's f/2.8, even better—the lower the number, the more out of focus your background will be). And, (2) zoom in on your subject. Just changing the f-stop to a low number won't be enough by itself, the zooming-in part is really important (so you might have to stand back quite a ways from your subject). Try this and you'll see what I mean. Go ahead and set your f-stop to its lowest number (say, on your lens, it's f/3.5), then shoot a portrait without zooming in—shoot it with a wide angle, like a 24mm. Now, take a look at the photo. Everything's in focus, right? Even though the f-stop is low, a wide-angle shot will make everything sharp. That's why the "zooming-in" part of this two-step technique is so important. Do both and you'll have a wonderfully soft, out-of-focus background.

Shoot in Portrait Orientation

Most photos are taken in horizontal (landscape) orientation, and that makes perfect sense, since cameras are designed that way—to be held horizontally—and that's why the shutter button is on the top right, right where your finger would naturally be. However, professional portraits are generally taken using a vertical orientation (that's why it's referred to as "portrait orientation," but that term is most often seen when you go to print something on your computer—you'll see a button for Landscape [wide] or Portrait [tall]). So, if you want more professional-looking portraits, turn your camera vertically and shoot in portrait orientation (of course, like any rule, there are exceptions, some of which you'll learn later in this chapter).

Shooting Portraits? Get a Battery Grip!

If you shoot a lot of portraits, you're going to be spending a lot of time with your camera flipped vertically, and before long you'll get tired of reaching over the top of your camera to press the shutter button. When that happens, you'll want to get a vertical battery grip. Besides enabling you to use two batteries, so you can shoot longer without recharging your batteries, there's another huge advantage to battery grips, and that is that most include a vertical orientation shutter button and dials for setting your aperture and shutter speed, so you're as comfortable shooting vertically as when you're shooting horizontally. Besides those advantages, most of the photographers I know swear that it makes the whole camera feel better and more substantial in their hands, even when shooting horizontally (and how a camera feels in your hands is very important). The best news is these battery grips are available for most DSLRs, and for all the advantages they offer, they cost less than you'd think (starting at around $50). Just one thing to look for when ordering yours: not all battery grips have the vertical shutter button, so check to make sure the one you order does.

MOST HIGH-END CAMERAS ALREADY COME WITH A VERTICAL SHUTTER BUTTON

If you've got a high-end digital camera, like a Canon 1Dx or a Nikon D3s or D4, they already come with a vertical shutter button built right in. Hey, ya pay that type of money, they oughta come with one, right?

The "Sun Over Your Shoulder" Rule Is Bogus

You may have heard of the "Sun Over Your Shoulder" rule, which basically states that when you're shooting people outdoors, you put the sun behind you (over your shoulder), so your subjects' faces are lit. This is a perfectly fine rule for people taking snapshots, but it is the worst thing you can do for your group portrait (besides the "tall people in the back" thing). If you want more professional-looking shots of people outdoors, the last thing you want is the bright sun blasting them straight in their faces (although that's exactly what your average person does), so everyone is squinting, trying to shield their eyes, and turning away from the camera. Worse, it puts harsh, direct, unflattering light on them. Instead, position your subjects with the sun behind them (not behind you), so it puts a nice rim light effect around them (outlining their hair), and then use just a tiny bit of flash (keep the brightness of your flash low) to put just enough light into their faces to make them blend in with the natural light that surrounds them.

Shoot Wide and Push in Tight

This is a concept—shooting on-location portraits with a wide-angle lens—that I hadn't considered for many years because of the time-honored rule that states: "Don't shoot people with a wide-angle lens because they look all distorted and weird." But it was one of the world's top shooters, the brilliant Joe McNally, who totally busted that myth and totally changed the way I shoot environmental portraits by turning me on to "shoot wide and push in tight." When you're shooting wide-angle and you get really close to your subjects (you're pushing in tight), they don't look distorted—only the stuff at the very edges of the frame looks a little "wide," but it's that stuff at the edge of the frame that shows the environment where the shot is taken. I was skeptical until Joe challenged me to pick up a *People* magazine and look at what most of the shots are—taken in tight with a wide-angle lens. I was shocked, but it's not just *People*, it's just about everywhere—from magazines to billboards to prints ads to the web. The pros are shooting wide and pushing in tight. You can, too!

NAME-DROPPING DISCLAIMER

Throughout this book, I wind up mentioning names of some famous photographers. The reason I do this isn't to drop names; instead, it's to give credit where credit is due. If I learned a tip or technique and I can remember who taught it to me, I think it's only right to give them the proper credit.

Shoot Profile Shots in Horizontal

So, now that we've learned the Shoot Portraits Vertically rule, let's break it! (That's the great thing about the photographic rules—once you learn 'em, you can break 'em, then it's cool. It's only uncool when you break the rules by accident because you didn't know any better.) Anyway, one place where we intentionally break this rule is when we're shooting a profile view of our subject. The reason is this: because your subject is facing the edge of the frame, if you shoot your subject vertically, they look boxed-in, and that's uncomfortable for your viewer. So, by breaking the vertical rule and shooting profiles horizontally, it gives your subject some visual breathing room and makes your subject look more comfortable within the frame.

Shoot Long for More Flattering Portraits

Have you ever seen a high-end photo shoot on TV (maybe a fashion or celebrity shoot), and have you noticed how far back the photographer is from their subject? That's because they're taking advantage of "lens compression" offered by a longer zoom lens (which is very flattering to portraits). The shots above really tell the story—the one on the left was shot with a 50mm lens, and the one on the right with a 70–200mm lens zoomed out to 190mm. Even though all the camera settings and lighting are identical (they were taken just seconds apart), her features in the shot on the right look much more pleasing. That's why you'll see many pro photographers shooting portraits at the far range of their zoom. By that I mean they shoot with the lens extended out as far as it can go. So, if they're shooting a 28–135mm lens, they're shooting out in the 100mm to 135mm range to get the best, most flattering look for portraits.

Scott's Pro-Speak TRANSLATOR

The phrase we use for shooting all the way out at the longest end of a telephoto lens (for example, shooting at 200mm on a 70–200mm lens) is "racked out." So, you might hear a photographer say, "I shot racked out to 200," which means he shot with his lens extended out as far as it can go—to the far end of its range (in this case, 200mm).

Why Diffusers Rock for Outdoor Portraits

When it comes to really harsh, unflattering light for portraits, it's a toss-up between which is worse: your camera's built-in pop-up flash or direct sunlight. Luckily, as you learned in part 1 of this book, if you're shooting portraits outdoors and there's an area with some shade nearby, you can shoot there. But what if you're out at the beach, or in the desert, or one of a thousand other places that doesn't have a shady tree nearby? Then you'll want to own one of these—a 30" Lastolite TriGrip 1 Stop Diffuser (the same one I mentioned in the flash chapter for diffusing harsh light from an off-camera flash—so it does double-duty here). Just have a friend hold this diffuser between the sun and your subject (as shown above on the right), and instantly you have soft, beautiful, natural light on location. It sells for around $70 at B&H Photo, and you'll want this lightweight lifesaver with you every time you leave the studio.

Making a Better Background for Portraits

The key to great backgrounds for portraits is "less is more." If you're shooting an environmental portrait (a photo taken on location in someone's home, office, etc.), to get that pro
look, it's not what you do to the background, it's what you take away from the background
that makes it work. You want to have as few distracting elements in the background as you
can, so either position your subject on a very simple, uncluttered background to begin with,
or if that's not possible, remove as many distracting elements (or knicknacks) as your subject
will let you get away with, as I did in the image on the right here. Don't take this lightly—to
create a really great environmental portrait, it can't just be the foreground that works. The
whole photo has to work together, and by choosing (or creating) a sparse, uncluttered
background, your chances of having a winner go way up.

Cropping Off the Top of Their Head

This is the next step past "Don't leave too much room above your subject's head" in portraits. In this composition technique, you actually cut off the top of your subject's head, and
while that probably sounds weird reading it here, it's a very popular pro technique that fills
your frame with your subject's head. Getting in tight like this makes for a very compelling
look, as you see above, and now that it has been brought to your attention, you'll see this
composition technique is everywhere and has become the mainstay of many top fashion,
beauty, and portrait shooters. (*Note:* Although it's perfectly fine to cut off the top of their
head, or side of their arms, shoulders, hair, etc., you shouldn't cut off their chin. People are
actually very used to seeing the top cut off and it looks natural, but seeing a shot where
the chin is cropped off makes for a very uncomfortable composition.)

Trendy Composition Tip

Since most photos you see are either horizontal or vertical, doing something different looks…well…different! And right now, a very popular technique for portrait photography is to turn the camera at an angle, which puts your subject kind of up in the corner. The technique couldn't be simpler—just rotate your camera to the left or right a little bit and then take the shot. It may take you a couple of tries to get your subject positioned right where you want them in the frame, but this look (which has been around for years) is getting very popular once again.

Group Photos Are Easier Outdoors

Lighting a group shot, and getting a consistent amount of light on each person, can be pretty challenging, which is why, when it comes to group shots, you'll usually get better results by moving the group outside. It's easier to light the group using available outdoor light, especially if you can get them in the shade (not deep in the shade, just on the edge of the shade, but without letting any dapples of light appear on them through tree branches or gaps between windows or buildings). If you're lucky enough to wind up shooting a group portrait on an overcast day, then your job will be pretty easy—just get them outside and the overcast sky will take care of your lighting woes, so you can focus on getting them posed. (By the way, professional-looking group shots never start with the photographer saying, "Okay, all the tall people in the back row.")

Tip for Posing Group Portraits

The next time you're shooting a group portrait, rather than lining everybody up in rows (which you already know doesn't look good), instead try to get them to rally around something—some object—and they'll arrange themselves naturally around it. For example, try posing people in and around a couch, a column, a chair, a car, a desk, or any object that can pull them together into a group that isn't just a bunch of people standing in straight lines.

Great Tip for Casual Group Shots

Want to make a more compelling look for a casual group shot? Put your subjects in a very tight pyramid shape (a triangle), but by tight I mean so tight that they're all touching—arms around one another, their heads very close together, with one person at the top of your frame, and one on either side of the bottom of the pyramid shape (as shown above), with the others all scrunched in the middle. Also, you'll notice their bodies are not in a straight line—they're kind of staggered, but they're all leaning into the shot, which gives the shot more energy and a sense of fun. I wouldn't try this for an executive group portrait, but if you've got a fun-loving casual group, this is a great way to visually say that about them.

DON'T USE ROWS—USE CLUSTERS

If you're shooting a large group, instead of posing everyone in those tired rows, group people together in small clusters—like mini-triangles within the group, with three or four people in each triangle. These little mini-clusters add closeness and energy, and then when you've got two or three groups put together, slide them all a little closer together to visually make one big group. (These mini-clusters don't have to touch each other—small gaps between them are okay.)

Get Couples Really, Really Close

When you pose a couple and tell them to get in nice and close to each other (which you definitely should), they never get nearly close enough to look "close" in a photo. When you put your eye up to the viewfinder, you'll see the gap I'm talking about, so you tell them to "get even closer" and they move in all of about 2 inches, but I've got a trick that fixes this every time. Go ahead and take a quick shot—with the gap between them—then take it right over and show them the gap on your LCD monitor. Once they see it (and how big the gap that they thought wasn't there actually looks), they'll really get in close, and it literally makes the shot. I've done this again and again, and it always works like a charm.

Want Better Portraits? Don't Count Down!

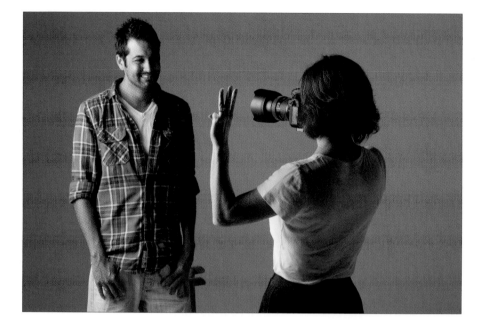

If you want that really posed look, then count 1-2-3 right before you press the shutter button. It's almost a guarantee that you won't have any natural expressions in your portraits. It's your job as photographer to find that moment when your subject looks natural, and capture that moment in time. Anyone can stand there and say "1-2-3" and push the shutter button at "4," and if you do that, you'll wind up with images that anyone can take. If you want something special, something more natural—a genuine smile or expression—then ditch the 1-2-3 cliché and instead just talk to your subject. Engage them, get them talking, laughing, smiling naturally in the course of a conversation, or even goofing around, and then when the moment is right—capture that moment. Then you'll be giving them more than a well-lit, totally posed photo. You'll give them something special.

Shoot Before & Between Shoots
for More Natural-Looking Portraits

A number of pros swear by this technique for getting more natural shots: they tell the subject not to pose yet, because they're just taking "test shots" to check the lighting. Since you're not really shooting, they're not really posing, and you're just talking to them, firing away the whole time. Once you tell the subject, "Okay, here we go," they change their demeanor, and begin "posing," so make sure you get lots of these candid, non-posed shots before the official shoot and between shoots, because they will probably be the most natural, un-posed shots of the day.

Don't Light Your Entire Subject Evenly

When people look at a photo, their eye is first drawn to the brightest thing in the photo, so you only want the brightest light falling where you want them to look, right? Right. So, if you're shooting a portrait, do you want the person viewing the portrait to look at your subject's face or their folded arms? Right. But most people light the entire portrait with the same exact light throughout, where the subject's hands at their sides have the same approximate light as the subject's face. If you want to create portraits that really lead the viewer to where you want them to focus, light your subject so the light is brightest on their face, and it gradually falls off the lower down their body it goes. This adds interest, drama, and a visual focus that you'll find so often in high-end portraits. By the way, this is another case for feathering your light (see page 61), so that the edges of the light are what light your subject's face, and below that the light falls off pretty rapidly (but don't let it get too dark—it should still have light, and detail, just not as much as their face).

DON'T LET TOO MUCH LIGHT FALL ON THEIR EARS

If there's a part of your subject that doesn't need to be well-lit, it's their ears. Ears are often distracting because they're poking out of what is usually a darker area (a person's hair), so they catch enough light to draw your attention. Since a person's ears are rarely their best feature, you don't want your viewer's eyes stopping on them first, so just be careful to not have some really bright ears in your portraits.

Window Light: Where to Position the Subject

Window light, especially light from a north-facing window, is among the most beautiful light for portraits anywhere (in fact, some pros insist on only using natural window light for all their portraits—period!). The window diffuses the light streaming in, and the larger the window, the more soft and diffuse the light. So, if you've got some nice window light, where do you position your subject to make the most of this beautiful light? You want to position your subject with their shoulder facing the window (so the light comes across your subject, creating soft shadows on the far side of their face). Then, place them about 6 feet from the window, so the light is very soft and wraps around your subject (if you get them any closer, that soft light could turn very contrasty fast). Also, position your subject a little bit back behind the window, so they catch the edge of the window light and not the direct sunlight. This edge light is very soft and gives you that wonderful, almost magical light that so many pros swear by.

Window Light: Where You Should Shoot From

When shooting a window-light portrait, you want to set up your camera right near the window, with your shoulder facing the window. Then, you'll aim back a little toward your subject, who should be positioned just past the window, about 6 feet from it (so basically, you're up against the window, shooting at a slight angle back toward your subject).

Window Light: Where to Position the Reflector

Since we generally use a reflector to bounce light into the shadow side of our subject's face, you might think that with window light you'd put the reflector on the shadow side of your subject's face. It makes sense, right? Right. And you can do that, but with window-light portraits, try this technique I learned from legendary portrait and wedding photographer Monte Zucker: bounce the light from the camera position (near the window) above your head, bouncing the window light down onto the dark side of your subject's face to open up those shadow areas.

Six Quick Tips for Fixing Facial Challenges

©ISTOCKPHOTO/DRB IMAGES, LLC

You can hide or greatly reduce many typical facial problems (like a big nose, round face, wrinkles, big ears, etc.) by how you pose and light your subject. Here are six quick posing tips to help you make your subjects look their very best: (1) If your subject is balding, shoot from a lower angle, and don't use any hair light whatsoever. (2) If your subject has lots of wrinkles, try lighting them straight on, because side lighting tends to accentuate the shadows and make the wrinkles more prominent. (3) If your subject has large ears, pose them so they're only showing one ear, then light them so that ear appears on the shadow side of their face (so basically, only one ear is showing, and that one is kind of hidden in the shadow). (4) If they have a big honkin' nose (that's a technical term, by the way), then have them turn their head straight toward the camera, have them raise their chin a bit, and shoot from a little lower angle, which will take much of the emphasis off their schnozz. (5) If your subject has a double chin, have them look straight at the camera, and extend their head forward toward the camera a bit. This stretches and tightens the skin under their chin. Also, if you light them straight on (with the light positioned directly above where you're shooting from), this puts a shadow under their chin and helps to hide the double chin. (6) If your subject has a round or fat face, make fun of them, and tell them to lose a few pounds. Then, when they burst into tears, you'll have some of the most natural-looking expressions of the day. Or, you can have them turn their face to the left or right, giving a ³/₄-view of their face, which will make their face look less round, but really—it's your call.

Don't Shoot with Their Shoulders Straight On

Everybody—women, men, kids—generally looks better when posed with their shoulders angled toward the camera. If their shoulders are straight toward the camera, it makes your subjects look very wide and flat, and even somewhat confrontational. But by simply having them turn one shoulder away from the camera, it makes them look thinner and generally gives them a more pleasing look by lessening the width of their shoulders and focusing more attention on their head. Remember: Their head can still face the camera—you're just turning their shoulders. Two exceptions: (1) If you want somebody to look very wide and flat (like a football player), then the straight-on look can look fantastic. And, (2) if you work with professional models, they are usually experts at posing, so they can get away with posing shoulders straight toward the camera, and it still looks great. But, for the rest of us, we generally look better with our shoulders angled.

Making Your Subject Look Slimmer

If you want to make someone's body look slimmer, keep their arms from touching their body—leave a little gap between their arms and their body, so their arms don't add to their body mass and make their whole figure look larger. You'll see this trick used often in celebrity and fashion shots, and you'll be surprised what a difference this little gap between the arms and waist can make (as seen in the before/after above). Another trick is to have your subject face their body away from the camera at an angle, and then just twist the upper half of their body toward the camera (leaving their lower half still facing away). Again, this is one of those little tricks that makes a big difference.

Using a Posing Chair

One of the best reasons to pose your subject in a chair is that people often feel more comfortable in a chair, and if they're comfortable, your chances of getting a relaxed, natural portrait go way up. If you have your subject standing alone in the middle of a studio, with all sorts of lights aimed at them, you're giving your subject every opportunity to be uncomfortable, and that usually translates to less-than-natural, uncomfortable-looking portraits. By the way, if you do shoot your subject seated, here's a tip to help get better-looking poses: have them sit near the end of the chair (being that far from the back of the chair almost ensures that they won't slouch or lean back), and it helps the overall look to have them lean a little forward, into the camera. So, the next time your subject looks really uncomfortable, offer them a seat, and watch them instantly become more comfortable, which usually results in better, more natural-looking portraits.

Keeping Your Subject "In the Zone"

When you're shooting a person's portrait, it's a very vulnerable, and often uncomfortable, position to be in, and in most cases the person you're shooting wants you, the photographer, to be happy with what you see and what's going on with the shoot. If they feel things aren't going well, they start to think it's their fault. You want them feeling great—you want them confident and happy, enjoying their time in front of the lens as much as possible, because that translates into better portraits. One way to keep them "in the zone" and engaged is to keep talking to them. All the time. The entire time. Talk about what you're doing, why you're doing it, talk about the weather—anything to keep them engaged. Anytime there's a period of silence, they start to get worried something's wrong, and that it may be their fault. They have no idea what you're seeing through the viewfinder, and if things get quiet, they start to get concerned and they start to get edgy, and within a minute or two they're totally out of the zone. When I'm shooting a portrait, I'm talking to them the whole time. If I stop to move a light, I tell them why (I know they don't care, but I'm keeping them engaged in the shoot). I keep giving them constant verbal encouragement ("That looks great. Fantastic! Right on the money! What a great smile," etc.) the whole time, and it makes them more comfortable and confident.

Avoid Dappled Light

If you read part 1 of this book, then you already know about putting your subjects in the shade to get better portraits outdoors (ideally, out near the edge of the shady area for the best light), but when you do this, there's something to watch out for—the dreaded "dappled light." That's those small areas of bright sunlight that break through the trees, causing uneven hot spots of light on your subject, which pretty much ruin the portrait (even if the dapples don't fall directly on their face). Luckily, the fix is amazingly easy—just reposition your subject in an area of the shade that doesn't have any of this distracting dappled light shining through. You can see how much better this looks in the image on the right here. Now, there are certain instances where dappled light works when you're shooting landscape photography, but when it comes to shooting people, dapples pretty much ruin any hope of a professional look, so be on the lookout for them anytime you're shooting under trees, or in a barn (where sunbeams can come through the cracks in the wood), or anyplace where small beams of sunlight can fall directly on your subject.

Gold Reflectors Are for Outdoors

One of the most popular color combinations for reflectors is silver on one side and gold on the other. The silver side is usually used when shooting indoors or inside a studio. The gold side is usually used outdoors, and since it's gold (and light picks up the color of whatever it hits), the light it throws will be very warm—like sunlight. So why wouldn't you use this warm reflected light in the studio? Because the light in your studio is usually very white balanced, probably from a flash, and you don't generally want to have white-balanced light from a flash on one side of their face and warm, golden light on the other side.

Minimizing Shadows Under the Eyes

If your subject starts to get shadows under their eyes (from overhead lighting indoors or outdoors), one way to reduce those is to put a silver or white reflector directly in front of them at their chest (or as high up as right under their chin), aiming up at them and reflecting some of the light back up into their eyes.

SHUTTER SPEED: 1/160 SEC   F-STOP: F/8   ISO: 100   FOCAL LENGTH: 16mm   PHOTOGRAPHER: SCOTT KELBY

Chapter Four

Shooting Landscapes Like a Pro

More Tips for Creating Stunning Scenic Images

In part 1 of this book, I had a chapter on shooting landscapes, and it turned out to be one of the most popular chapters in the book. So, when I started on part 2, I knew right then I would have to include another chapter with even more landscape techniques. And the only way to come up with new landscape techniques is to (you guessed it) shoot more landscapes, and what better place to shoot landscapes than at a landscape photography workshop? So, since I published the last edition of this book, I've taught at photography workshops in beautiful locations like Yosemite National Park, Cape Cod, Great Smoky Mountains National Park, and Glacier National Park, and then I just did some shooting in Maine this summer, and some other amazing places like Utah's Monument Valley, and the Grand Canyon, and a half-dozen other incredibly scenic spots. But when it's all said and done, do you know what all these places really meant to me? Tax deductions. That's right, because I went to these locations on business (the images will be used by me to teach photography), I get some really juicy write-offs for these trips. For example, you see that photo on the facing page? That's The Wave, which is just outside Page, Arizona, and not only is access to The Wave tightly restricted by the Bureau of Land Management, it was a grueling two-hour hike in scorching 112° desert heat over rocky mountains and hot desert sand, lugging all my camera gear, tripod (and bottles of water), and I have to be honest with you—there were times when I almost gave up, but you know what kept me going? It was the fact that if I didn't get there, and get a decent enough shot to make it into this book, I couldn't write my trip off as a tax deduction. See, I really do care.

The Secret to Shooting Sunsets

LOCATION: KAUAI, HAWAII

Because you're shooting into the sun, it can really throw your camera's built-in light meter way off, and what looked so beautiful when you were standing there comes out... well...pretty lame. Luckily, there's a simple trick to getting perfect sunset shots every time. The trick is to aim just above the setting sun itself (but make sure you can't see the sun itself through your viewfinder), then hold your shutter button halfway down, which tells the camera to set the exposure for just what it sees in the viewfinder right now. This gives you a perfect sunset exposure, but don't let go of that shutter button quite yet (keep it held down), then you can move your camera and recompose the shot as you'd like it to look. By keeping that button held down, you've locked in that perfect exposure, and once everything looks good to you, just press the shutter button down the rest of the way and take the shot. You will have nailed the exposure and captured the scene perfectly.

Cutting Reflections in Water

If you're shooting streams or lakes, or really anything with water, there's a filter you're going to want to use that does something very important—it removes the reflection of the sky from the water and lets you see through the water. That way, things like rocks below the shore or in a stream, fish in a koi pond, etc., all suddenly appear crystal clear, and that can make for some very compelling images. The thing that surprises most folks is that it's a filter that most photographers use to get bluer skies—a circular polarizer. As I mentioned in part 1 of this book, a polarizer is indispensable for getting those blue skies, but it's just as important for this overlooked double-duty of cutting reflections. Here's how it works: screw the filter onto your lens, aim at the water in front of you, and then rotate the circular ring at the end of the filter, and as you do, you'll almost magically cut through the reflections and see right through the water, as seen on the right here. It's one of those things you really just have to try to appreciate it, but believe me— you'll love it.

For Landscapes, You Need a Clear Subject

LOCATION: BIG SUR, CALIFORNIA

One of the things that kills a lot of landscape shots is that there's no clear subject, and for a landscape shot to really work, you have to be able to look at it and explain what you shot in one simple sentence. It's a lighthouse. It's that seagull on the rocks. It's that old barn. It's the palm trees on the beach. If you can't explain your landscape shot in a short sentence like that, you don't know what the subject is, and if you don't know, people viewing your image won't know either, and if that happens, the photo just isn't working. Keep this in mind when you're composing your landscape shots, and ask yourself the question, "What's my subject?" If you can't come up with a solid answer immediately, it's time to recompose your shot and find a clear subject. It makes all the difference in the world.

Using Your LCD Monitor Outdoors

If it's bright outside, you're going to quickly run into one of the biggest challenges of shooting outdoors, and that is you can't see anything on your LCD monitor—the sunlight washes everything out. In fact, it's often so hard to see anything that you might as well turn off your monitor and save your battery, but then your LCD monitor becomes about useless. That's why I've fallen in love with the Hoodman HoodLoupe Professional. You wear this around your neck (when you're shooting outdoors), then you simply hold it up over your LCD monitor and its soft rubber enclosure blocks out the sun and gives you a crystal clear view of your monitor. I carry this with me to all my outdoor shoots, and after you use it even once, you won't want to be without it. (*Note:* Even though it's called a "loupe," it doesn't really magnify your image like a traditional loupe—it just blocks the sun out, but really, that's all we need.) It sells for around $80 at B&H Photo.

A Trick for Shooting Great Rainbows

©ISTOCKPHOTO/PAUL GIAMOU

Want to really bring out the vibrance and color of your shots that have a rainbow in them? Then use a circular polarizer (now we've got three reasons to have a polarizer: [1] bluer skies, [2] cutting the reflections in water, and [3] making your rainbows "pop!"). Just turn the circular end of the filter while you're aimed at the rainbow and stop when the colors look their most vibrant. Easy enough to do, and the results are worth it. Now, beyond that, there's a wonderful tip I learned from my buddy, and renowned landscape photographer, Bill Fortney. Bill says, "If you see a rainbow, drive like the devil until you find something interesting for the rainbow to come down in." He doesn't mean drive until you come to the end of the rainbow, or all you'll get is a shot of that pot of gold. Just drive until you can find a gorge, or a water source, or something—anything interesting—for it to end with. Do those two things and you'll wind up with a remarkable shot.

A Timesaving Pano Trick

When you come back in from your shoot, if your shoot included some panos, you're going to quickly find out one of the hidden challenges of shooting panos: finding them. For example, when you open your images in Adobe Photoshop Lightroom, or Adobe Bridge, or in iPhoto, etc., you're looking at thumbnails of perhaps hundreds of images from your shoot, and it's a bit of a challenge to figure out where your panos start and end. In fact, numerous times I've been looking through thumbnails from a shoot, and I look at a shot and think, "What was I thinking when I took this one?" Only to find out later it was one frame from a 10-frame pano. Worse yet, if I'm shooting on vacation, it might be a week or more before I get home to look at the images, and I completely forget that there's even a pano included in a particular shoot, because they just don't jump out at you. Luckily, there's a simple trick that makes finding your panos a two-second job: Before you shoot the first frame of your pano, hold your finger up in front of your lens and take a shot (as you see in the first frame above). Now start shooting your pano. Once you finish shooting the last shot of your pano, hold two fingers in front of the camera and take another shot (as seen in the last frame). Now, when you're looking at your photos in a photo browser and you see one finger in your shot, you know there's a pano starting there. So, select all the photos that appear between your one-finger shot and your two-finger shot—that's your pano. Open those in Photoshop and let it stitch them together for you (we looked at this in Part 1 of this book series).

The Trick for Using a Fisheye Lens

Fisheye lenses are making a big comeback, and they actually can be very cool for a variety of landscape shots—you just don't want your final image to look rounded and distorted, like many fisheye shots you see. You only want a very wide field of view. The trick to doing that is to simply keep the horizon line in the center of your image. This limits the amount of fisheye-like distortion and makes a huge difference in the final look. The best way to test this is to actually tip your camera downward, then back up toward the sky, all while looking through the viewfinder. You'll see the edges of your image distort as you move up and down (as seen in the top image), but you'll notice that as your horizon line gets centered in the image, the fisheye distortion is at its very minimum (like in the bottom image), and it just looks like a really, really wide-angle lens. Give it a try—you'll see what I mean (by the way, this is the only time you really want the horizon line in the center of your image, as you learned in part 1 of this book).

When to Shoot Streams

LOCATION: GLACIER NATIONAL PARK, MONTANA

If it's a gray, cloudy, rainy day (I don't mean pouring rain—a light drizzle or soft rain), then head to a local stream, because you're about to make some magic. The overcast, cloudy, rainy sky does two things that make it ideal for shooting streams: (1) it makes the rocks, leaves, and everything sticking out of the stream nice and wet, which looks great in stream photographs, and (2) it makes the scene much darker (and the darker it is while still daylight, the better), which lets you use long shutter speeds, and it's those longer shutter speeds that give the stream that wonderful silky-water effect. Try shooting in aperture priority mode, and set your aperture (f-stop) to f/22 (or a higher number if your lens has it). With this darker sky, f/22 will leave your shutter open long enough to give you that silky-water look. The shot above was taken on a drizzly afternoon where there was literally nothing else to shoot, and shooting at f/22 in the forest, under that dark, cloudy sky, left my shutter open for 13 seconds (in aperture priority mode, you pick the f-stop and then your camera will leave the shutter open for however long it takes to get the right expo-sure—in this case, I stood there in the gentle rain for 13 seconds. How do you like the way that phrase "gentle rain" made the experience sound? Actually, I was cold and wet, but cold, annoying rain just doesn't paint a pretty picture—but the camera sure captured one).

Don't Stop Shooting at Sunset

LOCATION: SAND HARBOR STATE PARK, LAKE TAHOE, NEVADA

More and more people have totally embraced the golden rule of landscape photography, which is to only shoot when that wonderful, magical light is available, and that only
happens just before and during dawn, and just before and during sunset. However, a lot
of folks pack up their gear just a few minutes after the sun has gone down, and the sad
part is, they're about to miss what is often the most magical light of all. Around 20 to 30
minutes after sunset, sometimes the clouds turn bright orange, or deep red, or purple, or
if you're lucky, a combination of all three, and some of my all-time best shots have been
taken after everyone else has gone to dinner. Wait even longer (30 to 45 minutes or more
after sunset), and the sky will often turn a vibrant, deep blue (not black, like the night—
I'm talking blue—and it happens right before night). It only lasts for a few minutes (10 or
12 minutes usually), but what wonderful twilight photos you can get then. Try this blue
twilight-hour shooting when you have a cityscape, or bridge, or other lit object in the
background—it makes for a wonderful scene.

REMEMBER, YOUR CAMERA HAS SIMILAR SETTINGS

If I'm talking about white balance, and I'm showing the Canon white balance menu, but
you're not shooting with a Canon, simply breathe deeply and say to yourself, "It's okay,
my [insert your camera name here] also has a white balance setting and it works pretty
much like this one." Remember, it's about choosing the right white balance, not exactly
which buttons to push on your camera.

How to Shoot Fog

LOCATION: GREAT SMOKY MOUNTAINS NATIONAL PARK, TENNESSEE

I love the look of fog or mist in images. To me, it adds mystery and intrigue to the scene, but one unfortunate side effect is that it also is very hard for your camera's built-in light meter to read properly, so you get what you're seeing with your naked eye. Of course, like so many things, there's a trick of the trade that helps you get a good exposure that keeps that foggy look. Start by aiming at the fog itself, and then hold your shutter button halfway down (which tells your camera to take a reading of that area). Now, go to your camera's exposure compensation control and increase the amount of exposure by one stop (basically, what you're doing is disagreeing with what the camera read for the fog, and overriding it by increasing the exposure by one stop). On Nikon cameras, you do this by holding down the exposure compensation button on the top right of the camera (just behind the shutter button), and while you're holding that button down, turn the command dial on the top back of the camera to the right until you see +1 in your camera's viewfinder. On Canon cameras, you'll set the shooting mode to anything but manual, and then you'll spin the quick control dial (the big one on the back of the camera) to the right until you see +1 in the camera's viewfinder. Just one reminder: when you're done shooting your fog shots, set your exposure compensation back to zero, or you'll be shooting the rest of the day with every shot overexposed by one stop.

Getting Shots of Lightning (Manually)

©ISTOCKPHOTO/CLINT SPENCER

Shots of lightning can be very dramatic, because usually we only see lightning for a fraction of a second. If you can freeze that moment, it makes for a fascinating photo, but like many landscape shots, it requires a certain amount of timing (and luck). Now, before I share how to capture lightning with your camera, I want to make sure you don't capture lightning with your body. Don't stand in the rain, or under a tree, etc. Shoot from a very safe distance (because lightning will see you as a portable lightning rod) and exercise the same caution you would if you weren't a distracted photographer. Now, on to the technique. First, put your camera on a tripod (this is a must). Then, set your mode to bulb (the B setting on some cameras), which leaves the camera's shutter open for as long as you hold down the shutter button. Now, you can't actually press the button on your camera—for this to work properly you need to use either a shutter release cable (a cable that attaches to your camera with a shutter button you hold in your hand) or a wireless shutter release (you can find these for most camera makes and models at B&H Photo). The reason is: any minor vibration while your shutter is open, and the shot will be so blurry, it will be unusable. So, set up on a tripod, compose your shot (aim your camera in an area where you've been seeing lightning), use f/8 as a starting place, make sure your camera is set to bulb mode, then when you see a strike of lightning, press-and-hold the shutter release cable (or wireless) shutter button down and when you see a second strike, wait just a moment and then release the shutter button. It may take you a few tries at first, but you'll get it (hopefully the shot, not the lightning itself).

Getting Shots of Lightning (Automatically)

©ISTOCKPHOTO/CLINT SPENCER

If you try some lightning shots and fall in love with this type of photography, you might want to consider buying a Lightning Trigger (they're not cheap—so make sure you're truly "in love" first). This unit sits on your camera and it has a sensor that detects the bright flash of light from lightning, so it opens the shutter at exactly the right moment and gets the shot for you. In fact, you can pretty much set up your camera, set your camera to shutter priority mode (with your shutter speed anywhere from ⅛ to ¼ of a second), aim in the right direction, sit back with a cool drink, and wait for the magic to happen, knowing that your camera is doing all the hard work for you. Later, when you're showing off your amazing work, there is no obligation (from the manufacturer's point of view) for you to tell the people viewing your work that you used a Lightning Trigger. Hey, it's just another tool in your bag of tricks. Go to www.lightningtrigger.com for a model that works with most cameras (it runs around $329 direct from the manufacturer. Hey, I told you it wasn't cheap).

Where to Focus for Landscape Shots

LOCATION: LAKE LOUISE, BANFF NATIONAL PARK, ALBERTA, CANADA

When you're taking a landscape shot, where do you focus your camera's focal point (that red dot in the center of your viewfinder. Well, its default spot is in the center, but you can move that spot, so if you moved yours, get it back to the middle for this)? With landscape shots, the rule is: you want to focus about one-third of the way into the image. This gives you the widest possible range of focus throughout the image. Also, another trick you can use is to shoot big, sweeping landscape shots at f/22, which gives you the most focus from front to back in your shot.

GETTING THE CLEAREST LANDSCAPES POSSIBLE

Have you ever seen a landscape photo that just has incredible clarity throughout the image? I'm not talking about sharpness—I'm talking clarity (like a total lack of haze, or fog, or any other atmospheric effect). Well, there's a technique for getting that amazing clarity, and it's simple: shoot in winter. The air is the clearest during winter time, and it's the perfect time of year to get those amazingly clear shots that you just can't get any other time of year.

Find the Great Light First

LOCATION: SAND HARBOR STATE PARK, LAKE TAHOE, NEVADA

A few years ago, my friend, and landscape photography hero, Bill Fortney said some-thing that really had an impact on my photography and I'm going to pass it on to you. Bill feels that the single most important thing in a shot of any kind is the quality of light, and that the quality of light is so important that he'll search for great light first, and then once he finds that great light, he'll find a subject—something or somebody to shoot in that wonderful light. Essentially, if the light is great, you'll find a subject, but if you've found a great subject, you have to be very, very lucky for great light to just magically appear. In short: "It's all about the light." Once you get that, everything else falls into place. It's deeper than it sounds.

How to Shoot on a Gray, Overcast Day

LOCATION: DINGLE PENINSULA, IRELAND

This one might sound kind of obvious when I say it, but I can't tell you how many times I've been out shooting with a group and one or more people in the group has come up and said, "Well, the sky is totally messing up our shoot today." While a gray sky definitely stinks, there is something you can employ for shooting on gray-sky days, and that is simply to compose so little (like the shot you see here) or literally none of that gray sky winds up in your shots. If you go into the shoot knowing that you're going to do your best to avoid seeing much of the sky in any of your shots, you can then get all of the benefits that a gray sky usually brings, which are colors that are actually fairly saturated and softer shadows throughout your images. You probably won't be able to fully eliminate the sky from your photos, so just compose your shots so the amount of sky you do see is kept to a minimum. This simple technique has saved many a landscape shoot.

A Trick for Great-Looking Flower Shots

Want a great quick trick for some interesting-looking flower shots? Get down low, and shoot the flowers so they're backlit, with the sun behind them. The sunlight shining through the translucent petals creates a beautiful effect, and this is a popular trick employed by serious flower shooters that works every time. Don't forget to get down low (so low that you're either shooting straight on or up at the flowers) to get the most from this effect.

The Full-Frame Camera Advantage

The vast majority of today's digital cameras have a built-in magnification factor because of the size of the sensors in the camera. For example, most Nikon cameras have a 1.4x magnification factor, and what that means is if you put a 100mm lens on a Nikon digital camera (like a D3200, D5200, or D7100), that 100mm lens becomes a 140mm lens because of the sensor's magnification factor. Most Canon cameras have a 1.6x magnification (like the Rebel T3i, Rebel T5i, 60D, 70D, and 7D), which makes a 200mm lens more like a 320mm lens. Many sports shooters, birders, and a host of other photographers who routinely use zoom and telephoto lenses love this added reach from digital sensors, but when it comes to the wide-angle lenses landscape photographers use, it can somewhat work against us. For example, a 12mm wide-angle Nikon lens becomes a less-wide 16mm lens. For Canon shooters, a 14mm wide-angle lens becomes a 22mm equivalent. That's why some landscape photographers are drooling over the full-frame digital cameras, like Nikon's D4 or Canon's 6D (shown above), both of which are full-frame, and when you put a 12mm on the Nikon, it's that same, beautifully wide 12mm aspect ratio we used to enjoy back in the film days. When you put a 14mm on a Canon 6D, it's the same thing—a real 14mm with no extra magnification. I'm not saying you need to switch, or that you bought the wrong camera, I just want you to know what all the fuss is about for landscape photographers and other people who "go wide."

The Seven Deadly Sins of Landscape Photography

LOCATION: GLACIER NATIONAL PARK, MONTANA

Okay, in this chapter (and in part 1 of this book series), I've talked a lot about the things you need to do to make great landscape photos, but I haven't talked a whole lot about what to avoid when taking landscape shots. That's why in this new edition of the book I have included what I call "The Seven Deadly Sins of Landscape Photography," and one more I threw in just for good measure, but that last line isn't part of the official name because that would be really clunky. By the way, the shot you see above was taken in Glacier National Park in Montana (which is one of our largest national parks, spanning 1,013,322 acres) during a workshop I taught there with renowned landscape photographer Bill Fortney. Bill, who not coincidentally is one of but a handful of working photographers who happen to know the precise GPS location from which you can actually photograph this giant mono- lithic number seven (which soars more than 212 feet high at its peak), would be cringing right now if he read this because he would know that I obviously stuck that big seven there in Photoshop, after the fact (or he'd have a big seven in his shot, as well, which I'm pretty certain he does not). Nevertheless, this all makes a great (okay, decent) gateway to this new addition to the landscape chapter. If you can live your life avoiding these seven perilous pitfalls, your landscape shots will be blessed with the magical kiss of first morning light (not really, but they will certainly look a whole lot better).

Landscape Sin #1: Choppy Water

LOCATION: LAKE LOUISE, BANFF NATIONAL PARK, ALBERTA, CANADA

When we're shooting a lake or a cozy harbor, what we're looking for is that still, glassy water that creates a beautiful reflection. So, if you hike up to that beautiful lake with the snow-capped mountains off in the distance, but it's windy out that day and the lake looks more like the ocean…just keep walking. That's right, keep walking back to your car, drive back to your hotel, and try again the next morning at dawn. Dawn is your absolute best chance for having calm, still water (by mid-morning it's usually too late), and it's worth getting up early for (not to mention the quality of the light), because choppy water is instant death to lake and harbor shots. By the way, that telephone pole lookin' log there on the left isn't helping this photo much either.

Landscape Sin #2: Frozen Water in Waterfalls

LOCATION: NEAR HILO, ISLAND OF HAWAII, HAWAII

For a pro look to your stream and waterfall shots, you're looking for that smooth, silky water—the silkier, the better—and that means you have to keep your shutter open for a long time (the longer it's open, the smoother your water will be. See page 115). We're talking 30 seconds to 2 minutes here, and if you're snapping stream or waterfall photos in broad daylight, your shutter speed is going to be around $^1/_{1000}$ of a second at the minimum, but more likely $^1/_{2000}$ of a second or higher. This means two things: (1) frozen water, and (2) an amateurish looking shot. Don't let this happen to you.

Landscape Sin #3: Bald, Cloudless Skies

LOCATION: GREAT SMOKY MOUNTAINS NATIONAL PARK, TENNESSEE

Most people find clouds beautiful (I sure do), but when it comes to landscape photography, they're not just there to be pretty. They are there to hold the amazing colors of a sunrise or sunset, and without clouds, you get…well…pretty much what you see here—a whole lotta nuthin'. Now, picture this same shot with just an amazing sky of really interesting clouds that are red, pink, and purple. Then, look back at this one. See what I mean? So, even though you did the right thing by getting up early for the great light, and you got in place and were ready to shoot before dawn, and you were on a sturdy tripod, with a cable release, and you had a wide-angle lens on your camera, and you were at f/22, and you were at the top of a really cool ridge of mountains, if the clouds don't show, you won't look like a pro. Mother Nature is totally in charge of this one, and sometimes she delivers a spectacular cloud formation that makes you look like a star because all you have to do is literally press the shutter button, and sometimes she gives you squat! She's finicky that way.

Landscape Sin #4: Harsh, Midday Sun

LOCATION: DOUBLE ARCH, ARCHES NATIONAL PARK, UTAH

This shot really has it all. Sure, it has that trademark harsh, dried-out, awful, soul-sapping, direct midday sun look to it (even though it was actually shot around 10:20 a.m., so the light will actually get worse as the day goes on). But, it also has some bonus features, like an ugly dead tree, a bald, cloudless sky, and junk coming into the frame from the edges. (I ought to win some sort of bad light award for this one.) So, if you look around and the light on your landscape looks anything like this, you know one thing: you're in the wrong place at the wrong time. You should be at breakfast, back in your hotel taking a nap, feeding a gopher the contents of your purse, whittling a scale model of the U.S. Capitol building out of a dead tree branch, anything other than actually taking a photo. This light was designed to punish nature and the efforts of anyone who holds up a camera and aims it at any landscape.

Landscape Sin #5: A Crooked Horizon Line

LOCATION: CADILLAC MOUNTAIN, ACADIA NATIONAL PARK, MAINE

If there is one thing that drives people crazy when they look at a photo, it's a crooked horizon line. What's even worse, a lot of times people looking at an image with a crooked horizon line will tell you there's "just something about it that doesn't feel right," even if they don't realize the problem is the horizon line (it's easy to get distracted by beautiful colors and cool clouds, but the viewer will still perceive that something is wrong with the image, even if they can't articulate exactly what it is). Since just about every post-processing program out there has some sort of built-in straightening, there's no excuse for having a crooked horizon line. Hey, while we're here, although these clouds aren't spectacular or epic by any means, imagine this same shot without them, and instead you have a bald, empty sky. Really makes a difference, doesn't it?

Landscape Sin #6: Distracting Junk Near Edge

LOCATION: BIG SUR, CALIFORNIA

This one is particularly deadly because it's so easy to miss. When I teach landscape photo workshops, we do a class critique of shots from the participants in the workshop (the person who took the image always remains anonymous during the critique, unless we all really love the shot, then they usually stand up and shout, "Hey, I took that!"). Anyway, one thing that always stands out as a spoiler of some otherwise great images is that the image has a distracting element (also known as "distracting junk") in the photo. It can be a road sign, some seaweed on the beach, an empty beer can, some telephone wires, or quite often it's a tree branch extending into the photo. I've always felt that if it doesn't add to the photo, it takes away from it. There are three different ways you can deal with this "junk" that creeps into your photos: (1) Compose around it. When you're shooting, be very aware of what's in your shot, especially around the edges (we actually refer to this act of checking the outside edges of your frame as "border patrol"). Check all four sides of the frame (top, left side, right side, and bottom) for anything that you'll wish later wasn't there, and if you see something, change your composition to eliminate it. (2) Physically remove the distracting element (as long as you're not a photojournalist). If there's a beer can, a twig, some trash, etc., pick it up and move it out of the frame (be careful not to damage anything in nature—period!). Or, (3) remove it later in Photoshop or Lightroom, using the Healing Brush tool, the Patch tool, the Clone Stamp tool, or the Spot Removal tool. I've done a quick video clip for readers of this book to show you how to use these tools, and you can watch it at **http://kelbytraining.com/books/digphotogv2**.

Landscape Sin #7: No Foreground Object

LOCATION: LAKE LOUISE, BANFF NATIONAL PARK, ALBERTA, CANADA

If your shot doesn't have a strong foreground element, it's pretty much sunk. That's because one of the basics of landscape composition is that for a landscape shot to really work, it has to have three things: (1) something strong in the foreground, (2) an obvious middle ground, and (3) the background. This one has two out of three. It has a middle ground (the lake and the mountain). It has a background (the sky behind the mountains, although some might argue that the mountain and the sky are background elements, but it doesn't really matter because neither one of those is the problem here). What's missing is the strong foreground element, which is why this image looks so flat. If there were some large rocks at the bottom of the frame, or the tip of a canoe, or the shore, or a dock, or anything to show the depth of the image and lead the viewer into it, this shot would then have all three elements. It's kind of like a novel. If you skip the first few chapters and then jump in and start reading, you'll be missing key parts of the book, and you won't enjoy it nearly as much. You'll know you're missing something. Landscape photos are the same way—you shouldn't jump-in in the middle of the photo (or, in this case, the middle of the lake). You should start in the foreground and lead the viewer's eye throughout to the background. It's what gives landscape photos real depth and that big, epic feel. Don't start your photo in the middle of the lake, or the middle of the ocean, or in a flat, open desert. Find some object to include in the foreground and your composition will be much stronger.

And...Dead Trees and Tree Stumps...And...

LOCATION: MAUI, HAWAII

Okay, I said there were just seven, but since I had this extra page, I thought I'd add a couple more in. They're not nearly as deadly, but still worth avoiding like a festering boil. I'm just going to rapid-fire these off: Dead trees and tree stumps. I'm begging you, stop trying to make a good picture of these. And, no, converting your image to black and white won't help. There are beautiful living things found all over in nature. Stop shooting dead ones. Next, don't have out-of-focus things in your foreground. Not tree branches, or railroad crossing signs, or a big blurry rock. It's distracting to the viewer, who is programmed to try to focus on whatever is closest to them. Also, stop shooting really boring stuff just because you're standing in front of it. If you're looking at a scene and you realize that there's no chance anyone is going to look at the photo you're about to take and say, "Wow!" then here's what you do: move someplace else. It's like Joe McNally says, "If you want to take more interesting photos, stand in front of more interesting things." If you're standing in front of those ugly dead trees above, keep moving. Here's another: if you see a flat gray sky, avoid it like the plague. Another is if you're processing an HDR shot, or if you're adding tonal effects with a plug-in, keep this in mind: Clouds aren't black. They also don't have drop shadows or glows around them. Although you see incredibly vibrant colors in nature, don't make them all appear in your photo at once. Go easy on the saturation. Okay, now ya know, so there are no excuses for breaking the "Seven Deadly Sins."

SHUTTER SPEED: 1/80 SEC   F-STOP: F/6.3   ISO: 100   FOCAL LENGTH: 82mm | PHOTOGRAPHER: SCOTT KELBY

Chapter Five

Shooting Weddings Like a Pro

How to Get Professional Results from Your Next Shoot

Shooting a wedding is tricky business, and if you have friends (and they know you have a nice camera), it's only a matter of time before you're standing in a church yelling things like, "Okay, next I need the groom's grandmother and grandfather." Once you've said that line aloud in a church, you are officially ordained as a temporary wedding photographer. Now, just because you took the gig for free, as a favor to that guy you know over in accounting, don't think for a minute that the bride is expecting anything less than absolute pro-quality images. Worse yet, the nicer gear you have, the better they expect those images to be, and if, up until this day, you've been a sports shooter or a landscape photographer, all that goes out the window, because today you are a wedding photographer, which is arguably the single hardest photography job in the known world. The reason is simple: there is no reshoot. This particular wedding, the one you are responsible for shooting, only happens once. There is no, "Oh, my camera broke" or "I didn't bring enough memory cards" or "I forgot my charger for my flash," because if the bride hears anything even approaching one of those excuses, she will take her bare hands and squeeze your neck until either your lifeless body falls to the floor like a wet bag of cement, or a pack of AAA alkaline batteries pops out of you like a Pez dispenser. That's because regardless of whether you're getting paid or not, she has waited, dreamed about, meticulously planned, agonized over, and micro-managed this special day to death, and if you miss any one of those critical moments (the ring, kissing the bride, walking down the aisle as man and wife for the first time, cutting the cake, the first dance, etc.), then it's time for you to die. That's why this chapter is all about one thing: increasing your life expectancy.

Create a Shot List

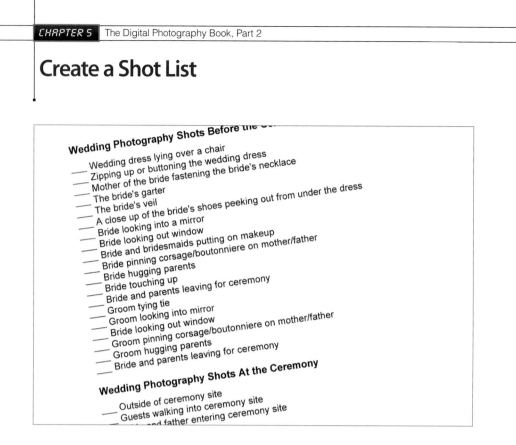

Wedding Photography Shots Before the Ce...

____ Wedding dress lying over a chair
____ Zipping up or buttoning the wedding dress
____ Mother of the bride fastening the bride's necklace
____ The bride's garter
____ The bride's veil
____ A close up of the bride's shoes peeking out from under the dress
____ Bride looking into a mirror
____ Bride looking out window
____ Bride and bridesmaids putting on makeup
____ Bride pinning corsage/boutonniere on mother/father
____ Bride hugging parents
____ Bride touching up
____ Bride and parents leaving for ceremony
____ Groom tying tie
____ Groom looking into mirror
____ Bride looking out window
____ Groom pinning corsage/boutonniere on mother/father
____ Groom hugging parents
____ Bride and parents leaving for ceremony

Wedding Photography Shots At the Ceremony

____ Outside of ceremony site
____ Guests walking into ceremony site
____ ...and father entering ceremony site

Before you even leave your office to head to the wedding, you should put together a shot list of photos you'll need to take for the wedding album, prints, etc. There are no redos at weddings, so you'd better be sure you leave with a list in hand of which shots you need, from bride and groom formals, to detail shots (the invitations, the rings, the bouquet, the bride's shoes, etc.), to reception shots like cutting the cake, receiving lines, place cards, and more. Without a written shot list, you're winging it, and it's almost an absolute lock that you'll miss one or more critical shots that your clients (the bride and groom) are going to expect to be in their album, so don't take a chance—this little bit of preparation can make a world of difference. Luckily, you can find wedding photography shot lists online for free at places like http://bit.ly/aboutshotlist or this article and shot list from Amazon.com at http://bit.ly/amazonshotlist (actually, there are literally hundreds of different shot lists available for downloading—just Google "wedding shot list" and you'll have a wide range of choices). Find a shot list that makes sense to you, and although you can get creative and do far beyond what it suggests, at least you'll have the most critical shots covered. Also, make sure you talk to the bride and groom before you finalize your shot list to ensure the specific shots they want are included (they may want shots with old friends from high school or college, or a special relative, and the only way to find out about these is to talk with the bride and groom in advance).

Have Backups for Everything!

Two Camera Bodies

Extra Flash Batteries

Extra Camera Batteries

Backup Flash

If anything can go wrong at the wedding you're shooting, it will. That's why the pros always take backups for everything, because there are no retakes, no redos, no "do overs." Go through each piece of your gear and ask yourself what you would do if it wound up missing or broke. I can tell you this, at the very minimum you need to have two camera bodies—one main and one backup (a friend of mine was shooting a wedding, his camera slipped out of his hands, and the shoot was over. He was lucky enough to have a friend race him a replacement camera, but if his friend wasn't available, or was shooting a wedding himself that day, or was at the movies, etc., he probably would have ended up in court). You also need backup batteries for your flash, and even a backup flash unit. You need extra memory cards and a backup lens (I recently saw a photographer pick up his camera bag, which he thought was zipped, and we all cringed at the sound of breaking glass). Also, don't forget to bring backup batteries for both of your cameras. It comes down to this: you don't want to put yourself in a situation where one piece of equipment fails, one piece gets dropped, or your battery dies, and your job is in jeopardy (not to mention the loss of future wedding gigs from the fallout of having a large public event like a wedding day shoot go belly up).

Silencing Your Camera's Beep

The last thing the wedding couple (or the clergy, or the guests) wants to hear during the ceremony is the distracting sound of your camera beeping as it locks focus. Before the wedding begins, go to your camera's menu and disable the audible beep sound. From that point on, use the focus symbol that appears in your camera's viewfinder to let you know when the autofocus has locked on. Once the ceremony is over, you can always switch back.

Backlighting Your Bride

A popular effect with wedding photographers is to backlight the bride—where a bright light rims the outline of the bride—and then add in just a little bit of flash to light the front of the bride, so she's not a silhouette (as shown above). This takes two flash units: one in front of the bride (in this case, I used an off-camera flash on a light stand, positioned to the left of the camera at a 45° angle), and a second flash on a light stand behind the bride (here, it was behind and to the right, just out of the frame). The flash of light from the front flash triggers the second flash behind the bride. The key is to make sure the flash behind the bride is much brighter than the flash in front of the bride (in the shot above, I lowered the power of the front flash as low as I could, but kept it bright enough so it would still trigger the flash behind her. It took a couple of test flashes to find out just how low that front flash could go). Another nice look (which is very dramatic) is to go ahead and let her just be lit with a flash behind her, then turn the flash in front off, so she actually is mostly a silhouette. If you do this, you'll have to set your front flash so it doesn't fire the full flash, but only a very low light pulse—just enough to trigger the wireless flash behind her, but so it doesn't throw any measurable light on the bride (Nikon's DSLRs with pop-up flash have this feature built in).

Don't Changes Lenses, Change Cameras

Once a wedding starts, things happen very quickly and you're not going to have a lot of chances (read as: none) to change lenses. So, if you're shooting with your zoom lens, and you suddenly need to switch to a wide angle, take a tip from professional sports shooters and don't switch lenses—switch camera bodies instead. That's right—keep two camera bodies around your neck (or one around your neck, one in your hand), and put a wide-angle lens on one body, and a zoom lens on the other. That way, switching lenses takes two seconds, not two minutes, and because of that, now you "get the shot."

ANOTHER TWO-CAMERA STRATEGY

Besides the zoom and wide-angle double-camera technique above, here's another one to consider: have one camera with a flash mounted on your hot shoe for when you need flash, and have your second camera with a really fast lens, like a 50mm f/1.8 or f/1.4 (see page 145) for when you can't use flash (or don't want to use it), so you can capture those intimate moments without being obtrusive.

Bring a Stepladder for a Higher Vantage Point

At weddings, you're going to be posing and shooting large groups (for your formals), and one trick the pros use is to carry a small, lightweight, collapsible aluminum ladder, like the Conair Travel Smart LadderKart, which doubles as a hand truck to help you move your gear (when you're not standing on it). It holds up to 300 lbs., and sells for around $61, but I've found other similar ladders online, as well. Being able to shoot the formal group portraits from a higher angle is a big help, because it enables you to see more faces and arrange your groups more easily. Also, it's great for shots during the reception, where a higher angle gives you a better view of the bride and groom on the crowded dance floor. Actually, you can put it to use anytime you want a different perspective, plus you can even use it as a posing stool in a pinch. You'll find this to be an indispensable tool (even if you only wind up using it for lugging your gear).

Why You Want a Second Shooter

Many pro wedding photographers bring a second shooter to their jobs (sometimes even a third shooter) as an insurance policy to make sure they cover all the most important shots, and the bigger the wedding, the more you need a second shooter. After all, you can't be everywhere, and if any little thing goes wrong (equipmentwise or otherwise), there's someone else to either keep shooting, or to deal with the problem so you can keep shooting. This second shooter also usually acts as an assistant, and in the fast pace of a wedding, they can be an absolute lifesaver. But, beyond that, the second shooter may (will) have a different style than you and can bring a different dimension (they can shoot zoom while you're shooting wide), a different camera angle, they can shoot from a different location in the church and reception hall, plus there's a good chance that if you missed "the shot," your second shooter will have gotten it (or vice versa).

When to Shoot in RAW

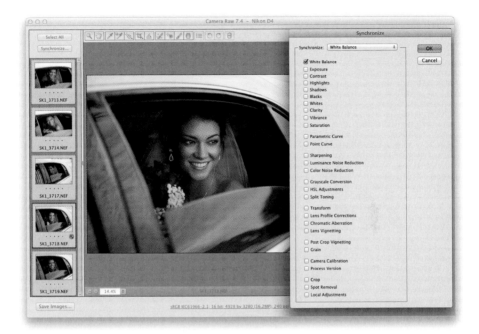

Although many wedding photographers choose to shoot exclusively in JPEG mode, when you get in a tricky lighting situation, your Get Out of Jail Free card is to switch to RAW mode. Here's why: when you shoot in JPEG mode, the white balance you set in the camera is embedded into the file. If you set it wrong (which can happen in tricky lighting situations), you've got a color correction nightmare. However, when you shoot in RAW mode, you have the option of changing the white balance to any one of the same white balance settings you could have chosen in the camera itself. Best of all, once you've fixed the white balance for one photo, you can apply that change to all the other images at once. If you use Adobe Photoshop, here's how: (1) Select all the RAW photos you want to adjust and open them in Photoshop's Camera Raw (it will open all your selected photos at once). (2) Choose the White Balance setting from the pop-up menu. (3) Click the Select All button at the top left. (4) Click the Synchronize button, and when the dialog appears, choose White Balance from the pop-up menu at the top, then click OK. Now the white balance you chose for the current RAW photo will be applied to all your other open RAW photos. If you use Adobe Lightroom, select the photos you want to adjust, then go to the Develop module and choose your new white balance. Click the Copy button on the bottom left. When the dialog appears, click the Check None button, turn on just the checkbox for White Balance, then click Copy. Now click the Paste button to paste that white balance setting to all your other selected photos. Also, if you want the best of both worlds, set your camera to Raw + JPEG, which captures a RAW image and a JPEG version at the same time.

Where to Aim Your Flash

Another one of the tricks the pros use to get just that little extra bit of light into their wedding photos (even ones taken in daylight) is to aim their flash head straight upward (as shown here). This works best if you're not standing too far from your subjects, and even if there's no ceiling to bounce the light from the flash off of, it still sends that little bit of light forward to light the face. This helps in adding catch lights in the eyes, but it does it without creating that "too much flash" look. To help make sure those catch lights appear, pull up your flash's bounce card to help direct more of that straight-up light forward (you can see the white bounce card pulled up in the photo above). So, if you've got a nice white ceiling to let the light from your flash bounce off of—great (but keep that bounce card extended either way). If not, still keep that flash aimed straight up most of the time, especially if there's already some existing room light, as the light from your flash will be subtle enough to nicely blend in.

Shoot in Lower Light Without Raising Your ISO

Since you'll be shooting on a regular basis in the low lighting of a church, there's a tool many of the top pros use that lets them get away with shooting perfectly exposed, sharp, handheld shots without using flash, or without pumping their ISO up to 1200. They buy an inexpensive 50mm f/1.8 lens (right around $100), or better yet, a 50mm f/1.4 lens (like the one shown above, which goes for around $469). These super-fast lenses let you shoot handheld in really low light, and you won't find a wedding pro that has one who doesn't swear by it. They're lightweight, surprisingly crisp (considering their low cost), and another tool in your bag of tricks to make sure you get the most important shots.

CHARGE EVERYTHING THE DAY BEFORE THE WEDDING

The day before the wedding, make sure you charge everything—including your cameras (both bodies). Make sure you have fresh batteries in all your flash units. If you're taking your laptop, make sure its batteries are charged. And just make certain that if a piece of your equipment has a battery, it's a fresh battery, or a freshly charged battery. Also, it's not a bad idea to fill your car up with gas now, too.

A Recipe for Balanced Flash in Church

When you're shooting the formals in the church (before or after the ceremony), here is a recipe you can use to get a natural-looking light balance between your flash and the available light in the church: set your ISO to 800, set your shutter speed to ¹⁄₆₀ of a second, and set your f-stop to f/5.6, or a lower number if possible (like f/4, f/3.5, or even f/2.8). By using a relatively low shutter speed like ¹⁄₆₀ of a second, it's a slow enough speed that your camera can properly expose the background (you see it lit with the available light in the room), and then your flash comes in to freeze the action. Once you've got those two settings in place, now all you have to do is take a test shot with your flash, and if it over-powers the room light (the background looks black), then lower the brightness (power) of your flash unit, so although your subject will be mostly lit with flash, you'll still see some of the natural light in the church. This gives a nice balance between the natural light (which should be around 30% to 35% of the light in the photo) and your flash (which should be 65% to 70% of the light).

Compose to Include the Church

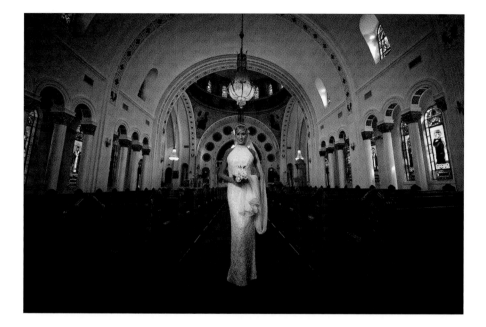

This is one of many tricks I learned from my friend, and wedding photography guru, David Ziser (a master wedding photographer and brilliant teacher): compose a decent number of the formal bride and groom portraits to include a lot of the interior of the church (as shown above). It's important to brides to see the church where the ceremony took place, and by composing it into the formals, it really gives the shots a sense of place (after all, if you compose them so tight that you don't see the church, you might as well have taken them the day before in the studio).

Tip for Posing the Bride

Another tip I picked up from David Ziser is a posing tip for formal shots of the bride that lowers the shoulder that's farthest from your light source, which creates a flattering diagonal line between her shoulders. To do this, have the bride stand with her feet in a staggered V-shape (as shown above), and then have her shift her weight to her back foot, which creates a much more dynamic look for your pose.

DEALING WITH THE "UNOFFICIAL" WEDDING SHOOTERS

When you're hired as the official wedding photographer, these days you're probably going to have to deal with a number of "unofficial" photographers (friends of the bride/groom with digital SLRs) who want to shoot over your shoulder while you're doing the formals. Well-known photographer and author Derrick Story shared a tip with me that might help give you some breathing room so you can get your job done. Derrick goes over to the unofficial shooters and asks that they let him get his job done first, then he'll hold the group in place for a few a moments so they can step in and get their shots. He finds that this usually does the trick, and they stay out of his hair while he's getting the formals taken care of.

Keeping Detail in the Bridal Gown

Since most bridal gowns are white, we have to be careful how we position the bride when shooting the formal bridal portraits, so we don't blow out the highlights on the gown and lose all the important detail of the dress (and that detail is very important to the bride). David Ziser taught me a great trick that works every time for keeping this critical detail, and it has to do with how you position the bride. You want the light from your flash (or from a window, if you're using window light) to cross the dress (so it accentuates the shadows and brings out detail), not hit it straight on and blow everything out. The easiest way to do this is simply to position your bride so her shoulder that is closest to the light source is angled toward the light source. That's it. This is important because if the shoulder closest to the light isn't in front, the flash hits the gown straight on and you lose the shadows and the detail. So, just make sure to angle the bride so her shoulder that's closest to the light is angled toward the light (as shown here, where you can see by looking at the bride, the flash is to the left of my camera, because she's much brighter on that side. The shoulder closest to the camera is aiming toward the light). Easy enough.

Getting More Flashes Per Wedding

Your flash is going to get a workout at a wedding, and you're going to be stopping to pop in fresh batteries on a pretty regular basis. Batteries must sense fear, because they always seem to die during absolutely critical moments in the wedding, so you want to be changing batteries as little as possible. (Plus, as your batteries start to wear down, it starts to take longer and longer for your flash to recycle so it's ready to fire again.) That's why many pros use a small external battery pack to double how long they can shoot with flash before having to change batteries. Better yet, it greatly cuts the recycle time between flashes. These packs are a little larger than a deck of cards, and run on six or eight AA batteries (depending on the model). You just connect the pack's cable to your flash, pop the pack into your shirt or suit pocket, and fire away. If you don't have a battery pack and your battery's getting low, try shooting at a higher ISO—it cuts the flash output and extends your battery life considerably.

Scott's Gear Finder

Canon Compact Battery Pack CP-E4 (around $150)

Nikon SD-9 High Performance Battery Pack (around $200)

Quantum Slim & Compact Turbo Battery Packs (around $350 and up)

How to Lessen Noise in Your Photos

When you raise the ISO on your camera (so you can shoot in lower light), there is a trade-off, and that is you increase the amount of noise (grain) in your shots. Depending on the make and model of your camera, this noise might be acceptable or it might be so visible that it kind of ruins the shot. If you have Photoshop CS5 or later or Lightroom 3 or later, they all have excellent built-in noise reduction (I used to have to use a plug-in for reducing noise, but not anymore). Here's what you do: Just open your noisy image in Camera Raw (or Lightroom's Develop module) and zoom in really tight, so you can see the noise (usually lurking in the shadows). Click on the Detail icon (panel) to get to the Noise Reduction controls, and then just use the Color slider to remove the color noise (those red, green, and blue color spots) and the Luminance slider to remove the luminance noise (those grainy-looking gray spots).

A TIP FOR OUTDOOR WEDDINGS

If you go a day early to scope out the location where you'll be shooting an outdoor wedding, make sure you're there at the exact same time of day that you'll be actually shooting the wedding. That way, you can see what the real lighting conditions will be when you're shooting the "real thing."

Tips for Shooting the Bride's Profile

Here are a few more tips I picked up from David Ziser for making perfect profile portraits of your bride: (1) Shoot horizontal. As I mentioned in the portrait chapter, this puts some breathing room in front of your subject, so they don't look squeezed into the frame. (2) Position the bride so it's a full profile shot, where you don't see any of the eye on the other side of her head, or any of the other side of her face at all. (3) Don't position your flash (or softbox) directly in front of her face—position it slightly behind her so the light wraps around her face. (4) Don't have her look straight ahead, or you'll see too much of the whites of her eyes. Instead, have her look just a tiny bit back toward the camera (don't let her move her head—just her eyes). That way, you see more iris and less whites. (5) If the shadow side of her face (the side facing the camera) gets too dark, use a silver reflector to bounce some of that light into that dark side of her face.

GET TO THE CHURCH EARLY AND SCOPE EVERYTHING OUT

The last thing you want during the wedding shoot is to frantically search for good light, good backgrounds to shoot in front of, or a power outlet to plug in your charger. Get there crazy early (or go a day before the wedding, if possible) and scope everything out in advance. That way, you're calm, prepared, and you have some great spots already picked out so the couple looks their best.

Wedding Zoom Effect Made Easy

Here's a popular effect for adding a sense of motion and energy to your reception shots (perfect for dance floor shots). It's a zoom effect that you create using your flash and zoom lens, and it's easier to get than it looks. First, set your camera to manual mode, and lower your shutter speed to around ⅛ of a second (or slower). Then, zoom in tight on the couple dancing, press the shutter button with your right hand, and then immediately zoom the lens out all the way to wide angle with your other hand. Because the shutter is open while you're moving the zoom lens, it creates that motion effect, and then your flash fires to freeze the motion. The key is to zoom out to wide just as soon as you press that shutter button. Try this just a few times and you'll "get it." (That's another benefit of digital photography—you can try the trick and look at the LCD on the back of your camera to see if you got the zoom effect or not. If you didn't, you can just try again.)

THROW SOME SNACKS IN YOUR CAMERA BAG

While everybody else is eating, you're expected to be shooting, so make sure you throw a few small snacks (energy bars are ideal) and some bottled water in with your gear. Even if the bride and groom have offered to feed you while you're there, you probably won't get a chance (once a reception starts, there's no break—too much is happening), so keep some snacks and water handy.

Add B&W to the Album

Another popular element in today's wedding albums is to include a number of black-and-white images. You'll still shoot these in color, and then you'll use Adobe Photoshop to convert some of your images into black and white. This enhances the "photojournalistic" look of the wedding album, it adds contrast to the album, and many wedding photos look just wonderful in black and white. If you have Photoshop or Lightroom, there is a black-and-white conversion tool that you can use to convert your color image into black and white (and it comes with some built-in presets—you just have to choose one you like). If you have Photoshop Elements, it can do the job, as well. While I do use Photoshop for converting images into black and white from time to time, most of the time I use Nik Software's Silver Efex Pro 2 black-and-white plug-in. Almost all the pros I know use it as well, and it's absolutely brilliant (and super-easy to use. You can download a free 15-day trial copy from www.niksoftware.com and see for yourself). I've created a short video clip to show you how to convert from color to black and white—you can find it on this book's download site at **http://kelbytraining.com/books/digphotogv2**.

Read David Ziser's *Digital ProTalk* Blog Daily

If you're serious about this stuff, do what I do: read David Ziser's *Digital ProTalk* blog every day. He is an absolute fountain of information for professional wedding photographers, and on his blog, he not only shares his tricks of the trade and hard-earned techniques, he also shares some of his amazing photography (including some wonderful non-wedding imagery). Plus, David does a lot of live speaking gigs, and if you ever get to see him in person, he will just blow you away. David speaks for me each year at the Photoshop World Conference & Expo, and the first time I sat in on his class (which was an on-location wedding shoot at a local church, complete with professional bride and groom models), I was amazed. When I came back to the conference hall, one of my buddies asked me how his workshop was, and I described it this way: "He was teaching more than just lighting and posing. He was teaching them the business of today's wedding photography, in such a meaningful and straight-to-the-point way that it was like he was running around stuffing money in their pockets. It was that good!" I find his blog as inspirational as it is informative. Check it out at www.digitalprotalk.com. Also, David wrote what many consider to be the Bible on wedding photography—it's called *Captured by the Light* (shown above). I worked with David on this book and I think he did just a wonderful job sharing his techniques and photography.

SHUTTER SPEED: 5 SEC   F-STOP: F/4.8   ISO: 200   FOCAL LENGTH: 68mm   PHOTOGRAPHER: SCOTT KELBY

Chapter Six
Shooting Travel Like a Pro
How to Bring Back Photos That Really Make Them Wish They Were There

When you come home from a really amazing trip, it's not enough to chronicle your trip through photos and show factual images that detail where you were. You want to move people. You want to create images that are so powerful that they make the person viewing them want to go there so badly that they're willing to risk a series of white collar crimes (mostly embezzling) to pay for their trip to that very same place. Now, if you took good enough shots, it won't be long before your friends are overcome with emotion (jealousy) and will have to go to the exact same location to experience that same amazing feeling once again. Now, if either of your two friends have DSLR cameras, it's helpful to understand right up front that they're not going to that spot because they trust your judgment on travel. They're going there because they think they can get better photos from that spot than you did. Then, once they come back and show off their images, all your mutual friends will say something like, "Did you see Rick's photos from Machu Picchu? Wow, his were much better than Sandy's" and at that moment—you've been blinged. Actually, this is what is known as an IB, or an "Intentional Bling," and it gives you some insight into just how shallow your friends really are. But as shallow as they are, you can drain a little more water out of the pond by pulling this quick and easy stunt: when they see a really cool travel shot of yours, and they ask you where you took it (which means they don't already recognize the landmark)—lie. They'll never know. For example, if you shot the Portland Head lighthouse in Cape Elizabeth, Maine, tell 'em it's the Nauset lighthouse in North Eastham, Massachusetts. By the time they catch on, they'll already be back home, and you can feign a mysterious illness.

In This Case, Less Gear Is More

I'm a total gear freak, but the one time I definitely don't want to lug around a lot of gear is when I'm doing travel photography. You're going to be lugging your gear all day long, hopping on and off of all sorts of transportation, and as the day goes on, your gear seems to get heavier and bulkier, and by the end of the day, you've all but stopped digging around in your camera bag. To get around that, take as little with you as possible—one or two lenses, tops. For example, for crop sensor cameras, Nikon and Canon make reasonably priced 18–200mm lenses, and Sony makes an 18–250mm lens, that let you leave your camera bag back in the hotel because you've got everything covered from wide angle to long telephoto in just one lens. For full-frame cameras, if you want the same type of range, Nikon, Canon, and Tamron make 28–300mm lenses that don't go quite as wide as the 18–200mm, but are amazingly small and lightweight. Also, there are some incredibly lightweight travel tripods available today, ranging from the Slik Sprint Pro II for around $90, to the Oben CT-3500 for around $350, to what is probably the best travel tripod on the planet, the Gitzo GT1542T Traveler carbon-fiber tripod (for around $680). When it comes to lugging around lots of gear in an unfamiliar city, travel photography is definitely a case of "less is more." Do yourself a favor and travel light—you'll find yourself taking more shots, because you're changing lenses and messing with your equipment less.

Working People into Your Travel Shots

LOCATION: AGRA, UTTAR PRADESH, INDIA

If you want to improve your travel photos, here's a simple trick: add more people to your shots. When you really want to capture the flavor of an area, don't just shoot buildings, cathedrals, and monuments—show the people of that area. Nothing conveys the character and soul of a city more than its people, and that's why so many of the top travel photo pros work people into the majority of their shots. The next time you're feeling disappointed with your travel shots, it's probably because you're looking at cold buildings and empty streets. Add people and everything changes (for the better).

HOW TO KNOW WHAT TO SHOOT

Before you travel to a new city, do some research to see what other photographers have shot there and where they shot it from. One great place to do this type of research is the websites of the big stock agencies (like Corbis or Getty Images), where you can do a search for the country or city you're going to. You'll see some amazing images, and you'll get lots of ideas for how the pros cover that area.

Getting People to Pose

LOCATION: AGRA, UTTAR PRADESH, INDIA

Candid shots of some of the locals make a nice addition to your travel shots, but if you have too many of them, they start to look less like travel photos and more like surveillance photos. To get those close-up, fascinating personal shots, you'll need to get some of the locals to pose for you. One of the best tricks for getting people to stop what they're doing and pose for you is to get them to let you take the first shot. When they see that I have a camera, I smile at them, hold up the camera with my finger on the shutter, and nod my head as if to say, "Is it okay if I take your picture?" Most of the time, they smile and nod back, and pause just long enough to let me snap one photo. Then I immediately turn the camera around and show them the photo on the camera's LCD monitor. Once they see that photo on your LCD, it kind of breaks down a barrier, because everybody loves a photo (especially if they're the subject), and they're usually more than happy to pose for a few more.

A SUREFIRE WAY TO GET THEM TO POSE (BUY STUFF)

If you're uncomfortable with the "lift-and-nod" technique I outlined above, here's one that can't miss—find somebody selling something and buy one. If you're in a market, and you buy something from a vendor, you can bet that they'll pose for a quick picture or two, because now you're not just some tourist with a camera, you're one of their customers. This one works like a charm.

What to Shoot on Overcast Days

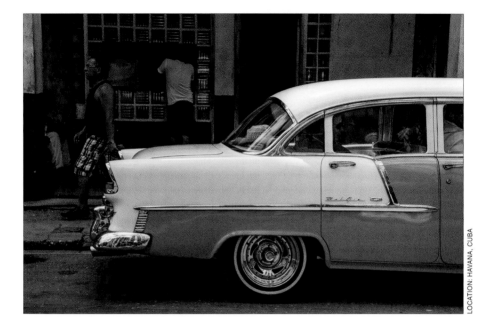

LOCATION: HAVANA, CUBA

When the weather gets cloudy and overcast, don't pack up your gear—this is the time to shoot people on the street, open-air markets, stained glass windows (which look great under cloudy skies), and close-ups of architecture (as long as you do your best to avoid including any of that gray, cloudy sky). Cobblestone streets are great to shoot right after it has rained, and flowers photograph great under the shade that comes from a cloudy sky. Plus, if the sky gets really nasty, it may be a great time to shoot the sky itself. If it's just a flat gray, it's boring. But if a storm is on the way, the dark clouds can make an interesting subject, or add to a boring subject just with the shadows and mystery they bring.

WHAT TO DO IF YOUR ROOM DOESN'T HAVE A VIEW

If you can't get a room with a view (see next page), try these: (1) See if there's a restaurant or lounge at the top of the hotel—you can bet it has plenty of great views, and they may let you shoot there at dusk, before they start serving dinner. (2) See if you can take a few shots from the rooftop. Strike up a rapport with the concierge (give him a big tip) and you'll be amazed at the doors that will open.

Shooting from Your Hotel Room

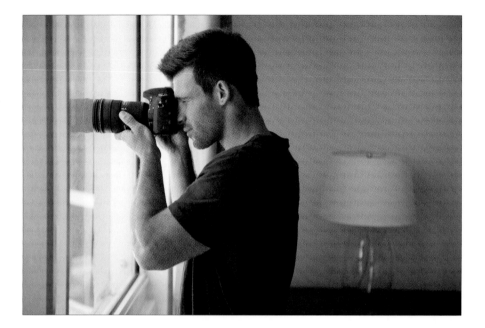

Everybody wants to have a "room with a view," and now you have even more motivation to ask for just that, because your hotel room can be a wonderful platform to shoot the city from. When you check in, ask for a room on the highest available floor and be prepared for some amazing opportunities to unfold right outside your window. If you don't have a balcony, or a window you can open, you can shoot right through the window if you follow these three rules: (1) Turn off any lights in your hotel room—they'll cause reflections in the glass that can show up in your photos—and (2) put your lens as close to the glass as possible (I keep a lens hood on my lenses, so I put the lens hood right on the glass itself. If you think you'll be doing this a lot, you can buy a rubber lens hood, which runs from around $5 on up). And, (3) you can often use a polarizing filter to cut the reflections in the glass, but since you lose some light, you might need to shoot on a tripod, which makes getting right against the glass that much trickier. (I'm not even going to count this last one as a rule, because I hope it goes without saying, but…don't use your flash.)

The Magic Time for Cityscapes

LOCATION: MONTMARTRE, PARIS, FRANCE

Great shots of cityscapes don't happen at 2:00 in the afternoon. If you want that killer shot of the city skyline, wait until about 30 minutes after sunset and shoot at twilight. The sky will usually be a rich, dark blue and the lights of the city will all be on, creating that magical photographic combination that creates the type of cityscapes you've always dreamed of taking. Now that you know what time to shoot, there's one more key to making this type of shot work, and that is you absolutely, positively must take this type of low-light shot with a tripod. Your shutter is going to have to stay open for a full second or more, and if you're not on a tripod, you're going to wind up with a blurry mess.

TAKING THE CITYSCAPE LIGHTS SHOT UP A NOTCH

If the city you're shooting is near water, try to position yourself so that water comes between you and the city (for example, try shooting from a bridge). That way, you see reflections of the city lights in the water, which can add a tremendous amount of visual interest. This is another one of those "can't miss" travel shots, and what an impact it makes when friends, family, and even other photographers see your city-at-twilight-reflected-in-the-water shot.

Get These Shots Out of the Way First

LOCATION: PIAZZA DEI MIRACOLI, PISA, ITALY

If you travel to a famous city, your friends and family back home will be expecting shots of that city's most famous landmarks. For example, if you go to Italy, you'd better come back with a photo of the Leaning Tower of Pisa or the Colosseum in Rome. If you go to Paris, you'd better come back with some Eiffel Tower shots (cliché as they may seem), because people expect it. If you don't come back with some Colosseum or Eiffel Tower shots, they'll be so distracted by what you didn't shoot that they won't pay attention to what you did shoot. So, get those out of the way first—shoot those for the folks back home now and get them "in the bag." That way, you can spend the rest of your time showing the city your way—shooting the people, the local flavor, the customs, and taking shots that speak to the photographer in you. One more thing: When you get back home, and friends and relatives tell you some of your shots look like postcards (and they will), just smile and thank them. Although photographers sometimes tend to look down on travel postcards, your average person doesn't, so if they tell you your shots "look like postcards," they're actually paying you a huge compliment.

One Landscape Rule Kinda Applies to Travel

LOCATION: ROSS CASTLE, KILLARNEY NATIONAL PARK, COUNTY KERRY, IRELAND

In Chapter 4 (the landscapes chapter), I talked about how important it is that you only shoot landscape photos twice a day—around dawn and around dusk—but landscape photos are all about having great light. Luckily for travel photography, we can pretty much shoot all day and night (look for tips about what to shoot during different times of the day here in this chapter). However, if we apply part of that landscapes rule to our travel photography, we'll have the opportunity to make travel photos that are truly spectacular, because just like landscapes look best in soft, beautiful dawn or dusk light, so do famous landscapes, monuments, cityscapes, castles, and charming old buildings. That doesn't mean we can only shoot travel at dawn or dusk (far from it), but if you really want to create some magical images, get up way before the tour bus arrives at your hotel and get some shots of the city in beautiful first-morning light. Or, plan your day so you'll have time after the bus tour to get in position in front of a beautiful landscape, or church, or monument (etc.), so you're in place at sunset to capture a shot that will make your photography friends back home totally jealous when they see it. Remember, beautiful light pretty much makes everything beautiful, so if you thought that fountain or majestic tower looked fascinating in the dry, harsh light of midday, imagine it wrapped in beautiful morning or evening light. Try it once—it'll make a believer out of you.

Air Travel with Camera Gear

Earlier, I mentioned that you want to travel with as little gear as possible, and here's another reason—you absolutely, positively want to bring your gear on the plane as a carry-on. If your camera bag is too big and bulky, there's a good chance it won't fit in the overhead bin, especially if at some point in your trip you wind up in a smaller regional jet or turboprop with little, if any, overhead space. If you're thinking of buying a hard case and checking your gear, I'd reconsider. A photographer I know once got *all* his checked gear stolen—lenses, camera bodies, flashes, the works! When he arrived at his destination and opened his case, it was completely empty. Keep your gear down to a minimum, take a small camera bag, and take it with you on the plane as a carry-on, and you'll avoid a lot of stress and complications, and possibly having to replace all of your gear. The camera bag shown above is the Airport International from Think Tank Photo. It's the best camera bag I've ever used.

BRING EXTRA BATTERIES

When you're in an unfamiliar city, the last thing you want to waste your time doing is searching for batteries (believe me, I learned this one the hard way), so make sure one thing you do bring with you is plenty of extra batteries for your flash unit and your camera (at the very least, recharge your camera battery every single night, because if your battery runs out, that's the end of the shoot).

Shoot the Food

Take a look at any great travel magazine and in every feature about a charming city, you'll always find a photo of its food. Trying new dishes is one of the most fun things about traveling to a new destination, so why wouldn't you include it in your photographs? Watch the expressions of people who look at your album when they come across a photo of a great-looking dish—do that once, and you'll always "shoot the food." Your best opportunities will be during the day, especially if you ask to sit near a window (to catch some of that gorgeous natural window light) or outside (preferably under an umbrella or awning, so you can shoot in shade). If you've got a white tablecloth (which is likely), you've got a great background to shoot on—just remove distracting items from around the dish as much as possible. Also, the classic food shots you see in these magazines generally have two things in common: (1) They generally use a very shallow depth of field (where the front of the plate is in focus and the back is somewhat out of focus). To get this effect, use the lowest f-stop possible (f/4, f/2.8, or even lower if you can). And, (2) shoot plates that have great presentation (in other words, shoot food that's beautifully arranged on the plate, which usually comes from higher-end restaurants). Desserts often are presented nicely, as are appetizers and sushi, and keep an eye out for anything served in a unique-looking dish.

Get a GPS for Your Digital Camera

Today, you can buy small, incredibly lightweight GPS units that sit in your camera's hot shoe or attach directly to your camera's 10-pin terminal, and each time you take a photo, they embed the exact location (longitude and latitude) of where the shot was taken directly into the digital photo itself. Then, applications like Lightroom can display that information (it appears in Lightroom's Metadata panel), and you're then one click away from seeing that location plotted on a Google map, and better yet, you can even see a satellite photo of that exact location while you're there. I use Dawn Technology's tiny GPS unit called the di-GPS that works with most digital cameras. They start around $150.

HAVE SOMEONE ELSE SHOOT YOU

If you're the one behind the camera, nobody's getting any shots of you in these fascinating, exotic, wonderful places. That's why you need to make it a point to get a friend or acquaintance you meet in your travels (even if it winds up being the waiter who serves you at a restaurant) to get at least a few shots of you. Although it might not mean much to you that you're not in any of your photos, it does mean something to your family and friends that you are in the shots.

Shooting Where They Don't Allow Flash

If you plan on shooting in museums, cathedrals, and other places that generally don't allow you to set up a tripod or use your flash, then I recommend buying an inexpensive 50mm f/1.8 lens. This is an old trick pro wedding photographers use (see the wedding photography chapter), and these super-fast lenses let in so much light that you can handhold shots where others dare not tread. Both the Nikon and Canon 50mm f/1.8 lenses sell for around $110–125 each, they take up little room in your camera bag, and they add very little weight to your bag, as well. If you can spring for an even faster lens (like an f/1.4, shown above, or an f/1.2), they let in an amazing amount of light, so you can fire away in incredibly low light (like candlelight situations) without having to raise your camera's ISO to 800 or more (which can greatly increase the amount of noise in your images).

WHEN THEY WON'T LET YOU SET UP YOUR TRIPOD

If you're in a place where they just won't let you set up your tripod, but the light is so low that your camera is going to leave the shutter open for a few seconds, try using your camera bag as a tripod. Turn your camera bag on its side, position it on a ledge, a counter, or any tall surface, then rest your camera on top. Put some spare batteries under the lens to support it and use the self-timer to take the shot.

Look for High Vantage Points

LOCATION: VENICE, ITALY

Your average person's view of a city is going to be from the city streets (or from a tour bus on those streets), so if you want a more compelling place to shoot from, look for a different vantage point—one above the city. Look for towers, observation decks, tall hotels, church towers, cable cars, a bridge, an office building, or mountains overlooking the city, where you can show the city from a completely different view that your average photographer wouldn't get. It's just another thing that keeps your travel photos from looking average.

THE PERFECT BACKGROUND MUSIC FOR TRAVEL SLIDE SHOWS

Want to find the perfect background music to put behind slides from your trip? Try this: buy the movie soundtrack from a movie that was filmed where you took your shots. For example, if your shots are from your trip to Italy, you can be sure you'll find instrumental background music that sounds very Italian in the movie *Under the Tuscan Sun*. If you shot in Paris, try the soundtrack from Disney's *Ratatouille*. If you shot in Russia, you can get some very dramatic Russian-sounding background music from the movie *The Sum of All Fears*. These all work so well because most movie scores are instrumental, which is ideal for your travel slide shows.

Give Yourself a Theme

THE DOORWAYS OF KENNEBUNKPORT

Once you've shot the classic local landmark photos, here is a great way to spark your creativity and show the city in a different light for a day: give yourself a mini-assignment. Pick a topic, spend part of the day focusing on that subject, and you'll be amazed at what you can come up with. For example, some of the mini–travel assignments I have given myself are: (1) shoot charming street numbers on the outsides of buildings, homes, and apartments; (2) shoot interesting doors and/or doorways; (3) shoot just things that are one vivid color; (4) shoot weather vanes; (5) shoot nothing but flowers; (6) shoot charming local barns; and (7) shoot close-ups of local architecture. Other ideas might be: shooting coffee cups; shooting those little food signs in local markets; shooting interesting columns, traffic signs or street signs, mailboxes, or things that are a particular shape (like only things that are round), or things of a particular color (only things that are red). You don't have to make one of these the only thing you do all day, just keep an eye out for it during your travels, and each time you see one of your assignment objects, make sure you get it. Then, you can present these all together in one print (an example is shown above).

SHUTTER SPEED: 1/500 SEC   F-STOP: F/5.6   ISO: 1600   FOCAL LENGTH: 300mm   PHOTOGRAPHER: SCOTT KELBY

Chapter Seven

Shooting Macro Like a Pro

How to Take Really Captivating Close-Up Photos

If you're one of those people who believes life is all about the little details, then have I got a style of shooting for you. It's called macro photography (macro is actually an acronym that stands for Man, Are Cows Really Obnoxious), and it's based on a special type of lens called a macro or close-up lens, which lets you focus on objects much closer than you'd normally be able to, and because of this close-up capability, you can often get close enough so that your subject completely fills your frame. Some of the most popular subjects for macro-loving photographers to shoot are flowers, leaves, ladybugs on leaves, bees on flowers, and other everyday things in nature that we're not used to seeing close up. That's one of the things that makes macro photography so captivating: you're often seeing images at a view or magnification we rarely, if ever, see with the naked eye. Now, because I was just able to work the word "naked" into the book, it's almost guaranteed that the book will be a bestseller. That's because, from now on, anytime someone goes to the web and searches for the word "naked" (so basically, most of my friends), one of the results they get back will be this book. Now, thinking that my book will have lots of nudie nakedness, these people will often buy it sight unseen, because apparently people who search for the word "naked" are also very loose with money—they'll buy any product that they feel will get them closer to actually seeing nudie nakedness. However, once they receive the book, they will soon realize, as you have (with great disappointment), that there is no nudie nakedness in the book, but if it makes you feel any better, I'm totally naked under my underwear (see that? I got the word "underwear" in now, too). Cha-ching!

Maximize Your Depth of Field

Macro lenses have a "sweet spot" where you get absolutely the most sharp results, and in macro photography, having tack-sharp images is critical. One trick to get the most sharpness out of your macro lens is to shoot with your lens aiming perfectly straight at the subject (in other words, don't angle your lens upward or downward toward your subject—try to shoot straight on for the best sharpness and clarity). So, for example, if you're shooting a bee on a flower, you'll need to lower your tripod to the point where you are aiming directly at the flower without having to tilt the lens, even a little bit (as shown above).

THIS IS TRIPOD TERRITORY

Although there are now macro lenses that have built-in image stabilization (IS) or vibration reduction (VR), if you're serious about macro, you're going to be serious about how sharp your images are, which means you seriously need a tripod. This is absolutely tripod-land for sure, and a tripod may well be the single most important piece of your "making great macro shots" puzzle, so although you can cut a lot of corners in other areas, shooting on a tripod is one thing you absolutely, positively should do. They haven't yet come up with a built-in stabilization device that holds a camera as steady as even the cheapest tripod.

Why You Should Turn Autofocus Off

By now, you've learned that one of the big challenges of macro photography is getting things sharp and in focus. You're about to come to one of the things that can be the most frustrating, and this is using autofocus when you're as close in on your subject as you are with macro shooting. If I can give you one tip that will lower your frustration level by a hundred, it's to turn off the autofocus on your camera's lens and manually focus instead. I know, you hate to give up the autofocus feature because, honestly, on today's cameras it's really amazingly accurate. That is, until you shoot macro. What will happen is your camera will try to find a focus point, and you'll hear the whirring of the lens as it tries to snap onto something, anything to focus on, and while it's getting frustrated—so are you. Just switch over to manual focus, and you'll both be better off.

Don't Touch That Shutter Button!

If you're going through the trouble of putting your camera on a tripod (and you absolutely should), you can still get a "less-than-tack-sharp" photo from the vibration that happens when you push the shutter button. That's why, when shooting macro, you should either use a shutter release cable (a cord that attaches to your camera that lets you take a shot without touching the shutter button on the camera itself) or use your camera's self-timer, which takes the shot for you about 10 seconds after you press the shutter button, so any vibration caused by your pressing the shutter button will be long gone.

FOCUS ON THE EYES

In portrait photography, we always focus on the eyes to get the sharpest image. Same thing in wildlife photos. Same thing in macro shots of insects or butterflies, or any little critters that wind up in your viewfinder.

Which f-Stop Works Best

Is there an f-stop that works best for macro shots? Well, yeah. It's f/22. Because the depth of field of macro lenses is so shallow (meaning, the front of that flower you're shooting can be perfectly in focus and the petal just one inch behind it can be totally out of focus), you need to get as broad a depth as possible, and that comes when your aperture setting is at something like f/22. You could get away with f/16, or maybe even f/11, but to get the maximum amount of your subject in focus, try f/22 (or higher if your lens will allow). The higher the number, the more of your photo will be in focus.

Point-and-Shoot Macro Photography

Most compact point-and-shoot cameras these days actually have a macro lens built right into them—you just have to know how to engage it (so to speak). You do that by switching your mode to macro (its icon is usually a little flower). This sets up your camera so you can get very close to your subject (like a flower, an insect, etc.) and still focus the camera (you can't get as close as you would with a dedicated macro lens on a DSLR, but you still can get surprisingly close for a compact digital camera). Once you've got this mode turned on, you can shoot using all the rest of the rules in this chapter, like shooting on a tripod, not shooting in even light wind, etc.

A Trick for Visualizing Macro

©ISTOCKPHOTO/NAIVE

When you're out shooting and you're looking at something and thinking, "I wonder if that would make a good macro shot?" you don't have to pull out all your gear and test it (especially because you probably won't). Instead, just carry a small magnifying glass (you can get thin plastic ones that fit in right in your wallet), then pull it out, go up to the object you're thinking about shooting, and you'll see right then and there whether it makes a good macro subject. Also, you can use this magnifier to try out different angles (think shooting flowers from way down low) before you go crawling around on your stomach with all your gear.

SIMPLE BACKGROUNDS ARE BEST

The same background rule we follow in portrait photography is also true in macro photography, and that is: keep the background simple. It may even be more important with macro than with portraits, because you're in so close your background will play a bigger role, so make sure your background is as simple as possible.

Why You Might Want to Shoot Indoors

A lot of nature macro photography is actually done indoors, rather than outside (in most cases, you're going to be so close in, you don't have to worry much about anyone realizing that you're in a studio). One of the main advantages of shooting macro indoors is that there's no wind. This might not seem like a big deal at first, but when you set up your camera with a macro lens outdoors and look through the lens, you'll see firsthand that the tiniest bit of wind—wind that you don't really even notice is there—is moving your flower (leaf, twig, etc.) all over your frame, which means your photos are going to be soft and out of focus. It'll really throw you, because you'll back away from the lens, and you'll swear there's no wind, but then you'll look through the viewfinder and know right away—you're hosed. Another advantage of shooting indoors is that you can control the light (especially if you're shooting under studio strobes), and the key to lighting macro shots is to have nice even lighting across the entire image. You don't want drama and shadows—you want nice even light, and getting that in the studio is easier than it is outdoors by a long shot.

Buying a Macro Lens

If this macro thing sounds really interesting, there are three ways you can dip your toe into the close-up shooting world: (1) Check to see if you already have a telephoto or zoom lens that has macro capability built right in. (2) Buy a macro lens—both Canon and Nikon make great macro lenses (that's a Nikon lens above), and you can get a Sigma 105mm macro lens for around $769. Or, (3) add a close-up lens attachment to one of your existing lenses. These screw on the end of your lens and turn any zoom lens into a macro lens (I have one of these, and it's small enough and lightweight enough that it goes with me everywhere I go). When it comes to macro lenses, the higher number the lens, the closer your subject will be in the frame (so a 65mm macro lens might get you the entire bee, but a 105mm will get so close you can get just the bee's head).

CREATE YOUR OWN WATER DROPS

Use a tip from part 1 of this book, and that is: don't wait for rain—bring a water bottle on your shoot and spray water on your flower petals (or leaves) to create the look of fresh raindrops, which look great in macro photography. Plus, if you get close enough, you'll be able to see reflections in the water drops themselves. Cool stuff.

Perfect, Even Light for Macro Shots

When it comes to lighting close-up shots, your goal is to get as even lighting as possible, and there's actually a special flash, called a ring flash, that's designed to do exactly that. It's actually not one flash, it's a series of flashes attached to a ring that slides over your lens, and because these flashes light your subject from all sides, it creates that very even light you're looking for.

Scott's Gear Finder

Sigma EM-140 DG Macro Flash (around $379)

Canon MR-14EX Macro Ring Lite (around $549)

Nikon R1C1 Wireless Close-Up Speedlight Flash w/SU-800 (around $719)

Making Your Lens into a Macro Lens

COURTESY OF GRADUS GROUP LLC

The more space you put between your camera's sensor and your lens, the closer you'll be able to focus, and because of that, companies make extension tubes. These extension tubes attach between your lens and your camera (they look like a thin extra lens) to move the lens farther away from your camera's sensor, which cuts your minimum focus distance big time, so you can get in there and shoot nice and close (like you had a true macro lens). The advantage of these extension tubes is: they're much less expensive than a dedicated macro lens, starting around $83. (By the way, if you have a macro lens already, an extension tube can make your macro focus even closer. Sweet!)

SHUTTER SPEED: 1/4000 SEC   F-STOP: F/2.8   ISO: 200   FOCAL LENGTH: 300mm   PHOTOGRAPHER: SCOTT KELBY

Chapter Eight

Pro Tips for Getting Better Photos

Tricks of the Trade for Making All Your Shots Look Better

There are some tricks of the trade that just don't fit under any of the existing chapters, because they're not really just about getting better-looking portraits or more luscious-looking landscapes—they're about being a better photographer and getting better shots. And getting better shots is what it's all about, right? This is something we're all very passionate about, and if we get to the point where we're actually starting to sell our work (maybe as fine art prints, or through assignment work with a magazine), and are turning our passion into profits, then we're really living the dream—doing something we truly love for a living. Speaking of dreams, I haven't made a big deal about this on my daily blog (http://scottkelby.com) or in any of my live classes yet, because I don't want it to come off like bragging, but I recently signed a year-long contract with *National Geographic* that I'm pretty psyched about. In the terms of this agreement, I get 12 monthly issues for only $15, which is 74% off the newsstand price, so as you might imagine, I'm very excited. Anyway, in this chapter, we're going to focus on lots of those little tricks of the trade that you can apply to a wide range of photography to make everything you shoot look that much better. Now, one last thing: You might have heard I run with a dangerous crowd. We ain't too pretty, we ain't too proud. We might be laughing a bit too loud, but that never hurt no one. (I just wanted to see if you're still reading this after that whole *National Geographic* scam I pulled on you above. Come on, you have to admit, I had you going there for just a second or two, didn't I?)

Which Mode to Shoot In

Not sure which mode you should be shooting in? Here are some tips:

Aperture Priority (A or Av): I recommend this mode for both portrait photographers and landscape photographers, because it gives you control over your background. You get to choose whether you want your background out of focus (by choosing lower numbered f-stops, like f/4 or f/2.8) or totally in focus (by choosing higher f-stop numbers, like f/11, f/16, and higher), and no matter your choice, your camera will automatically choose the right shutter speed to give you a good exposure.

Shutter Priority (S or Tv): I recommend this mode if you're shooting sports, where you generally need to freeze the action. This lets you choose to shoot with very high shutter speeds (provided you're shooting in bright enough light—like daylight), and then your camera will automatically choose the right f-stop for you to give you a good exposure.

Manual (M): If you're shooting with studio strobes, you need to shoot in manual mode, because in aperture priority or shutter priority, you won't get a proper exposure, as they won't take into account the fact that you're using strobes.

Program (P): Shoot in this mode when you want to be in point-and-shoot mode, but don't want the flash popping up. Perfect for when you need to quickly capture a moment and don't want to mess with any settings.

Choosing the Right ISO

Our goal is to shoot with our digital cameras set to the lowest possible ISO (ideally 100 ISO) for one simple reason—it offers the lowest amount of noise (grain) and gives us the sharpest, cleanest images possible. The only reason to raise your ISO is to be able to handhold your camera in low-light situations. So, for regular daylight or brightly lit situations, we shoot at 100 ISO. If you raise your camera's ISO setting to 200, it lets you handhold your camera in a little lower light and still get a sharp photo, but the trade-off is a tiny increase in visible noise. At 400 ISO, you can handhold in even lower light, but with more visible noise. At 800 ISO, you can handhold in the low light of a church, but with even more noise, and so on. It comes down to this: the higher the ISO, the lower light you can handhold your camera in, but the higher the ISO, the more noise you get, too. That's why we try to use tripods as much as possible. When our camera is on a tripod, it's perfectly still, so we can shoot at 100 ISO the whole time without worrying about getting blurry photos in low light.

Which Format to Shoot In (RAW, JPEG, or TIFF)

Most digital cameras these days (and all DSLRs) offer at least these three main file formats: RAW, JPEG, and TIFF. Here's when to use each:

JPEG: Shoot in JPEG if you're really good at nailing your exposure every time. If you're dead on (or really close) on your exposure and white balance, and don't think you'll need to tweak it much later (or at all) in Photoshop, then JPEG is for you. The file sizes are dramatically smaller, so you'll fit more on your memory card, and they'll take up less space on your computer.

RAW: Shoot in RAW mode if you don't nail the exposure and white balance most of the time, and think you might need to tweak your images later in Photoshop or Photoshop Lightroom. In RAW mode, you can control every aspect of the processing of your images, so if the image is underexposed, overexposed, or has a color problem—you can fix it easily. RAW offers the highest-quality original image, too, and offers maximum flexibility.

TIFF: Shoot in TIFF if you're loose with money. This is a great format for people who have money to burn, people who shoot to huge 32-GB memory cards and have plenty of 'em handy. TIFFs are also perfect for anyone who has lots of spare hard drive space and lots of spare time, because TIFF files are huge to deal with. Outside of that, I can't think of any really compelling (or remotely reasonable) reason to shoot in TIFF format.

Which JPEG Size to Shoot In

I recommend shooting at the largest size and highest quality setting that your camera will allow, so if you're shooting in JPEG format, make sure you choose JPEG Fine and a size of Large, so you get the best-quality JPEG image possible. If you choose a lower size, or JPEG Norm (normal), you're literally throwing away quality. The only trade-off is that JPEG Fine photos are a little larger in file size. Not staggeringly larger (those are TIFFs or RAW files)—they're a little larger—but the increase in quality is worth it. If you're serious about getting better-looking photos (and if you bought this book, you are), then set your image size to Large and your JPEG quality to Fine, and you'll be shooting the exact same format many of today's top pros swear by.

WHIMS Will Keep You Out of Trouble

Let's say you're going out shooting landscapes one morning. Do you know what your camera's settings are? They're whatever they were the last time you went shooting. So, if your last shoot was at night, chances are your ISO is set very high, and your white balance is set to whatever you used last. I've gotten burned by this so many times that I had to come up with an acronym to help me remember to check the critical settings on my camera, so I don't mess up an entire shoot (I spent a whole morning in Monument Valley, Utah, shooting at 1600 ISO because I had been shooting a local band the night before). The acronym is WHIMS, which stands for:

W: White balance check

H: Highlight warning turned on

I: ISO check (make sure you're using the right ISO for your surroundings)

M: Mode check (make sure you're in aperture priority, program, or manual mode)

S: Size (check to make sure your image size and quality are set correctly)

Before you take your first shot that day, take 30 seconds and check your WHIMS, and you won't wind up shooting important shots with your camera set to JPEG small (like I did when shooting one day in Taos, New Mexico).

How to Lock Focus

This is another one of those things that has snuck by a lot of people, and that is how to lock your focus. For example, let's say you're lying down, shooting a landscape through some tall grass, and you want the blades of grass in front of you to remain in focus, but when you lift the camera up to get the rest of the scene, the camera refocuses on the background. You can force the camera to keep its focus locked onto those blades of grass by simply holding the shutter button down halfway. While that shutter button is held down, your focus is locked, so now you can recompose the image without your camera trying to refocus on something else. I use this a lot on photos of people who may not be in the center of the frame (it keeps me from having to move the autofocus dot—I just point at the person, hold the shutter button halfway down to lock the focus, then recompose the shot the way I want it. When it looks good, I just press the shutter button down the rest of the way to take the shot).

Moving Your Point of Focus

You know how you look through your viewfinder and, in the center of your viewfinder, there's a red circle or a red rectangle? That's your camera's autofocus (AF) point, and what that point hits winds up being what's in focus. Well, something a lot of people don't realize is that most cameras let you move that focus point up or down, left or right. That way, if you've composed a shot where your subject is standing over to the left side of your frame, you can move the AF point over, right on them, so they wind up being perfectly in focus. On Canon cameras, you move your AF point by using the tiny multi-controller joystick or the dial on the back of the camera. On Nikon cameras, you move the AF point by using the multi-selector on the back of the camera.

Zooming in Close? Fast Shutter Speeds Help

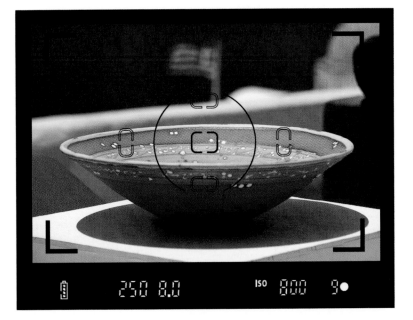

If you're using a long zoom lens, like a 200mm lens, there's something you should know to help you make sure you get sharp photos, and that is: the closer in you zoom, the more any tiny little movement of your lens is exaggerated. So, if you're handholding your camera, and you're shooting zoomed in to 200mm, any little movement on your part and you're going to have some blurry photos. Now, if it's a bright sunny day, you'll probably be shooting at some very fast shutter speeds, which will pretty much neutralize your movement, so you can sidestep that problem. However, if you're shooting in the shade, or really in anything where your shutter speed falls below 1/250 of a second, the best remedy is to put your camera on a tripod (even though it's during the day) or raise your camera's ISO enough to raise your shutter speed to at least 1/250 of a second. That way, you can shoot out at 200mm all day long and not worry about some tiny movement on your part causing a serious loss of sharpness in your shots.

When It's Okay to Erase Your Memory Card

If you only have one memory card, it won't be long before you have to erase that memory card so you can get back to shooting. I have a pretty simple rule I use to know when it's actually okay to erase a memory card, and that is I erase it when I know I have two backup copies of the images that are on it. In other words, I have one set that I copied onto my computer, and then I copied that folder of images over to an external hard drive, so I have two copies. Then, and only then, I feel comfortable erasing that card and shooting again. Remember, when you have just one copy, you're working on the negatives. If your computer's hard drive crashes, those images are gone. Forever. That's why you gotta make a second backup copy, because I've seen people lose their work again and again, year after year, because they didn't make that second backup copy, but don't let that happen to you—back up twice, then erase that card!

DON'T JUST DELETE YOUR PHOTOS, REFORMAT THE CARD

You've probably heard horror stories of people who have done an entire shoot, only to have the memory card go bad and they lose all their shots (if you haven't heard this story, I've got dozens). Anyway, one thing you can do to avoid problems is to not just delete the images on the card (once you've backed up twice), but to format the card in the camera, which erases all the files in the process. Yes, it's that important.

Why You Need to Get in Really Close

This is probably the single simplest tip in the whole book, and the one that has the potential to make your photography the best, but it's also the one people will resist the most. The tip is: move in close to your subject. Really close. Way closer than you'd think. If you search the Internet, you'll find dozens of references and quotes about how much you can improve your photography by simply getting in closer to your subject. You'll find the famous quote (I'm not sure who it's attributed to) that says (I'm paraphrasing here), "Get your shot set up to where you think you're close enough—then take two steps closer." Or my favorite quote, which I think really sums it up nicely, from famous photographer Robert Capa, who once said, "If your pictures aren't good enough, you're not close enough." The pros know this, practice this, have embraced it, and have passed it on to their students for who knows how long, and yet your average photographer still tries to get "the big picture." Don't be an average photographer, who gets average shots. Take two steps closer, and you'll be two steps closer to better-looking photos.

What to Use Your Histogram For

Today's DSLRs can display a histogram (which is a graphical reading of the tonal range of your photo) right there on the camera's LCD monitor, but if you don't know how to read one (or didn't know it's there), it doesn't do you much good. I only use my camera's histogram for one thing, and that's to make sure I haven't clipped off any important detail in my highlights. So, what am I looking for when I look at my histogram? Two things: (1) I don't want to see the histogram's graph touch the far right wall. If any of that graph hits the far right wall, I'm losing detail. So, what I'm really hoping to see is (2) a small gap between the end of the histogram and that far right wall (as shown above). If I see that gap, I know I'm okay, and that I'm not clipping any highlights. I can look at my histogram and immediately see if this has happened, and if I have clipped off important highlight information, I will generally use the exposure compensation control on my camera to override what my camera read, and lower the exposure by 1/3 of a stop, then I take the shot again and check my histogram. If I'm still clipping, I lower the exposure compensation to –0.7 and then shoot again, and check again. I keep doing that until my clipping problem goes away. Now, the histogram can only help so much, because what if there's a direct shot of the sun in my photo? That sun will clip big time, and there will be no gap, but that's okay, because the surface of the sun doesn't have any important detail (well, at least as far as I know). So the histogram can help, but it's not the bottom line—you still have to make the call if the area that's clipping is (here's the key phrase) important detail, so don't get hung up on histograms—at the end of the day, you have to make the call, and the histogram is just a helper, not your master.

Leave Your Lens Cap Off

My buddy Vinny calls your lens cap "The Never Ready Cap," because whenever that magical once-in-a-lifetime moment happens while you're out shooting, don't worry— it will be long gone by the time you stop and take your lens cap off. I definitely recommend putting your lens cap on when you're storing your gear back in your camera bag, but if your camera is out of that bag, your lens cap needs to be off your camera. If you're worried about scratching your lens, then buy a lens hood (or use the lens hood that came with your lens), but keep that cap off once that camera comes out of your bag.

Removing Spots and Specks After the Fact

If you have a dust spot, smudge, or speck on either your lens or your camera's sensor, you're going to see that spot (or smudge or speck) again and again once you open your photos in Photoshop (or Lightroom, or Elements, etc.). If you want a quick way to get rid of that junk, try Photoshop's (or Elements') Spot Healing Brush tool. All you do is choose it from the Toolbox, then click it once over any spot or speck, and it's gone. That's all there is to it. Now, if you have Photoshop, you can fix a bunch of spots all at once (because, after all, if you have a spot on your lens, every shot from your shoot will have that same spot in that exact same location, right?). So, here's what you do: STEP ONE: Select all the photos that are in the same orientation (for example, select all your horizontal shots) and open them in Adobe Camera Raw. STEP TWO: Get Camera Raw's Spot Removal tool (from the toolbar up top) and click it once right over the spot. This removes that spot from your current photo. STEP THREE: Press the Select All button (on the top left) to select all your other photos, then click the Synchronize button. STEP FOUR: When the dialog appears, from the Synchronize pop-up menu up top, choose Spot Removal, and then click OK. This removes that spot from all your other selected photos automatically. Click Done to save your retouch. STEP FIVE: Open all the photos you took with a tall orientation and do the same thing. Now, all your spots are gone from all your photos in less than two minutes. If you shot 300 or 400 photos—that's sayin' something!

What Looks Good in Black & White

Some subjects just look great when you convert them from color to black and white, so when you're out shooting, keep an eye out for anything with lots of texture, like the peeling paint on the side of an old building, rusty old machinery, anything with an interesting shape or lots of contrast (because you don't have the crutch of color, you have to look for other things to lead the eye), objects with a lot of metal, old barns, old cars, old abandoned factories, and also consider cloudy days with dark menacing skies a perfect subject for black and white. In fact, any gray nasty day can wind up being a field day for black and white because you don't have to worry about avoiding the sky since it's not a nice, blue, sunny day. In black and white—it's all gray.

Recompose, Don't "Fix It" in Photoshop

I love Photoshop. I think it totally rocks, and I've written around 35 books on Photoshop. That being said, it's much faster and easier to get it right in the camera than it is to fix it later in Photoshop. If you see something distracting in your viewfinder, like a telephone line or a road sign, that's ruining your shot, you certainly could remove either one later in Photoshop. It probably wouldn't take you more than 10 minutes or so to remove that telephone line or road sign in Photoshop. But it probably wouldn't take you more than 10 seconds to move one foot in either direction to recompose your shot so you don't see the telephone wires (or the road sign) at all. Getting it right in the camera is just so much faster, and besides—you want to save your time in Photoshop for finishing your photos, not fixing them. Do yourself a favor, and compose so those distracting elements aren't in your frame, and you'll spend a lot more time shooting and having fun, and a lot less time on tedious cloning and repairing in Photoshop.

Want to Be Taken Seriously? Start Editing

If you want to be taken seriously as a photographer and you want people to start to view you as a pro-quality photographer, then take a tip from the working pros, which is: only show your very best work. Period. One thing that makes a pro a pro is they're really good photo editors—they're really good at picking, and only showing, their very best stuff. You don't see their so-so shots or the shots that would have been great, if only…. You also don't see them showing seven or eight similar shots of the same subject. Only show your best of the best. That means if you went on a trip and you took 970 shots, you don't come home and show a slide show of 226 images. If you want people to think you're good, show your best 30. If you want people to think you're great, show just your best 10. Think about it: If you took 970 shots, maybe 400 are decent. Out of those decent shots, maybe 80 are pretty good. Out of those 80, maybe 30 are really good. Out of those 30, maybe 10 are outstanding. Now, just show those 10—and blow people away. (Just ask yourself what you would rather see—80 pretty good shots, or 10 outstanding shots.)

HOW TO BE A GREAT PHOTO EDITOR OF YOUR OWN WORK

Your shots have to stand on their own, without you telling a story about why you like the shot. If you have to explain to someone why you chose it or why you think it's special, it doesn't belong in your portfolio.

Label Your Memory Cards

This is another tip I picked up from Derrick Story, and he tells the true story of how he left a memory card in a taxi cab, but because he always puts a sticker on his cards with his name and address, he was able to get that card returned to him with all the photos still intact. That's right, he lost his memory card in a taxi and got it back. This obviously didn't happen in New York. (I'm totally kidding. You knew that—right?)

Go Square

Today's digital cameras all produce an image that is rectangular, so no matter whose photo you see, it's either a tall rectangle or a wide rectangle. Want to make your photo stand out from the pack and have more of a "fine art" look when you print it? Then "Go square!" That's right—just crop your photo to a perfect square (as seen above), and then position that perfect square with plenty of nice white space around it, for a nice fine art, gallery look, like the layout you see here. It's a simple little thing, but they're all little things, right?

Tip for Shooting at Night (Long Exposure Noise)

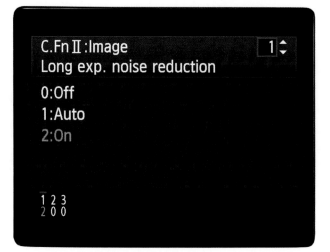

If you're shooting at night, your shutter is going to wind up staying open long enough for you to make a good exposure, and depending on how dark it is where you're shooting, it could open for ¼ of a second, 4 seconds, or 40 seconds. If you start to have long expo-sures, like 40 seconds, chances are you're going to start to get some serious noise in your photo (even if you were shooting at 100 ISO). One thing you can do to help is to turn on your camera's Long Exposure Noise Reduction feature (Nikon, Canon, and Sony DSLRs all have this feature). This kicks in your camera's built-in noise reduction to combat the kind of noise that shows up in long exposures like these, and they actually do a surprisingly decent job, so they're worth turning on (just in these long exposure instances—this is *not* for everyday use).

The Very Next Book You Should Get

You've heard me mention legendary assignment photographer Joe McNally here in the book, and Joe has a book that I truly believe is the most important photography book in many years. It's called *The Moment It Clicks: Photography Secrets from One of the World's Top Shooters* (from New Riders), and what makes the book so unique is Joe's three-pronged "triangle of learning" where (1) Joe distills the concept down to one brief sentence (it usually starts with something along the lines of, "An editor at *National Geographic* once told me…" and then he shares one of those hard-earned tricks of the trade that you only get from spending a lifetime behind the lens). Then, (2) on the facing page is one of Joe's brilliant images that perfectly illustrates the technique (you'll recognize many of his photos from the covers of your favorite magazines), and (3) you get the inside story of how that shot was taken, including which equipment he used (lens, f-stop, lighting and accessories, etc.) and how to set up a shot like that of your own. There's just never been a book like it. The photography is so captivating, you could buy it just for the amazing images (think, coffee-table book), but his insights on equipment, technique, and the fascinating backstory behind the shot let the book totally stand on its own as a photographic education tool. This book combines those elements as it inspires, challenges, and informs, but perhaps most importantly, it will help you understand photography and the art of making great photos at a level you never thought possible. I worked as an editor on the book, and I have to tell you—it blew me away. It will blow you away, too!

Chapter Nine

Photo Recipes to Help You Get "The Shot"

The Simple Ingredients That Make It All Come Together

The chapter from part 1 of this book that I probably got the most emails on was this last chapter—the photo recipe chapter. In this chapter, I show some of my shots, and then give the details for how to get a similar shot, including what kind of equipment you'd need, what time to shoot (if it's relevant), where to shoot it, where to set up your lights, tripod, etc., so it's kind of a photo recipe cookbook. Although there are a lot of shooters that do anything to get "the shot," you'll be happy to know—I'm not one of them. In fact, I've often toyed with the idea of starting a trade association for people like me and calling it "The International Society of Convenient Photographers" (or the ISCP, for short). Our credo would be, "Any shot worth getting, is worth driving to." Our ideal situation would be we drive up to a location, roll down the window, take the shot, and drive off. It doesn't get much more convenient than that. There would be special recognition for members who abide by our 50-ft. Cone of Convenience rule, which states: "If a once-in-a-lifetime photographic opportunity presents itself, the member may venture as far as 50 ft. from the member's vehicle, in any one direction, as long as they leave the car's engine running and the air conditioner turned on." But then I realized this was very limiting, because it would exclude most studio photographers. So, we added a special dispensation for them, in rule 153.45, Section B, which states: "A studio photographer should avoid changing their subject's pose, as doing such could force an inconvenient repositioning of the light, which breaks with the sacred tenets of our group." Sure, it's a small group, but we really get around.

The Recipe for Getting This Type of Shot

LOCATION: YOSEMITE FALLS, YOSEMITE NATIONAL PARK, CALIFORNIA

Characteristics of this type of shot: A sweeping shot with a silky waterfall effect, with lots of detail front-to-back and a real sense of depth.

(1) To get this type of sweeping look, you need to use a very-wide-angle lens. This was shot with a 12mm wide-angle (it's not a fisheye lens—just a super-wide-angle).

(2) To get the detail from front to back, shoot in aperture priority (Av) mode and choose the highest number f-stop you can (this was shot at f/22, which keeps everything in focus from front to back).

(3) You absolutely need to shoot on a tripod for a shot like this because you're shooting at f/22, which means your shutter will be open long enough that even a tiny bit of movement will make the photo blurry.

(4) Another benefit of shooting at f/22 is that since your shutter stays open longer, the water in the waterfall looks silky (you might remember this trick from part 1 of this book—how to get that smooth, silky water effect). You'll also want to use a cable release (or your camera's self-timer function), so you don't add any blur when pressing the shutter button (yes, it makes a difference).

(5) The final key to this shot is shooting it right around dawn. This does two things, the first being that since it's darker outside, your shutter will stay open longer and your water will look silkier. You couldn't get that silky water look at 1:00 in the afternoon. The second thing is even more important: the quality of the light and the nice soft shadows only happen like this around dawn (and around sunset), so get up early and get the shot!

The Recipe for Getting This Type of Shot

Characteristics of this type of shot: Very shallow depth of field (the front of the plate is out of focus, so is the back). The subject looks very sharp and the lighting is just great.

(1) The biggest challenge in getting a shot like this in a restaurant is having enough light to make the shot look great. The secret is, of course, to ask to sit outside (dining alfresco) or near a window, so you can use natural light to light your food (this shot was taken at a table outside, so there was plenty of light, but the umbrella over the table kept the light from being too harsh). Next, position the food so the light is coming from either behind it, so it's backlit (my first choice), or from the side.

(2) The second technique for capturing a shot like this is to use a long lens, so you can zoom in really tight on one part of the plate (for this shot, I used an 18–200mm f/3.5–5.6 lens zoomed in all the way to 200mm). By zooming in tight and locking focus (in this case, on the appetizer right in the center), it puts the rest of the food out of focus at the top and bottom of the image, which is what you want.

(3) The last part is the compositional part, and it's perhaps the most important one (well, besides the light, anyway). Don't try to capture the entire plate of food. Pick one part of it and zoom in tight on that. It's okay to include the curve of the plate, but if you do, just show that one side.

(4) If you're shooting indoors, even near a window, you might need a very small table-top tripod (I use a Manfrotto tabletop tripod, barely big enough to hold my camera). To minimize any blur, use your camera's self-timer feature to take the shot.

The Recipe for Getting This Type of Shot

LOCATION: ST. NICHOLAS GREEK ORTHODOX CATHEDRAL, TARPON SPRINGS, FLORIDA

Characteristics of this type of shot: A large, wide, sweeping shot of a cathedral with lots of detail in all the ornate objects in the scene.

(1) In many ways, this shot was taken like it was a landscape shot—it was designed from the outset to have that big, sweeping look. Shoot a church like this with a wide-angle lens (this was shot with a full-frame camera, which means it was extra-wide compared to a cropped sensor camera, and it was shot with a 14mm lens).

(2) Churches generally have low light, and even though the ceiling of this church was white and there was natural light coming in through the windows, it was still dark enough that, at f/4, my camera needed to keep the shutter open $1/13$ of a second, which is way too slow to handhold. So, you'll absolutely have to be on a tripod.

(3) This is the beautiful St. Nicholas Greek Orthodox Cathedral in Tarpon Springs, Florida. I'm positioned in the center aisle between the pews, right at the first pew, so there are no obstructions (pews) between the camera and altar.

(4) Compositionally, I used a trick that helps make it look like a big, sweeping shot: I collapsed the tripod legs, so the tripod was only about 18" tall (if that). That way, you see a lot of the marble floor leading up to the altar, which creates its "bigness."

(5) To bring out the detail, you finish off this shot in Photoshop (or Elements or Lightroom) using a plug-in filter that creates a tonal contrast effect, like Nik Software's Color Efex Pro, onOne's Perfect Effects, or Topaz Labs' Topaz Adjust—all offer one-click presets for that effect (you can download fully-functional, free trial versions of all three from their websites).

The Recipe for Getting This Type of Shot

Characteristics of this type of shot: A soft, dramatic, backlit silhouette of a bride taken with just one small light.

(1) This was shot using only one light with a small (24x24" square) softbox attached. Start by making the room she's standing in so dark that the only thing lighting her is the light from the softbox. Set your camera to manual mode, so you can control the shutter speed and aperture separately. Set your shutter speed to the highest number that will still sync your camera/flash (for most studio strobes, that's $^1/_{200}$ of a second. For most hot shoe flashes, it's $^1/_{250}$ of a second). By using a high shutter speed number like this, it lets in less existing room light.

(2) Keep your flash turned off, set your f-stop to f/8, take a test shot, and then look at the image on the back of your camera. If you can clearly see the bride, raise the f-stop to f/11, and take another shot. Keep doing this until you're pretty much getting a solid black image (no bride, no detail, no nuthin'). Now, turn on your flash.

(3) You're going to position the flash with the small softbox behind her, but not directly behind her. You want to position it off to one side behind her, so it is coming from behind but aiming back at her at an angle. Next, position her so her head is turned a little toward that light, so some of that angled back light reflects back onto her face (here, you can see some of the light reflecting off the flowers back into her face). Now, your job is to keep the power of the flash low (like $^1/_4$ power or less) to keep it looking dramatic.

(4) When you're done, convert the photo to black and white and add a brown tint in Photoshop or Elements (use a Photo Filter adjustment layer), or Lightroom (use a Develop preset).

The Recipe for Getting This Type of Shot

Characteristics of this type of shot: Dramatic portrait, nicely suited for male subjects, with lots of drama to the lighting.

(1) This was taken with an inexpensive hot shoe flash on an inexpensive 6' light stand.

(2) I used a roll of black seamless paper for the background (around $25 for a 53" roll).

(3) To get directional light like this, you have to get the flash off the camera, and to get it off the camera this far, you have to use either a wireless flash or a really long sync cable (but, try not to use a long sync cable—at some point you'll trip over it).

(4) To get the softness and wrapping quality of the light from the flash, you'll need to either fire the flash through a diffuser or use a small softbox made for hot shoe flash (that's what I used for this shot. It was a 27x27" hot shoe softbox from Impact. Lastolite makes a softbox like this, too, and there's even a Joe McNally signature version of this handy hot shoe softbox that folds up flat like a reflector).

(5) Position the flash to the right of the camera, up about one foot higher than your subject, at about a 45° angle aiming down toward them. Put it about six feet back from your subject. If you're using a small softbox, you're all set. If you're using a diffusion panel, position it as close as you can get it to your subject without actually seeing it in the photo. Put your flash about one foot behind that panel.

(6) No reflector is necessary (you want the dark shadows on the far side of his face) and no tripod is necessary because the flash will freeze your subject and stop any movement.

The Recipe for Getting This Type of Shot

LOCATION: SAND HARBOR STATE PARK, LAKE TAHOE, NEVADA

Characteristics of this type of shot: Glassy, still water; a beautiful gradient of colors in the sky; and a wide, interesting vista.

(1) The key to this shot is when you shoot it. This type of shot needs to be taken before sunrise, not just for quality of light, but perhaps more importantly, to get the glassy, still water. The best time for this is at dawn. About an hour later and, in most cases, that water won't be still and glassy any more.

(2) While the sky does have a nice color gradient, it has something really important missing—clouds. Clouds are what make the sky interesting, so when you have a bald, cloudless sky like this, compose the shot so the horizon line is up in the top third of the frame. That way, you don't show much of the sky at all.

(3) In low dawn light like this, you need to, of course, shoot on a tripod and use a cable release or your camera's self-timer to minimize any camera shake. Because you're on a tripod, you can shoot at your lowest ISO (here, that was 100 ISO) to minimize any noise.

(4) You'll need to use a wide-angle lens to capture this wide a view (this was taken with a 14–24mm f/2.8 lens set at 14mm).

(5) This is another one of those occasions where you want to use a high f-stop number to keep as much in focus, front to back, as possible. I used f/22 (my go-to f-stop for landscapes).

(6) For a landscape shot to be successful, you need a strong foreground element (like these rocks, and to accentuate them, I put my tripod way down low).

The Recipe for Getting This Type of Shot

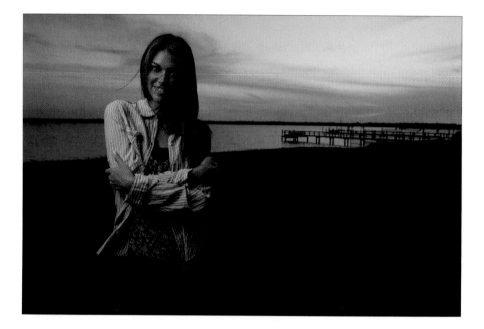

Characteristics of this type of shot: A simple sunset portrait using hot shoe flash.

(1) Start by positioning your subject with their back to the setting sun.

(2) Make sure your flash is turned off, because you first want to meter as if you're taking a regular ol' natural-light photo with no flash. Switch your camera to manual mode, set your shutter speed to ¹/₁₂₅ of a second (that's important), then aim at your subject, and hold the shutter button down halfway so your camera takes a meter reading of the scene. Look inside your camera's viewfinder, and you'll see a meter graph (on a Nikon, it's on the right; on a Canon or Sony, it's on the bottom). You're going to adjust *only* your f-stop until the meter reading reads 0 (zero; the proper exposure). So, move the dial to adjust your f-stop and, as you move it, you'll see that meter move, as well (keep it aimed at your subject while you're doing this). Once you've got the meter set to 0, look at your f-stop (let's say it's f/5.6, for example). Your job is to underexpose (make darker) the scene you're about to shoot by about 2 full stops (or more). So, if you were at f/5.6, you'll go two stops higher to f/11. Now, take a test shot. Does your subject look like a silhouette against the sky? If not, darken the scene more—try f/13 and take another test shot. When your subject looks like a silhouette, your settings are good to go.

(3) Turn on your flash with a *very* low flash power setting, like ¹/₄ or ¹/₈ power, and put an orange gel over your flash so the light isn't white (see page 26). Use a diffuser or softbox to soften the light and take a test shot. If the flash is too bright, lower the power. If it's not bright enough, raise the power, but keep it natural looking—don't "over-light" your subject.

The Recipe for Getting This Type of Shot

Characteristics of this type of shot: A natural-light shot taken in direct sunlight, with a soft, out-of-focus background and a shallow depth of field.

(1) This shot, taken in the garden area between the church and the church office, was in direct sunlight. To get soft, beautiful light in a situation like this, we have to diffuse the light (use something to make the harsh, direct sunlight soft and beautiful), so standing just to her left (from the camera position) is a friend holding up a diffuser right over her head (see page 84 for more on diffusers). You basically put the diffuser between the sun and your subject and it spreads and softens the light in a big way (as you can see above).

(2) To make the diffused light even softer, have your friend hold the diffuser as close to the top of your subject's head as possible without actually being visible in the frame itself. The closer you get the diffuser to your subject, the softer the light (in fact, you can almost see a glow as the diffuser gets really close).

(3) By looking at the photo, you can probably figure out the f-stop I used, because the background is way out of focus, and you've learned that f-stops that do that are "wide open" f-stops with low numbers, like f/1.8, f/2.8, f/4, and f/5.6 (in this case, it was f/2.8).

(4) If you remember back to page 77, then you also know that f-stop alone won't give you that out-of-focus background look like this—you have to use a longer lens and zoom in (in this case, it was a 70–200mm zoomed in to 200mm).

The Recipe for Getting This Type of Shot

Characteristics of this type of shot: A bright, clean, dreamy look using softened natural light.

(1) This shot was taken in the worst light possible, at "high noon" (well, at 12:07 p.m. to be exact), in an empty lot near downtown, but still the light is just gorgeous. The trick is simply to make the sunlight soft (you learned that trick back on page 84), which is to put a diffuser between the sun and your subjects. We used an inexpensive Westcott diffuser (part of their 5-in-1 reflector/diffuser kit for around $40) and I had a friend hold up the diffuser over their heads to block the harshness of the light, making the light source larger by spreading and diffusing it.

(2) At high noon like this, the sun is usually straight overhead, but if it's not (you're shooting earlier or later in the day), just remember to position the sun behind your subjects (so their backs are facing the sun). That way, any sunlight from behind them just creates a nice rim light around them and doesn't spill onto their faces.

(3) To create a soft glow with your diffused light, have your friend (or assistant) hold the diffuser right over their heads, as close to your subjects as possible without actually seeing the diffuser itself in your frame.

(4) Now, give the entire image a soft glow effect in Photoshop (or Elements). Just duplicate the Background layer and apply a 50-pixel Gaussian Blur filter to this layer. Lower the Opacity of this layer to 30%, and then, at the top of the Layers panel, change the layer's blend mode from Normal to Soft Light. Lastly, convert the photo to black and white.

The Recipe for Getting This Type of Shot

Characteristics of this type of shot: A bright, backlit, blown-out look shot with visible motion to give the sense of speed.

(1) In sports photography, you normally try to freeze the action, which means getting a shutter speed of $1/1000$ of a second or faster. However, there are times (and certain sports, like cycling and motorsports) where you want to create a sense of motion and speed, so the athletes (cars) appear to be moving (and not parked in position, ready for the race to start). To do this, shoot at a slow shutter speed and pan with your subject (in this case, the cyclist), which keeps most of the bike in focus, but makes the wheels and background show motion.

(2) To do this, shoot in shutter priority mode (S) and set your shutter speed to $1/60$ of a second (far below the $1/1000$ you'd use to freeze motion), and then turn on Continuous High-Speed mode (on a Nikon) or Continuous Shooting (on a Canon or Sony), so it takes multiple photos when you press-and-hold the shutter button.

(3) When the athlete is nearly to you, lock your focus on them (I usually aim my center focus point at their helmet), and then track along with them, firing in continuous mode, taking a series of photos as they go by. Hold that shutter button down until they are well past you.

(4) Many of the shots will be terribly out of focus and that's normal, but in that burst of shots, you'll usually find one that looks just right (and that's the only one you need).

(5) Lastly, to get the popular blown-out look, take your lens hood off your camera, position the athlete between you and the sun, and fire away. Lens flare will come.

The Recipe for Getting This Type of Shot

Characteristics of this type of shot: A tight, close-up shot of the wedding rings with a glassy reflection.

(1) Getting something as small as two wedding rings to fill the frame, like these do, and still look really sharp means using a lens that was made for this type of shot: a macro lens. If you have a macro lens, you're all set. If not, there are three alternatives that can help: (a) Use a Canon Close-Up lens, which screws onto the front of your regular size lens like a filter, turning it into a macro lens. It's cheaper and smaller and does the trick. (b) Many zoom lenses have a Macro mode, in which case you're already set. Or, (c) you can use an extension tube (see page 183).

(2) The reflection comes from just placing the rings on a shiny surface (in this case, ivory piano keys. You can also place the rings on a black area of the piano for a more mirror-like reflection). On the off chance that neither the church nor the reception hall has a piano, then head out to the parking lot to see who has a shiny white or black car (maybe the bride and groom hired a limo, or someone in the wedding party has one). Just put the rings on the hood and—voilá—instant reflection (of course, ask permission before you put things on someone's hood or a reflection may become the least of your worries).

(3) If you have a tripod, this is the time to pull it out, because you'll be shooting at an f-stop that will help keep as much in focus as possible, like f/22. You'll need this because the depth of field for macro lenses, even at f/22, is so small that the front of the rings will be in focus, and the back will be a little out of focus.

The Recipe for Getting This Type of Shot

LOCATION: PARIS, FRANCE

Characteristics of this type of shot: A sweeping view of a city skyline at sunset.

(1) The first key to this shot is the high vantage point. To get a rooftop skyline shot like this, you have to be up at least as high as the average building height. This shot was taken from the roof of the ultra modern L'Institut du Monde Arabe in Paris, along the Seine River, just behind Notre Dame. It has an open rooftop where you can even set up a tripod for a beautiful view of Notre Dame at night. However, this shot was taken on the opposite side of the building where there is no open rooftop and no clear view of the Eiffel Tower, which is what made getting this shot a bit of a challenge. But, I used the technique from page 162 on shooting through the glass window in your hotel. By the way, I used this same technique for the opening shot for this chapter, except it was pressed against the glass window of a moving tour bus.

(2) Near the elevators on the opposite side of the building is a patterned facade facing the building's courtyard. It covers the entire side of the building, but the pattern had a circular hole in the center of each square—just big enough for me to press my lens up firmly against the glass to minimize glare. That was total luck, but there's more to it than this. The way it's constructed, I couldn't use my tripod to hold the camera, but of course, it's sunset and low lighting (not to mention the fact that I'm now shooting through what I imagine is tinted glass). So, I had to raise the ISO on my camera to 800 ISO. This raised my shutter speed above 1/60 of a second, which is a fast enough shutter speed where I could handhold the shot and not get a blurry photo.

The Recipe for Getting This Type of Shot

LOCATION: PARIS OPERA HOUSE, PARIS, FRANCE

Characteristics of this type of shot: An empty hallway with a wide, long look, lit with natural light, with lots of detail visible throughout.

(1) There were two keys to this photo: The first was patience. There is nothing that kills a shot faster than one filled with tourists, and this is a hallway in the Paris Opera House, which is open to the public all day for self-guided tours. Loads of tourists were walking right in front of me from this vantage point, going to the balcony outside to the left that overlooks the street below, and even more people were walking down the hallway itself straight toward me. The only way to get a shot where it was not packed with people was to stand there, camera in hand, and literally just wait. I stood there for nearly 25 minutes to get this shot (you can still see a few tourists way off at the other end, but for the most part, they blend into the background).

(2) The other key was kindness and a smile. As soon as I started to set up a tripod (it doesn't look like it, but the light was pretty low), a security guard immediately came up to me and told me it was "not allowed." I smiled and said "just one quick shot." He shook his head, "No." But, I was really nice about it, and then said, "I'll just take one quick shot—this hall is so beautiful, and I'd love a quick shot." He paused and then said, "Well…I'm just going to walk into this next room and if you take a quick shot with the tripod, just don't let me see you do it." He smiled. I smiled. And, I didn't abuse it—when the time was right, I unfolded the legs, took the shot, and then packed it up. I smiled, winked, and gave a thumbs up as I left. He smiled back. Kindness and a smile go a long way.

The Recipe for Getting This Type of Shot

Characteristics of this type of shot: A simple two-light food shot using a couple of little tricks that make the food look more appetizing and the shot look better.

(1) This was actually shot in the restaurant (I was hired by the restaurant to shoot different dishes for their menu), but they set us up in a dark back corner in a part of the restaurant that wasn't being used. We used a dining table as our shooting platform.

(2) I used two continuous, always-on lights from Westcott (see page 46), which are perfect for food and product shots like this. I placed one light behind the food, at an angle off to the right, with a small softbox, and another in front of the food, off to my left, with a small softbox.

(3) This is taken with a macro lens (to get that super-shallow depth of field, where only part of the food is in focus). This means shooting on a tripod with a shutter release, and keeping the barrel of the macro lens pretty straight (not tipping it down too much—see page 174).

(4) To keep the food looking moist and fresh, we kept a small bowl nearby with vegetable oil and we brushed it liberally on the food to give it that shine.

(5) To make the highlights really pop, we used four very small, inexpensive (we bought them at the local pharmacy) tabletop swivel vanity mirrors, and we bounced light from the back light into areas where we wanted an extra kick of light in front (that swivel comes in really handy for this—with continuous lights like we're using, you can literally see the beams of light from these mirrors as you swivel them up/down).

The Recipe for Getting This Type of Shot

LOCATION: MAUI, HAWAII

Characteristics of this type of shot: A misty, almost cloudy sea with beautiful clouds above to make a classic sunset scene.

(1) A key part of this is simply luck. The next day I could have come to this same location, at the same time, with the same equipment, and been faced with a bald, cloudless sky. But this particular night, I got lucky with a beautiful, cloud-filled sky, which is exactly what you need to create a beautiful sunset image.

(2) For a sweeping landscape like this, you need to use a wide-angle lens (this was taken with a 28–300mm zoom lens, set at 28mm—its widest angle). To keep a decent amount of focus throughout the shot, you should choose a higher number for your f-stop (f/14, f/16, f/22, etc.).

(3) Since you're shooting around dusk, the light will be low, so you absolutely need to shoot this type of shot on a tripod or your shot will be blurry. Also, use a cable release or your camera's self-timer to minimize any camera shake. Since you're on a tripod, you can shoot at 100 ISO for the cleanest image.

(4) But just shooting a f/22 alone won't get you that misty, cloudy water you see here—you're going to need a filter to darken the scene even more, so your shutter can stay open for 30 or 40 seconds or longer (longer is better). It's called a Neutral Density (or just ND, for short) filter. It screws onto your lens and darkens the scene by 2 stops, 4 stops, or even 10 stops (the more stops, the longer your shutter stays open). Here's a link to a video tutorial I did on using ND filters: **http://bit.ly/173lgGL**.

The Recipe for Getting This Type of Shot

Characteristics of this type of shot: Nice, soft, beautiful light on the bride and brides-maids, even though it's taken outside at "high noon."

(1) Have you noticed a theme in this chapter? It's all about getting soft, beautiful light, and once you have that, the rest all falls into place. Here, we have a shot of the bride and bridesmaids, taken outside when the sun is its harshest, and all it took to get this shot was to make sure all of them were fully under an awning in front of the reception hall. By simply having them under an awning, so they're in the shade, the light is soft and beautiful. For softer, more beautiful light, move them toward the edge of the shade (I had them move a few steps forward, toward the camera, until they were almost in the sun without any of it actually hitting them directly).

(2) To have the background behind them a little bit out of focus, you want to use an f-stop that makes the background soft and out of focus, like f/2.8 or f/4. It's not super-out-of-focus because I wasn't able to zoom in tight enough (I would have had to use a really long lens and stand across the street to zoom in tight and fit four people in the frame).

(3) To add a little more energy to the shot, I tilted the camera to its side a bit (you might hear some photographers say, "Oh, not that cliché tilty trick," but clients still love it, and that's who you want to make happy)..

Index

Today, the 61 point autofocus
is completely on her.

Meet the 5D Mark III, a camera designed specifically for your creativity. With a 61 Point High Density Reticular autofocus and an extended ISO range of 100-25600, there is no limit to your creative vision.

EOS 5D Mark III

pro.usa.canon.com/5DMarkIII

Canon

The **Shoot** Like a **Pro** Tour

WITH SCOTT KELBY

See the concepts, images, & ideas from Scott Kelby's Digital Photography book series come to life—LIVE!

a full day of LIVE training for only $99

NAPP members pay $79

From day one,
KelbyTraining.com
has specialized in **creative,**
artful and **inspired**
Photography taught by
the best **Photographers**
in the world. Teaching
great photography is
our **passion** & it's all
we do!

photo by Lindsay Adler, KelbyTraining.com instructor